Fawlty Towers

Fawlty Towers

The Story of the Sitcom

GRAHAM McCANN

HODDER &
STOUGHTON

First published in Great Britain in 2007 by Hodder & Stoughton
An Hachette Livre UK company

1

Copyright © Graham McCann 2007

The right of Graham McCann to be identified as the Author
of the Work has been asserted by him in accordance with
the Copyright, Designs and Patents Act 1988.

A CIP catalogue record for this title is available from the British Library

Hardback ISBN 978 0 340 898116
Trade paperback ISBN 978 0 340 898123

Typeset in Bembo by Hewer Text UK Ltd, Edinburgh
Printed and bound by Mackays of Chatham Ltd, Chatham, Kent

Hodder & Stoughton policy is to use papers that are natural, renewable
and recyclable products and made from wood grown in sustainable
forests. The logging and manufacturing processes are expected to
conform to the environmental regulations of the country of origin.

Hodder & Stoughton Ltd
338 Euston Road
London NW1 3BH

www.hodder.co.uk

For
Dick, Silvana and Vera

Contents

Acknowledgements

I am very pleased to have the opportunity to thank my agent, Mic Cheetham, for her advice, encouragement and faith; I genuinely could not have completed this book without her kindness and guidance. Nick Davies, my editor at Hodder, was more patient, trusting and tactful than I deserved, and I will not forget his support.

Among interviewees and advisers, I am particularly indebted to John Howard Davies, Prunella Scales, Andrew Sachs, and Ballard Berkeley's son, Peter. I am also grateful to the staff of the following institutions: the BBC Written Archives Centre (especially David McGowan); the National Archives; the London Metropolitan Archives; the British Library, Newspaper Library and Sound Archive; the Theatre Museum; the Margaret Herrick Library; the National Film and Sound Archive of Australia; the British Film Institute Library; and the University of Cambridge Library. I am pleased to acknowledge, in addition, the assistance of several other people at Hodder – Rowena Webb, Nicola Doherty, Eleni Fostiropoulos, Josine Meijer and Hugo Wilkinson – as well as John Ammonds, Eddie Braben, Sir Bill Cotton, Penny Isaac, Richard McCann, Irene Melling and Robin Williams.

Finally, my heartfelt thanks also go to Vera McCann, Silvana Dean and Dick Geary. Their kindness, and company, helped me see the project all the way through to its conclusion.

*England, you know, is a nation
of small hotel keepers, not shopkeepers.*

JOHN CLEESE

CHECKING IN

Qué?

Look: if we can attract this class of customer, I mean . . . the sky's the limit!

The television is on, and it is Fawlty. A lean, lanky, moustachioed man with clenched fists, clenched hair and a clenched heart is raging at the whole of the world: stuffing cheese down the windpipe of an innocently verbose spoon salesman, shouting at an elderly semi-deaf person, ranting at a middle-aged German person, slapping a little Spanish person, lashing out about kippers, ducks and salads, administering a damned good thrashing to a stationary car and depositing an outsized garden gnome inside an incompetent Irish builder. This is Fawlty, and it is faultless.

Watch as the latest visitor wanders through the forecourt, climbs up the steps, comes into the lobby and rings the bell at reception:

FAWLTY: Yes, yes? Well – *yes?*
VISITOR: Er, well, I was wondering if you could offer me accommodation for a few nights?
FAWLTY: Well, have you *booked?*
VISITOR: I'm sorry?
FAWLTY: Have you *booked*, have you *booked?*
VISITOR: N–no.
FAWLTY: Oh *dear!*
VISITOR: Why, are you full?

FAWLTY: Oh, we're not full. We're not *full*. Of *course* we're not *full!!*
VISITOR: Well, I'd like . . .
FAWLTY: One moment, one moment![1]

Now move on to the dining room and see someone try to ask for a little assistance:

GUEST: Excuse me . . .
FAWLTY: Yes?
GUEST: Er, look, we've been waiting here for about half an hour now, I mean, we gave the waiter our order . . .
FAWLTY: Oh, *him!* He's *hopeless*, isn't he?
GUEST: Yes, well, I don't wish to complain, but when he does bring something, he's got it wrong.
FAWLTY: You think I don't know? I mean, you only have to *eat* here. We have to *live* with it![2]

Next, turn back into the lobby, sneak upstairs and spy on the poor bewildered guests who are in the process of being expelled:

FAWLTY: I'm sorry, but you'll have to go. We made a mistake – all these rooms are taken. I'm so sorry. Well, actually, I'm *not* sorry. I mean, you come here, just like that, and, well, to be perfectly blunt, you have a very good time at our expense! Hmmm? I mean, I think you know what I mean. *Hmmm?* I mean, you have had a very, *very*, good time, haven't you? Well, not *here* you don't! Oh no! Thank you and good night![3]

Finally, slip back down to reception and observe another couple struggle to pay up and check out:

FAWLTY: Yes?
GUEST: Er . . . could we have our bill, please?
FAWLTY: Well, can you *wait* a minute?

GUEST: Er . . . I'm afraid we're a bit late for our train – we didn't
get our alarm call.

FAWLTY: *Right*. I was up at *five*, you know, we *do* have staff
problems, I'm so sorry it's not all done by magic![4]

This is the place we all know as Fawlty Towers – the hotel we
can switch off any time we like, but never want to leave.

Fawlty Towers was only on our television screens for twelve
half-hour episodes – six in 1975 and another six in 1979 – but it
has stayed in our lives ever since. It was a truly great sitcom, and,
like all other great sitcoms, it gave us a central character – like a
Hancock, a Steptoe, a Mainwaring or a Wilson – who was so
vivid, so funny, so flawed and so weirdly real that he very rapidly
became positively adjectival: after this man came into view, so
many other people we knew seemed, all of a sudden, 'just like
Basil Fawlty' or even eerily 'Fawltyesque'. You laughed at him,
and sometimes you laughed with him, or at least sympathised
with him, and you even, in an odd sort of way, *cared* about him.
He was not just a comical bit of fiction; he was also a figure who
seemed to live and breathe and struggle to cope with all of his
many inadequacies – just like you, or me, or, as you and me
would probably prefer to think, that awful person whom we
both happen to know.

There was more to the show, however, than Basil Fawlty.
There was the classic 'trapped relationship' between Basil and his
shrewishly sybaritic wife Sybil, which gave us a marriage
between a man who was afraid of women, and a woman
who loved being feared by men even more than she loved
being adored by them. There was poor Polly, who had so much
unfulfilled potential, and the dotty old Major, who had so much
unread newspaper, as well as the hapless Manuel, who was from

Barcelona. There were also the weekly wild cards: the procession of peculiar guests, with their range of deceptively banal requests, who sparked off each new gloriously manic storyline. All of these elements combined to create a sublimely rich, distinctive and supremely well-crafted comic fiction that mesmerised in order to amuse. Structurally, the show moved from moment to moment with the cruel and remorseless logic of a Feydeau farce; emotionally, it twitched, twisted and tensed like a classic little Freudian fable.

It all added up to the kind of sitcom that did so much more than merely use up another thirty minutes with mechanical babble and bustle. Week after week, *Fawlty Towers* kept on setting itself fresh challenges – in terms of pace and plot and personae – and never failed to see them through. There were no blank pages in its scripts, no aimless moments, no loose threads, no spare flesh. The chaos worked like clockwork: each episode was elegantly elaborate, cleverly self-contained and thrillingly driven and direct. The end might have been inevitable, but the means were unpredictable. It was always Fate that Fawlty fought, but, even though we knew that his fight was hopeless, we were fascinated to watch the various ways whereby he failed to evade that final slap in the face.

We were left wanting more – much more. After just two short series, when the inspiration was still at its height, it was gone, and its absence was keenly felt. It still is. *Fawlty Towers* was, and remains, very special indeed. It was 'event' television, 'water-cooler' television, 'appointment television'. Whatever the voguish phrase, whatever the current buzz word, the salient point is that, whenever *Fawlty Towers* was on, you had to watch it, and then you had to discuss it, and laugh about it, and love it. It was never a chore. It was always a pleasure. It was comedy at its very best.

Success – in both the popular and critical senses – came rather slowly at first, as word of its very special magic took time to spread, but it then proceeded, very rapidly, to grow and grow and grow. In 1976, the first series won the Broadcasting Press Guild 'Best Comedy' award, the BAFTA 'Best Situation-Comedy' award and the Royal Television Society 'Outstanding Creative Achievement' award, and then, in 1980, the second series won the BAFTAs for 'Best Situation-Comedy' and 'Best Light Entertainment Performance'. The plaudits kept on coming long after the run was done.

During the decades since the original shows were first aired, *Fawlty Towers* has been shown repeatedly in more than sixty countries – from Tonga to Bosnia, from China to Pakistan and from Latvia to Malta (and, in a 2004 poll, it was voted the most popular British sitcom seen by non-British viewers[5]). There have also been volumes of scripts, vinyl records, audio cassettes, CDs, videos, DVDs and even an interactive CD-ROM and UMD to meet the needs of the most avid of fans, but still the appetite appears to remain unsated (in 2007, for example, a *Radio Times*-sponsored 'Great British TV Survey' named the show as the one that most people wanted to see brought back to the screen[6]). Similarly, as far as the vast majority of the critics are concerned, the benchmark set by the show still remains unsurpassed: in an industry poll conducted by the British Film Institute in 2000 to determine the nation's 100 best-ever television programmes, *Fawlty Towers* ended up right at the top of a very distinguished list.[7]

This is why the show is still worth recalling, analysing and celebrating. It was a great event, it had a huge impact – and it is still as funny as ever. *Fawlty Towers* is therefore well worth a return visit and a relatively leisurely stay.

I

When Python Met Sinclair

A satisfied customer – we should have him stuffed!

Things first started going slightly Fawlty in the middle of May 1970, when the *Monty Python's Flying Circus* team checked into a perfectly ordinary-looking, four-star hotel on the outskirts of Torquay.[1] They were in the area for a fortnight to film a few sketches and sequences for the second series of the comedy show that sought to provide people with something completely different. The BBC had chosen this hotel as a suitable base for the troupe.

The hotel in question was the Gleneagles, situated in Asheldon Road in the Wellswood area of Torquay, overlooking the pretty little Anstey's Cove (where the novelist Agatha Christie used to go for quiet moonlit picnics) and the nearby Redgate Beach, with panoramic sea views across the bay towards Seaton, Sidmouth, Exmouth and Lyme Regis. Bright and clean and neat, the converted Georgian mansion had acquired a reputation in the area for the beauty of its ocean views, the comfort of its rooms and, alas, the exceptional short-temperedness of its proprietor.

The proprietor in question was a skinny little Irish-born Englishman named Donald William Sinclair (a thrice-torpedoed former Commander in the British Navy), who had been co-managing the Gleneagles with his much taller, and even more formidable Aberdonian wife, Beatrice (known to most as 'Betty'), for the past seven years (prior to which he had managed the nearby Greenacres – now defunct – throughout the 1950s). Now aged sixty, he considered himself far too old, too busy and too important to suffer any fools either gladly or glibly. The problem was that, by Donald Sinclair's exacting standards, most of the people who happened to venture inside his hotel seemed like utter and insufferable fools.

Often combining (grudgingly) the roles of manager, porter, night porter, receptionist, lunchtime bar person, still-room assistant and tea-maker, he was invariably behind schedule, highly stressed and extremely irascible. What kind of things exacerbated his anger? Most kinds of things did the trick.

It was not unusual, for example, for him to bring down the shutters on the bar abruptly and prematurely at 9.00 p.m. because he had already grown tired of those whom he was still supposed to be serving (snapping at anyone brave enough to complain: *'Tough!'*). He once halted breakfast and began interrogating certain guests when a teapot meant for four was found sitting on a table meant for two. He also ejected several residents from the lounge at lunchtime when they inquired politely if any sandwiches might possibly be available ('Right, that's it – *out!*²).

One evening at around 10.45 p.m., when a young mother pressed the night porter service button at reception to request a flask of hot water to heat her baby's bottle, Sinclair finally appeared (following a delay of about fifteen minutes) in his dressing-gown and proceeded to berate her for getting him out of bed for such a maddeningly 'trivial' request. Similarly, when a large number of guests, who had been made to wait for more than an hour for the arrival of the band to commence the evening's scheduled formal dance, at last grew impatient and started to complain – Sinclair, without offering any explanation, marched silently into the room, dumped an old record player, with no records, in the middle of the floor and then stormed off into the night. Then there was the newly arrived visiting academic who, upon finding no more than a couple of sheets of lavatory paper hanging limply from the roll in his en-suite bathroom, found the courage to ask, in the meek manner of a grown-up Oliver Twist, 'Please, sir, I want some more' – and was startled to hear Sinclair moan in response, 'What on earth are you *doing* with it?'[3] On yet another painful occasion, he ejected some late-arriving visitors for daring to question, quite mildly, the hotel's less-than-superlative standard of service.[4]

Hell, for Donald Sinclair, was having to put up with other people inside his own hotel. Every new guest, therefore, represented a fresh threat of unbearable chaos.

None of the Pythons knew anything about this when they first checked in to the Gleneagles – but they soon found out that something was not quite right. Something was not quite right about Donald Sinclair. 'He was completely round the twist, off his chump, out of his tree,' an exasperated Graham Chapman would recall. '[Sinclair] did not like guests and even thought that Eric [Idle's squash] gear, which was in a bag, and which Eric had just left outside the hotel, was in fact a bomb.'[5] The bag in question ended up being hidden seventy yards or so away beyond a tall white wall by the hotel swimming pool just in case it blew up ('We've had a lot of staff problems lately'[6]); but the madness had only just started.

When the Pythons first sat down together for dinner, Sinclair noticed that Terry Gilliam, who was an American, was using his cutlery just like an American would do (cutting all of his meat with his knife, then picking up his fork with his right hand in order to transfer each morsel to his mouth). 'We don't eat like *that* in this country!' barked Sinclair, all stiff-shouldered and staring-eyed, before moving on like a patrolling policeman.[7] The sound of an increasingly angry kerfuffle then filtered through from the bar, where a number of thirsty guests had been left high and dry while Sinclair – who, for some unknown reason, was the only member of staff he was allowing to serve drinks on this particular evening – continued to supervise the distribution of dishes in the dining-room.[8] Later that evening, Michael Palin mustered the courage to ask this curmudgeon if he could book a wake-up call: Sinclair simply stared at him, his eyebrows shooting up skywards with surprise, and then asked incredulously, '*Why?*'[9] 'Everything we asked for,' Palin would recall, 'seemed to be the most unforgivable imposition'.[10]

All of the Pythons were shocked and appalled at such an ill-mannered attitude, but one of them, John Cleese, was not only shocked and appalled but also strangely intrigued and enthralled. He had found himself in a few bad hotels before, and was no stranger to poor service, but this was so much worse that it was actually strangely hypnotic. 'He was the rudest man I've ever met,' he would say of Sinclair. 'He was wonderful.'[11] While most of the others, therefore, escaped after just one traumatic night to the nearby, and infinitely more welcoming, Imperial Hotel (but only after Mrs Sinclair had tried to charge them personally for the whole two weeks that had been booked by the BBC[12]), John Cleese stayed on at the Gleneagles, unable to let Mr Sinclair stray very far out of his sight.

Each subsequent day was filled with filming – a rugby match between Derby Council and the All Blacks at the local stadium

('And the Lady Mayoress has scored!'); a spoof general election results broadcast at a mansion in Paignton ('Well, this is largely as I predicted, except that the Silly Party won – I think this is mainly due to the number of votes cast . . .'); a parody of French cinema's *nouvelle vague* with a shaky camera and a piece of lettuce at a nearby rubbish dump ('*Venez-vous ici souvent?*'); a one-sided football match at a recreation ground between eleven largely immobile Long John Silver impersonators from Bournemouth and a team of frenetic gynaecologists hailing from Watford; a comic epic called 'Scott of the Sahara' ('From the same team that brought you *Lawrence of Glamorgan* . . .') shot on Goodrington Sands; and some bits and pieces involving psychiatrists and a milk float on a quiet suburban street ('. . . and a pot of yoghurt, please'). Each night, as far as John Cleese was concerned, was best spent ensconced back in the lounge at the Gleneagles – observing, overhearing and collecting gossip about the increasingly incredible Donald Sinclair.

Over at the five-star Imperial, the other Pythons were being pampered while they relaxed out in the sun beside a heated sea-water pool, sipping a steady succession of gin and tonics, before heading off for a gourmet meal and a bottle or two of lightly chilled Meursault, Sancerre or a good old Château de Chasselas ('Very passable, this, eh? Very passable') in the hotel restaurant. At the Gleneagles, meanwhile, Cleese (who had by now been joined by his wife and occasional *Monty Python* supporting artiste, Connie Booth) was relishing each one of Sinclair's maniacally tetchy little episodes. 'When you walked down the steps into reception,' Cleese would later recall, 'he'd be just sitting at the desk, staring into space. But the moment that he saw somebody coming, he'd immediately pretend that he was very, very busy. And then you'd come up and stand there on the other side of the reception desk and he would ignore you as though you'd suddenly been rendered invisible. So eventually you'd say, "Er, excuse me . . ." and he'd say, "Oh, *WHAT?*" '[13] Nothing, it seemed, was ever too little trouble. 'Could you possibly call me a taxi, please?' Cleese asked him on one occasion. 'I beg your pardon?' Sinclair replied, sharply. 'Could you call me a taxi, please?' Cleese repeated. 'Call you a *taxi?*' Sinclair exclaimed. 'Yes,' said Cleese. 'Oh, I *suppose* so,' sighed Sinclair, sounding as though he had just been asked to drop everything else and construct the taxi himself out of bits of hotel cutlery, learn the 'Knowledge', acquire a licence and then drive the passenger all the way from the hotel to some distant and difficult destination during the rush hour.[14]

If Cleese still harboured the suspicion that Sinclair was just having an exceptionally taxing and trying summer season, and perhaps was not normally quite so awful as this, then other guests, and the odd member of staff, would surely have been quick to disabuse him. This, they would have confirmed, was par for the course for Donald Sinclair. It would not get any better – and indeed, if anything, it might well get even worse.

Years later, shortly after Sinclair's death in September 1981 (at the age of seventy-two from a combination of 'myocardial infarction' and 'hypertension'[15]), his loyal (and similarly irascible) widow, Betty, would defend him angrily to the Press, claiming that, although he had indeed been a strong and impatient disciplinarian, he had also been a 'highly intelligent man and very efficient and courteous at his job' – and nothing at all like the 'neurotic eccentric' that John Cleese (whom she said she regarded as a 'complete and utter fool') had gone on to make him out to be.[16] 'Donald didn't want the Python team to stay at the Gleneagles,' she protested. 'They didn't fit into a family hotel and Donald came to me and said they should go. He said they would upset the other guests.'[17] Mrs Sinclair's well-meant attempt to revise her late husband's reputation backfired somewhat, however, because her comments only succeeded in prompting others who had known him to come forward with a fresh set of unflattering anecdotes.

Rosemary Harrison, for example, wrote a letter to the *Daily Telegraph* recalling her own brief experience of working at the Gleneagles, on a break from her training as a hotel management student, during the summer of 1973. Her former employer was, she insisted, 'bonkers': 'I have never come across anyone quite like Mr Sinclair. He was a square peg in a round hole.' After noting how he failed to delegate any duties, but still shouted at anyone who tried to urge him, very tactfully and discreetly, to speed up, she confirmed that he 'was just rude to the guests, and where possible staff kept out of his way.'[18] She added in a subsequent interview: '[The hotel] almost had the mentality of a prison camp in that guests and staff alike pulled together and talked and laughed about Mr Sinclair as a way of surviving.'[19]

There was more to come. There was much more.

One account was provided by a former customer, Roy Browning, who stayed at the hotel with his wife and two friends for what they had hoped would be a relaxing week on the so-called English Riviera. On their first evening, he reflected, they wandered into the bar for a pre-dinner drink only to be told very brusquely by Mr Sinclair: 'You'd better drink up, my wife doesn't spend her life in the kitchen preparing good food to have it spoilt because you can't get here on time.' Browning, understandably, was rather startled, but tried to dismiss such rudeness as an isolated incident. Two days later, however, events took a turn for the worse. 'Mr Sinclair explained there would be two sittings for dinner,' Browning recalled, 'because they had a dinner dance, and said if we didn't mind having the second, we could pre-order to ensure we received our choice.' The party agreed to the request and then wandered off to explore Torquay. When, however, they returned to the bar for another pre-dinner drink, there was an even stronger sense of tension in the air: 'The band was in a heated discussion with Mr Sinclair, after which two of them packed their instruments and left.' The foursome took their seats, somewhat nervously, in the dining room, only to be told that several of their pre-ordered choices were now inexplicably unavailable. Browning, his patience now perilously close to snapping, complained to Sinclair, only to be told that 'the kitchen was not his responsibility and I should speak to his wife. When we did so it was clear our requests had not been passed on.' Seeking to drown their shared sorrows, Browning and his fellow diners ordered some wine – or at least they tried to: 'It took three attempts before we found a wine on their list that they actually had in stock.' By the following morning, therefore, the holiday had turned into such a disaster that all four of them decided to cut their losses and leave early: 'We calculated what we owed, paid up and left.' Several weeks later, however, a court summons was slipped through Roy Browning's door: 'He was suing us for the full cost of the week, even though we had stayed only three days.' The Brownings eventually won after a court declared that they had not received the service they had a right to expect, but the painful memory of their stay would remain with them for ever.[20]

Something depressingly similar happened to Richard Saunders during his stay there on a family holiday. His polite request at the bar for a post-prandial gin and tonic prompted Sinclair to slam down the shutters and shout, 'The bar is *closed!*' A colleague who was staying at another hotel nearby – The Queen's – suggested that a drink could be drunk there freely in peace, so Saunders got up and set off: 'As I was walking out, [Sinclair] said to me, "And where do you think *you're* going?" And I said, "Oh, I'm just popping down to the Queen's to have a drink with my friend – *you* won't serve me!" He said, "If you go out, and you're not back by eleven o'clock, the door will be closed!"' Saunders strode off, shaking his head at such surly 'service', and, as the G&Ts slipped down, he resolved – as a matter of principle – to flout the curfew by a few symbolic minutes. 'And when I came back, the front door was closed. Locked. Couldn't get in. So I thought, "This is ridiculous – my wife and daughter's in there!" So I thumped on the door. Suddenly, a window went up, and [Sinclair] poked his head out the window with his pyjamas on. He said, "I told you you'd be locked out!" I said, "If you don't open this door I shall *bash* it in!"' After three or four minutes, a reluctant Sinclair opened the door, let Saunders in and then slammed it shut again – thus waking up most of the other guests in his hotel.[21]

It was not only former customers who offered their recollections; several former contractors did, too. One builder, for example, recalled a bizarre incident in the early 1970s involving Sinclair and an innocent-looking sign: 'At that time we were constructing additional bedroom accommodation, and one morning whilst working on the roof [we heard] a commotion taking place in the car park below. At one side, sign specialists were assembling a glass fasciaboard signifying the "Hotel Gleneagles" in readiness to be fixed over the front entrance, but little did they know that they wouldn't complete their job that day. Out of the hotel, in rather a hurry, came Donald Sinclair in an attempt to avoid abuse being directed at him from reception. He jumped into his car, slammed home the gear and reversed right over the corner of the new glass-fronted sign. He then moved forward, realigned the car, and again, this time with obvious intent, proceeded to completely demolish the remaining part of the sign, much to the amazement of the onlookers.'[22]

Few details, it seemed, would prove too small when it came to the risk of causing another commotion. One guest, who stayed at the Gleneagles one summer during the early 1970s, recalled how she and her husband tried in vain to order fresh strawberries and cream from the hotel menu for four nights in a row. 'The first night we were told they were off, the second we were told they were finished, the third night we were told they were off and on the fourth night we were told they were finished. On the fifth night we gave up on the whole idea. My husband had a row with him over it but he didn't really care.'[23] Sinclair, she said, was 'Fawlty to a "T".'[24]

Even the odd well-intended gesture often ended up going horribly awry. Barbara DePaulis, who used the hotel for her daughter's wedding in the early 1970s, would describe how one of her guests had to be rushed to hospital with a broken nose after crashing into a door that failed to open, and then her husband ended up being persuaded by a harassed Sinclair to spend most of his daughter's special day serving customers in the restaurant. 'It was the first wedding reception that the Gleneagles had had,' she would recall. 'They did not have enough staff or food. It was just hysterical. In the end we had to laugh.'[25]

Another anecdote came from Colin Bratcher, a bass player in a local band that often used to play at the Gleneagles. 'One evening,' he reminisced, 'there was no chair for the organist on the bandstand, so I opened the dining-room door and took one from there. It was already well past dinnertime and I didn't think it would be a problem. Shortly after, a note was passed to me from Mr Sinclair asking me to switch the chair because it didn't go with the others on stage. I don't know how he could even see it because someone was sitting on it, but he was fastidious. He used to serve at the bar while we played and he would often pass us notes with orders on them. We would be playing away quite merrily when an instruction would come: "The guests look half-asleep, play a samba." The guests seemed happy with our peaceful tunes, but he liked to be in control. He was totally eccentric.'[26]

Sometimes, Donald Sinclair's remorselessly belligerent attitude tipped his victims right over the edge and straight into frenzied acts of revenge. On one such occasion (long after he and his wife had retired from the hotel business), he became embroiled in a predictably fractious dispute with a couple of labourers over the quality of their handiwork (one of them had been laying carpets, the other had been hired to spruce up some of the décor). After yet another angry day of accusations, insults and threats, Sinclair woke up the following morning, peered out through his bedroom window and was horrified to find that his car, swimming pool, garden furniture, doors, walls, lawn, trees and bushes had all been painted the same shade of battleship grey during a long silent night of stealthy retaliation. 'They were not happy with painting the car,' his wife wailed about the workmen, 'they had to paint the windscreen as well.'[27]

Perhaps the most damning anecdote of all was the claim by an old colleague that, on more than one exceptionally fraught occasion, Mrs Sinclair herself became so exasperated by her volatile husband that she locked him in their own flat after his shrill and eccentric demands on their staff had become absolutely unbearable for all concerned ('Now don't let him out,' she ordered the others, 'he's only going to upset you!').[28] There was, as Eric Morecambe might have said, no answer to that, so Mrs Sinclair withdrew back into haughty obscurity, and her late husband went on being recalled and roundly mocked.

Back in the kinder, gentler world of the summer of 1970, however, such a risible legend seemed unlikely ever to commence. After the fortnight of filming in the area was over, John Cleese and Connie Booth had gone straight back to London with the rest of the Pythons, Donald Sinclair had stayed put in Torquay, and the odd little interlude that they had shared appeared to be over for good. There were no immediate schemes to tease; there were just plenty of sighs of relief. Cleese soon found, however, that he could not stop thinking, talking and laughing about the attitude and antics of the very strange man called Donald Sinclair. He simply could not shake the character from out of his head.

The normal writing routine was resumed, and, to the few who were 'in the know', faint traces of Sinclair could soon be discerned in the emerging scripts. It started out as no more than a line here or a gesture there (such as in the extended sketch that Cleese wrote that autumn for a forthcoming edition of *Six Dates with Barker*, which had Ronnie Barker playing a psychiatrist who is visited by an eccentric prospective patient so fearful of being diagnosed with mental problems that he pretends initially to be a gas man who has only come in to read the meter[29]), but, after just under a year, the temptation to try something more substantial grew too strong for Cleese to resist, and a semblance of the whole man crept back into the comical view. In a script for an episode – broadcast on 30 May 1971 – of *Doctor At Large* (the follow-up to the popular LWT sitcom *Doctor In The House*) entitled 'No Ill Feeling!', Cleese found a place for Mr (and Mrs) Sinclair in his own little fictional world.

Since the sitcom's central character, Dr Upton (played by Barry Evans), was now newly qualified and out and about in search of work, Cleese had him check in for a short stay at a Gleneagles-style seaside hotel – the humdrum Bella Vista – while gaining experience as a locum under the supervision of a provincial GP. Timothy Bateson played the role of the establishment's tetchy manager, George Clifford – a short, scrawny, somewhat Crippen-like man, with flat, shiny, centre-parted hair and round little National Health spectacles. Eunice Black played his hectoring wife: a tall and broad woman in frilly chiffon (a sort of English Edna Everage), who looked as though she might smack you and then kiss you and then punch you on the nose. The other guests included a trio of eccentric old ladies, a few paunchy middle-aged men in pinstripes and a tiresome self-styled 'wag'.

Just like Donald Sinclair had 'greeted' the puzzled Pythons, Mr Clifford introduced himself to Dr Upton with a brusque, 'What *is* it?' Interrupted repeatedly by distant barks from his bossy wife ('George – you haven't done the sprouts yet! Why haven't you done the sprouts?') and irritated by Upton's repeated ringing of the reception bell during his absence ('I *do* know you're *here*, you know!'), Clifford sighed, snapped and tut-tutted his way through the process whereby Upton was booked in and accorded a room ('Let's *try* and get this thing quite clear, shall we?'). The young doctor was then hurried through into the cramped little dining area by Clifford's redoubtable wife: 'This *is* a hotel, Dr Upton – we do ask our guests to be *prompt* for meals!'

Things were just as awkward the following morning, when Upton came down to brave a quick breakfast:

CLIFFORD: Cereal?

UPTON: Er, no, thanks, just—

CLIFFORD: Kipper or sausage?

UPTON: Would the kipper be quick?

CLIFFORD: I beg your pardon?

UPTON: Er, would the kipper be quicker?

CLIFFORD: Well, it'll be as quick as it can be. It can't be quicker than that, can it? I mean, how quick can a kipper be? I've got to *cook* the wretched thing!

UPTON: Er, y-yes.

CLIFFORD: Do you want it *cold?*

UPTON: No, no, I—

CLIFFORD: Look: I've got to make the *beds* by eleven o'clock!

'How quick can you cook a kipper?' – *coh!*[30]

Little more was seen of Clifford during the episode, apart from a final scene in which, out of sheer frustration, he poured a bowl of minestrone (pronounced so as to rhyme with 'home, sweet home') over the head of one of his guests ('I *hate* you!'), but, nonetheless, the character certainly made an impact on those who were watching the show.

Humphrey Barclay, the programme's producer (and a Cambridge contemporary), told Cleese enthusiastically, 'There's a series in that hotel.' The writer merely thought, 'Bloody television producer, can't see a programme without thinking about a series.'[31] After all, Cleese was far too preoccupied at that time with numerous other projects to take such a comment seriously; apart from contributing to the increasingly popular *Monty Python's Flying Circus* on television (and various other media) and the long-running *I'm Sorry I'll Read That Again* on radio, he was also writing for several other TV shows, including *The Ronnie Barker Yearbook*[32] and *The Two Ronnies*,[33] as well as acting in the odd edition of Les Dawson's *Sez Les*[34] and such one-off productions as *Elementary, My Dear Watson* (an edition of *Comedy Playhouse* – scripted by N. F. Simpson – in which he played Sherlock Holmes opposite Willie Rushton's Dr Watson).[35] In addition to all of this, Cleese (who was still in need of extra cash – 'I'd lost some money in an investment – I put some money into a gym and set a man up, and about three months later he died. Most extraordinary! I'd lost quite a bit of money on that'[36]) was also now involved in planning, writing and acting in projects for Video Arts, a new production company (co-founded in 1972 with Anthony Jay, Peter Robinson and Michael Peacock) that made short training films for the business world (teaching people how to avoid being as inefficient, bad-mannered and tactless as the likes of Donald Sinclair).[37] The last thing that he needed, therefore, was the strain of creating a new sitcom.

Life thus went on as normal (or abnormal), with Cleese slipping in and out of a wide variety of *Monty Python* comic personae, including an esurient cheese eater; a fish slapper; a bereaved parrot fancier; a fruit-fearing martinet; an upper-class twit; a psychotic chef; a minister for silly walks; an argument coach; an Australian philosopher called Bruce; Attila the Hun; Inspector Tiger of the Yard; Professor Enid Gumby; loud-mouthed bore Brian Equator; the quiz show host Michael Miles; the broadcaster Alan Whicker; an unfortunate member of the public by the name of Eric Praline; the entrepreneurial Dr E. Henry Thripshaw; a highwayman called Dennis Moore; and a taunting French guard from the Middle Ages. The characterisations, inevitably, were sketchy but as sketches they were very well done, and further enhanced Cleese's already heady reputation as one of the funniest men in the country.

The memory of the hotelier from hell, however, showed no signs of fading off into the past. As obdurate as the man himself, the idea of him kept on niggling away, waiting impatiently to take centre stage. It was just a matter of time.

2

Morning, Fawlty!

And now for something completely different . . .

At the end of 1972, after completing three series of *Monty Python's Flying Circus*, John Cleese told the rest of the troupe that he felt that he needed to leave.[1] He wanted, he said, to do something different, and he wanted to write with his wife.

It was a bold step for him to take, as the phenomenon that was *Monty Python* was still far from achieving its full potential, but, as a glance at the story of his life up to that point would have shown, the decision did conform to a certain sort of dogged logic. Coming from a relatively conventional, closely knit and quietly desperate 'lower-middle with pretensions to middle-middle'-class English background,[2] where a wardrobe full of pinstripe and a choice between law or accountancy for a career were considered to be practically *de rigueur*, he had grown used to seeking out new challenges instead of waiting for them to stroll up to his door.

Born on 27 October 1939 at 6 Ellesmere Road in Uphill, Weston-super-Mare, John Marwood Cleese (to give him his full name) was the only child of Reginald Cleese, an 'insurance official' (as he put it, rather grandly, on various forms and questionnaires, or a 'travelling insurance salesman', as everyone else was more likely to have described him), and Muriel Cross, a dutiful homemaker. Reg was a well-meaning but somewhat stuffy, starchy, literal-minded sort of individual (he once sent a letter of complaint to the humorous magazine *Punch* when he failed to find one of its cartoons sufficiently funny[3]) who had changed his name from Cheese to Cleese in 1915, shortly before he joined the Army, because he had already grown well and truly cheesed-off at being teased. Muriel was, ostensibly, an eminently 'proper' and conservative individual, but, in her own discreet and subtle manner, was quite capable of principled acts of rebellion (the most significant of which had seen her defy her stern father's disapproval to marry Reg – who was deemed to have been somewhat 'beneath' her – in a register office[4]), as well as the occasional angry outburst. (Whereas Reg was sometimes known, in the privacy of his own home, to behave in a mildly playful sort of way, Muriel was usually much more moody, depressed and perhaps even somewhat neurotic.[5]) Baby John arrived six days after his parents' thirteenth wedding anniversary, when Reg was forty-six and Muriel had just turned forty ('Life there is, of course, entirely free of sex,' their son would say of his birthplace. 'Occasionally, people are born in Weston by parthenogenesis'[6]).

The dawning of war caused the Cleese family to commence a fairly peripatetic period of existence, moving, as soon as the bombs began falling, first to rooms eight miles away in a large, detached Victorian farmhouse called Hillside House in the village of Brent Knoll, and then on for short spells spent in several other nearby places before eventually returning home, once the war was over, to Weston-super-Mare. It was at this stage, it seems, that Reg Cleese, anxious to protect the family finances from the hazards of an age of austerity, grew increasingly – and, at least in his son's eyes, rather comically – 'careful' with his pennies. 'For instance,' John would recall fondly, 'if my mother had asked him to buy some ham, he would always come back in and she would look at what he had bought and say, "This isn't the usual ham." He would say, "No, they have some special Norwegian ham this week. They recommend it very highly. They said it's better than the ordinary stuff." In reality it was just cheaper.'[7]

Thanks, however, to a relatively small but nonetheless very welcome inheritance that Muriel had recently received, John was still able to attend three good schools in the area – first, briefly, a private preparatory school in Burnham-on-Sea, then St Peter's Preparatory School in Weston and, finally, Clifton College public school in Bristol (an institution, as he later put it, 'in the middle of the middle of the middle of the public-school hierarchy'[8]) – and proved himself a pupil of real academic promise as well as, considering his spindly frame (described by his PT master as 'six foot of chewed string'[9]), a fairly decent player of football and cricket ('I had fantasies,' he would recall, 'of being a famous cricketer, scoring centuries for Somerset'[10]).

He was already six feet tall by the time that he was twelve ('His clothes and his feet,' said his mother, 'were a great worry'[11]), so there was a nagging sense of awkwardness that had to be overcome: 'The thing about being tall,' he would reflect, 'is that you cannot shrink into the background. And [. . .] I didn't find mixing very easy. But I discovered that by making the rest of the class laugh I could get acceptance and become rather popular.'[12] Outside of school, he spent countless hours at the movies, marvelling at the style, grace and wit of his hero, the Bristol-born Cary Grant – one of the least awkward human beings on the planet: 'Even as a boy,' he would say, 'when my pals worshipped Western movie stars such as Roy Rogers and Gene Autry or thrilled to the adventures of exotically caped comic book characters such as Superman and Batman, my idol was a suave man in a pinstripe suit. Regularly during the Nineteen-forties I would make the twenty-mile journey from my home in Weston-super-Mare to a little fleapit cinema on the outskirts of Bristol on a sort of holy pilgrimage to watch Cary Grant movies.'[13]

As an only child, Cleese continued to be somewhat cosseted by his caringly conservative parents, who would always make sure that he went out wrapped up in the appropriate combination of thick vests, woolly jumpers and warm coats, and, much to his irritation, refused to let him risk any injury by riding something quite as sensational as a bicycle: 'We were both anxious for him,' his mother later admitted. 'I suppose it was our age. We could see dangers he couldn't see.'[14] At school, however, as a contributor to school plays (such as a version of Molière's *Tartuffe*) and end-of-term revues, he acquired more confidence in himself and began to relish the chance to assume a more forceful sort of demeanour. He was still no show-off, but he was starting to make the most of his singular moments.

As a footballer, for example, he became notorious for one particular party piece, which saw him contrive to torment the opposition by drifting into a corner of the pitch and then indulge, for as long as was possible, in intricately aimless passing routines with two or three of his similarly mischievous teammates. In 1958, the school's unintentionally suggestive in-house magazine, *The Cliftonian*, reported of one such performance: 'Cleese, the self-styled schemer, has fiddled the ball, himself, his opponents and his fellow forwards into a state of neurotic frenzy!'[15]

As a cricketer, young Cleese went considerably further, playing for the school's highly competitive 1st XI and making a name for himself locally both for his exhilarating rashness as a batsman (his manic dashes between the wickets seemed designed primarily to summon up a sorry pair of run-outs) and his inscrutability as a slow off-spinner (his great height meant that his bowling arm cleared the sightscreen, making him unusually hard to 'read'). He even began to catch the eye of the national newspapers, with *The Times* including in its report on the 1957 match at Lord's between Clifton and Tonbridge an affectionate description of the 'long-legged Cleese' (who, when not indulging in his 'habit of finishing short runs on his stomach', gave 'the quaint impression of running on stilts'[16]). He attracted further coverage the following year, when, during an exhibition match on the college sports ground – The Close – in Bristol, he produced an off-spin delivery to the recently retired Middlesex and England great, Denis Compton, that was smacked straight into the hands of the waiting Ken Whitty at mid-on, thus earning the bowler the enviable line on the scorecard: 'Compton, D. C. S., c. Whitty b. Cleese, 22'.[17] (For his pains, poor Compton would end up getting a name-check in an episode of *Fawlty Towers* entitled 'The Builders': 'Well, whose fault is it then, you cloth-eared bint – *Denis Compton's??*')

After achieving three suitably sober-sounding science A-levels (in Mathematics, Chemistry and Physics) at Clifton, Cleese spent two years teaching at his old prep school, St Peter's, before entering Downing College, Cambridge, in 1960 to read Law. Sporting a newly grown, Jimmy Hill-style beard that made him look, according to a fellow fresher, 'like some weird blend between the sailor on the Players [cigarette] packets and an up-ended toothbrush',[18] he wandered back and forth through the well-manicured grounds of his bright-bricked college, sat dutifully through all of his lectures (which included regular sessions on Roman Law with R. W. M. Duff, International Law with R. Y. Jennings, Constitutional Law with E. C. S. Wade and Contract and Tort with J. A. Jolowicz), listened carefully to his tutors, put in the hours of study in the old Squire Library in Trinity Lane and kept himself on course for a decent conclusion (an Upper Second) to the first leg of his Tripos.

It was as a member of the university's Footlights Society, however, that Cleese at last found an outlet for his budding comedic talents – but only after surviving an embarrassingly inauspicious start. Keen to follow in the footsteps of the recently graduated Peter Cook (whose influence 'was so thick in the air for two or three years you could cut it with a knife'), Cleese, like many would-be entertainers, set off at the start of his first term in search of the Footlights stand at the annual Freshers' Fair: 'They said, "Well, what do you do? Do you sing? . . . Do you dance?" Well, of course, if there's anything I'm worse at than singing, it's dancing. So I said, "No," and they said, "Well, what *do* you do?" and I said, "I make people laugh" – and I blushed the colour of beetroot and ran – literally.'[19] Eventually, however, he passed an audition and soon established himself as a prominent presence at the club's HQ (based in those days on the first floor of premises secreted in the shadowy Falcon Yard, above the back of MacFisheries in an area of town known as Petty Cury[20]), collaborating with such kindred spirits as Graham Chapman, Tim Brooke-Taylor, Bill Oddie, David Hatch, Humphrey Barclay, Jo Kendall, Trevor Nunn, Tony Buffery and Miriam Margolyes on a succession of high-profile revues.

Blessed with a sharper ear than an eye for comedy – 'I'm not very good at observing people but at the end of a conversation I can remember a great deal of what they have said and probably know how their mind works. But I don't think I know what kind of person they are'[21] – Cleese started producing clever little verbal exercises that were shaped in part by the interrogatory customs of his legal training, as well as by his instinctively rigorous style of thinking. 'By the time I was halfway through my second year,' he would say, 'I was beginning to show one or two glimmerings of talent. By the time I got to my third year, I was writing some sketches that were really quite good.'[22] The best of them all was probably an ensemble piece entitled 'Judge Not' (written when he was aged twenty-one), which anticipated the kind of communication problems that would inspire so much of his later comedy:

BARRISTER: You are Arnold Fitch, alias 'Arnold Fitch'?
DEFENDANT: Yes.
BARRISTER: Why is your alias the same as your real name?
DEFENDANT: Because, when I *do* use my alias, no one would expect it to be the same as my real name.
BARRISTER: You are a company director?
DEFENDANT: Of course.
BARRISTER: Did you throw the watering can?
DEFENDANT: No.
BARRISTER: I suggest that you threw the watering can.
DEFENDANT: I did not.
BARRISTER: I put it to you that you threw the watering can.
DEFENDANT: I didn't!
BARRISTER: I submit that you threw the watering can!
DEFENDANT: No!
BARRISTER: *Did you or did you not throw the watering can?*

DEFENDANT: *I did not!*

BARRISTER: YES OR NO? DID YOU THROW THE WATERING CAN?

DEFENDANT: *No!*

BARRISTER: *ANSWER THE QUESTION!*

DEFENDANT: I – I *didn't* throw it!

BARRISTER: So – he *denies* it! Very well – would you be surprised to hear that you'd *thrown* the watering can?

DEFENDANT: Yes.

BARRISTER: And do you deny *not* throwing the watering can?

DEFENDANT: Yes.

BARRISTER: *HAH!*

DEFENDANT: NO!

BARRISTER: Very well, Mr Fitch – would it be true to say that you were lying if you denied that it was false to affirm that it belied you to deny that it was untrue that you were lying?

DEFENDANT: *Ulp* . . . Er . . .

BARRISTER: You hesitate, Mr Fitch! An answer, please – the court is waiting.

DEFENDANT: Yes!

BARRISTER: What?

DEFENDANT: Yes!

[The barrister tries desperately to work out if this is the right or the wrong answer]

BARRISTER: No further questions, m'lud.[23]

After graduating in the summer of 1963 with an eminently respectable Upper Second Class degree ('He would have made a remarkably good barrister,' recalled a contemporary. 'Those glaring eyes would have won him many a case'[24]), he abandoned plans to pursue a career at one of the City of London's most venerable law firms, Freshfields (solicitors to the Bank of England), in favour of a £1,500 per year job in BBC Radio as a trainee writer/producer (beginning by 'taking jokes out of scripts that were too gaggy',[25] before writing his own material for the likes of Brian Rix and Terry Scott – a seasonal special called *Yule Be Surprised* – Dick Emery and Deryck Guyler – a series entitled *Emery At Large* – and Ronnie Barker and Cyril Fletcher – for a series called *Not To Worry* – as well as contributing the odd line to television's first satirical current affairs show, *That Was The Week That Was*).

Within a few months, however, he had taken leave from the BBC to rejoin his former Footlights colleagues in the West End for a version of their final university revue, *A Clump of Plinths*, now under the new title of *Cambridge Circus*. The production proved popular enough to prompt a six-week summer tour of New Zealand, where Cleese first experienced spectacularly poor service on a daily basis: 'The New Zealanders, in those days, were a little bit out to lunch and almost nothing in New Zealand worked. The only thing was, because they were New Zealanders, they'd never been anywhere where things did work. So, if you criticised them, they thought you were mad!'[26]

After the short stay in New Zealand, however, came an offer to visit the United States of America. At the start of October 1964, the company embarked on a run in New York – first, for twenty-three performances, at the Plymouth Theatre on Broadway (where a critic for the *New York Times* judged the cast 'engaging' and 'appealing' while wishing that 'the level of their material was consistently higher'[27]), and then, for the remainder of the year, at a cosier café theatre on West Fourth Street in Greenwich Village (where another, more contented critic reported that 'John Cleese dominated some of the skits with a talent for portraying innate cruelty'[28]).

It was while Cleese was in America that he first met the

woman who would become his wife: Connie Booth. Born in Indianapolis in 1944, Booth – the daughter of a wealthy Wall Street magnate and a frustrated actor – had grown up in New Rochelle, New York, in a Celtic-American household that was as raw and raucous as Cleese's had been refined and repressed. So loud were some of the shouting matches between her mother and her father that, on more than one occasion, the police had been summoned to restrain them. 'My family was given to affection and anger and it was expressed with less restraint than in England,' Booth would recall. 'You could easily get smacked or spanked.'[29] Her mother, however, encouraged her early ambition to act, and Connie first trod the boards at the age of fourteen in junior high school; by the time that she was nineteen, she had started to attract a small measure of attention as one of New York theatre's many budding talents, even though she was still working mainly as a waitress to support her nascent career.

It was in November 1964, while she was combining her waitressing chores with a stint as an understudy in a Broadway show, that she first encountered John Cleese. He was dining with friends at a Second Avenue café (styled to resemble an upmarket brothel) called The Living Room, and she – dressed, or rather *un*dressed, in the obligatory staff 'uniform' of a black leotard with fishnet tights – was busy serving the clientele. He barely muttered to her when she first came to his table (in spite of the fact that she gave him an extra-large helping of fruit salad), but, when he returned for a second visit a few nights later, they struck up a conversation (about, amongst other things, Virginia Woolf) and he invited her to see him perform on stage.

She went, was impressed, and then joined him for supper after the show. 'It was our mutual lack of self-confidence that drew us together,' Cleese would recall.[30] 'He was so articulate and funny and I felt overwhelmed and intimidated,' Booth reflected. 'I felt out of his league – but I did make him laugh now and again.'[31] They made for an odd-looking couple: she was a slender, pretty, fine-boned five-foot-three-inch woman with ash-blonde hair and cornflower-blue eyes, and he was a skinny, six-foot-five-inch black-haired, greeny-brown-eyed man who resembled, as one journalist put it, 'a professional pall-bearer hooked on embalming fluid'.[32] A connection, however, had been made, and an intense relationship commenced.

Cleese proposed to Booth, he would later say, 'more or less immediately', but 'failed miserably'.[33] She panicked, particularly when he mentioned he might end up swapping show business for the Foreign Service: 'I thought that would be the end, marrying a diplomat.'[34] Undeterred, Cleese, when his *Cambridge Circus* colleagues returned to England soon after the start of 1965, stayed on in America, touring for six months as the upper-class twit 'Young Walsingham' in a US production of the Tommy Steele musical *Half A Sixpence*, followed by a short spell on the political desk at *Newsweek* and then a similarly brief period as part of a touring company of satirists from Peter Cook's London Establishment Club, while, in his spare time, he continued to pursue Connie Booth. Although lured back to Britain at the end of the year to start work on several new writing projects, the courtship continued back and forth across the Atlantic.

Cleese started writing for, and performing in, *The Frost Report* (BBC 1, 1966–7), *The Frost Programme* (ITV, 1966–8), *I'm Sorry I'll Read That Again* (BBC Radio, 1964–73) and *At Last the 1948 Show* (ITV, 1967–8 – the show, featuring Cleese, Graham Chapman, Tim Brooke-Taylor and Marty Feldman, that was responsible for such memorable sketches as 'The Four Yorkshiremen'). Booth, meanwhile, continued to struggle to find acting jobs in and around New York, and kept on filling up her free days with waitressing. Eventually, however, the bond between them proved too strong, and the periods apart too painful, for the procrastination to continue: he proposed once again, and this time she accepted. The couple finally married on 20 February 1968, and she gave up her New York-based career to come to live with him in London (initially in a flat next to Harrods in Basil Street before moving a few years later into a more capacious modern townhouse development at Woodsford Square in Holland Park).

This was an increasingly busy period professionally for Cleese. Apart from teaming up in 1969 with Graham Chapman, Michael Palin, Terry Jones, Eric Idle and Terry Gilliam on television to make *Monty Python's Flying Circus*, he was also contributing to several movie screenplays (including Terry Southern's 1969 social satire *The Magic Christian*, and Peter Cook's 1970 political satire *The Rise and Rise of Michael Rimmer*) and acting in a few big-screen projects as well (including minor roles in the 1968 romantic-drama *Interlude*, Denis Norden's 1969 Victorian satire *The Best House in London* and the awkwardly *à la mode* 1970 David Niven comedy *The Statue*) – and he was already earning enough money to have treated himself to a smart second-hand Bentley S3 and several other eye-catching investments. He was also already sufficiently popular with the more youthful sections of the viewing audience to beat the likes of the writer and broadcaster Alistair Cooke, the astronomer Patrick Moore and the actor Derek Nimmo to being elected Rector of the University of St Andrews in 1970,[35] and well-known enough more generally to be invited on to BBC Radio 4's *Desert Island Discs* the following year (his choices included

Elgar's 'Nimrod', Groucho Marx's 'Show Me a Rose' and Tchaikovsky's 'Romeo and Juliet Fantasy Overture', as well as a book of recipes by Vincent Price and, as his luxury, 'a life-sized *papier-mâché* model of Margaret Thatcher, and a baseball bat'[36]).

Cleese's career was therefore now definitely on the ascent, and Connie Booth was soon drawn into his professional orbit. Between 1969 and 1974, for example, she was sometimes to be seen playing minor roles (such as Michael Palin's disappointed girlfriend in the lumberjack sketch and song) in certain episodes of *Monty Python's Flying Circus*, and she also joined some of the team for the odd live revue. In 1974, she and Cleese co-wrote and co-starred in the delightful forty-minute movie short, *Romance with a Double Bass* – an adaptation of a story by Anton Chekhov about a humble musician and a beautiful princess (both of whom respond to a hot summer's afternoon by skinny-dipping in a secluded lake, only to have their clothes stolen by a passing thief, thus causing the musician to attempt to smuggle the princess back into her castle by hiding her in the case of his double bass).[37] There was even an attempt to collaborate on a pilot script for a television thriller[38] which, even though it came to naught after a couple of months of struggle, encouraged both of them to remain open to new ideas.

There was, however, a crisis on the horizon: Cleese was becoming more and more irritable and depressed. *Monty Python*, he felt, was part of the problem. It was still building a large audience (both in the UK and abroad[39]), and (responding to what Michael Palin noted somewhat uneasily was 'a comfortably receptive market'[40]) was also branching out with books, albums and theatre tours, but it was grinding Cleese down. Tired of having all of his writing edited by a committee, unhappy with what he saw as a general decline in standards ('I was only happy with five out of the last fifty or so sketches,' he would say. 'The rest were sausage machine – permutations and combinations of old stuff'[41]) and dismayed by the increasingly fractious internal politics ('It was like the history of the Balkans – millions of alliances, constantly breaking up and reforming'[42]), Cleese declared that he wanted out. He was three or four years older than most of the other Pythons, with a longer career in television, and, as Michael Palin acknowledged at the time, 'He's ahead of us in the disillusionment stakes.'[43]

Monty Python, as a television series, was definitely undermined by his leaving. The critic Alan Coren, for example, mourned his absence at the start of the following series in the autumn of 1974, lamenting the loss of 'that rock-founded maypole of manic sanity around which the lesser madmen danced and who was an iron control, both on the screen and behind it, upon the daft extravagances to which the others are prone and which can lead to the ultimate dissipation of a good funny idea'[44] – and the show petered out after a shorter-than-usual (six-episode) run. From Cleese's perspective, however, the decision helped prevent him from going completely 'potty'.[45]

The split allowed him to stand back and reflect on the other possible factors that were responsible for dragging him down. 'Life seemed almost pointless. I felt very cut off from everything – including my body,' he said.[46] For long periods during each of the past two or three years, for example, he had been suffering from nagging flu-like symptoms that had undermined his spirits. 'Like a good public school chap,' he would say, 'I assumed [the condition came from] physical causes and had it checked out a couple of times by all the specialists and they could find nothing wrong. Then, to my astonishment, a very nice Australian doctor had me fully checked out physically and then suggested afterwards it might have a psychological/psychosomatic basis.'[47] Although alarmed, initially, by such a suggestion – 'I was very rigid, very Weston-super-Mare,' he would later say of himself at this stage in his life. 'I had a very British attitude towards therapy. Couldn't see what it would achieve'[48] – he ended up acting on the advice of a friend and went to see a psychiatrist, Robin Skynner, and joined the psychotherapy group that Skynner ran with his wife, Prue, every Thursday afternoon in his rooms at Montagu Mansions.

The therapy sessions helped, but so, too, did the greater freedom he now had to write the kinds of things, in the kinds of ways, that he wanted. Having deconstructed conventions with *Python* until the deconstruction itself became a new convention ('I'm fed up with having to turn up at eight a.m. on Monday morning on Wakefield railway station dressed as a penguin'[49]), Cleese wanted to create something more obviously substantial with his comedy craft. 'There comes a time,' he would later explain, 'when it's much more satisfying to work on something with a storyline and real characters.'[50] He had enjoyed the experience of 'huddling together for warmth' with his five old colleagues and 'producing a new style of television humour' (on the periphery, relatively speaking, 'at odd times, with few viewers around'), but he now relished the challenge of producing something equally worthwhile within the mainstream.[51] What he most wanted to write next, he decided, was a genuinely top-quality peak-time comedy.

Cleese had spent his childhood loving the sort of comedies that boasted that kind of decent mass appeal: home-grown radio shows such as *Take It From Here, Ray's A Laugh* and *The Frankie Howerd Show*, and star-vehicles from the US featuring the likes of

Jack Benny, Fred Allen, Groucho Marx and the husband-and-wife double act of George Burns and Gracie Allen, as well as such hugely popular television series as *The Army Game*, *Early To Braden* and *The Phil Silvers Show*. Although, therefore, he always adored the invention, imagination, irreverence and sheer audacity of Spike Milligan's writing for *The Goon Show*, he had also grown up revering the rigour, realism, richness and sensitivity of Ray Galton and Alan Simpson's scripts for *Hancock's Half-Hour* and *Steptoe and Son*. Recalling, for example, how keenly each new episode of *Hancock* had been anticipated, he later remarked: 'Say it went out on Friday: you began to think about it on Sunday night – you'd think, "Ooh, there'll be another *Hancock* on Friday!" I think, probably to a greater extent than almost any other comedy show I can remember, people arranged their week round *Hancock*.'[52] It was that same very special combination of high quality and broad appeal that Cleese now hoped to achieve.

He wanted to achieve it via a collaboration with his wife, Connie Booth. His previous writing partnership, with Graham Chapman, had grown increasingly fraught and unbalanced over the course of the decade or so that they had shared since coming together at Cambridge. Although the union had quickly established a distinctive and effective style – 'Our sketches would consist of people coming on and abusing each other out of thesauruses,' said Cleese. 'We both would find abuse very, very funny and we loved people arguing and fighting and being rude to each other'[53] – certain tensions developing within had ended up diminishing the quality, as well as the quantity, of their joint output. Barry Cryer, who knew and worked with both of them, described their respective approaches to the actual business of crafting a script: Cleese, he said, was methodical, disciplined and fastidious ('John wants to start at page one, and start going line by line, word by word'), whereas Chapman was far more mercurial and intuitive (when told during a short stay in Germany that a scheduled visit to Dachau clashed with 'early closing day' at the camp, he shouted out, 'Tell them we're Jewish'[54]), as well as prone to numerous booze-induced distractions ('Graham would pace about, light his pipe and twiddle his sideburns and gaze out of the window and say: "Oooh, they're open!" in the quaint old days when you waited for the pub to open. "Oooh, shall we have an early one?" Graham used to say, and I'd think: Oh, boy, there goes the day . . .').[55] By the early 1970s, Cleese, though still extremely fond of Chapman as a friend, had grown tired of thinking, as his co-writer, 'there goes the day', and was looking forward to forming a much steadier and more reliable partnership with Connie Booth.

Ironically, however, it was only after their marriage had started to founder that their writing partnership started to flourish. Booth had come to feel, by her own admission, increasingly aimless and peripheral as she watched her husband and his fellow Pythons ascend to ever greater heights of fame while she remained at home caring for their baby daughter, Cynthia (who was born in 1971). 'I just didn't have the incentive to go out and start a new career all over again,' she would reflect. 'I felt very out of things.'[56] Cleese, meanwhile, had come to feel more and more burdened by the sense of having to live up to other people's expectations, and had grown progressively edgier and more aloof: 'My worst fault,' he would say, 'is that if I get stressed I very much turn inwards. I lose my sense of humour and tighten up. People around me say that I just cut myself off from them, and that's probably what happened with Connie.'[57] Problems within their marriage had begun to become apparent to others as early as the summer of 1973, when Cleese joined the rest of the *Monty Python* troupe on a short tour of Canada. '[H]e was just so unfriendly to everyone,' Carol Cleveland, the Pythons' solitary female regular, would recall. 'I hadn't realised quite what was going on with him until we got there and I was taking it personally at first – I thought, "Oh, no, he doesn't like me any more, what have I done?" And they were, "No, Carol, he's going through one of the questioning periods in his life," like what's life all about, and of course he was going through his [difficulties] with Connie.'[58] Cleese would later confirm how much of a struggle it was: 'I remember looking into a black abyss that was terrifying. It was a very painful period and I had about two-and-a-half years of being depressed a lot of the time.'[59]

Tensions between the couple had tended to undermine the odd attempt to collaborate at any length on a script, but, after a trial separation was reluctantly agreed (with Cleese temporarily moving out of their Woodsford Square home and into a rented apartment about five minutes away in Hyde Park Gardens), the pair found that, whenever they had reason to meet and talk about their respective ideas, the atmosphere was reassuringly amicable. An emotional weight seemed to have been lifted from their shoulders: they no longer lived so easily together, but now they could write together surprisingly well. It was a bitter-sweet discovery, but it offered a way forward that, professionally at least, was simply too propitious for either of them to resist.

Booth, felt Cleese, had the potential to be as inspired, in her own way, as Graham Chapman had been when sober. Her strengths seemed to complement his strengths. 'She's enormously fertile with funny ideas,' Cleese would say. 'Only Michael Palin compares with her for funny ideas. I'm good at the carpentry, saying, "let's shift that line up, move that section down a bit". I take a script along obvious lines, moving towards farce, but Connie stops me from doing the obvious.'[60] Booth, in turn, valued Cleese's relentlessness and rigour: 'I'm all over the place. John ties [all of the ideas] up. We know at once what the good lines are. We hear them like hearing the same music.'[61] It seemed, they agreed, an excellent partnership for shaping a comedy project that was witty and intelligent as well as attractive and accessible.

The BBC, eager to keep hold of John Cleese post-*Python*, was happy to encourage such an ambition. A lunch was arranged at a West London restaurant called The Gun Room, and Cleese agreed to attend. He recalled: 'I went and talked to Jimmy Gilbert, who was the Head of Light Entertainment, and I said that I'd like to do something with Connie. And he said, "Fine, come back with an idea." And I went back to Connie and said, "They'd like us to do a pilot, what shall we do?" '[62] The two of them spent about twenty minutes or so weighing up and evaluating a variety of formats and themes ('We soon decided that it was pointless doing sort of Mike Nichols and Elaine May,' Cleese later explained, 'because [Eleanor] Bron and [John] Fortune had already done it better. There was no point in trying revue stuff because Python was obviously superior'[63]) before they settled on the idea of writing a sitcom.

It was quite a brave decision, in a way, because, in the mid-1970s, British television seemed close to saturation point with sitcoms. In 1973 alone, for example, the likes of *Porridge*,[64] *Some Mothers Do 'Ave 'Em*,[65] *Man About the House*,[66] *Last of the Summer Wine*,[67] *Whoops Baghdad*,[68] *Open All Hours*[69] and *Whatever Happened to the Likely Lads?*[70] had all made their debut, and they would soon be joined by *It Ain't Half Hot Mum*, *Rising*

Damp and *No Honestly* (in, respectively, January, September and October, 1974) and *The Good Life* (in April 1975). When Cleese and Booth proposed their idea of creating a sitcom of their own, therefore, there were already more than fifty home-grown examples of the genre (as well as several foreign imports) currently being shown at peak time on British screens. It was thus the most competitive market in comedy, but, nonetheless, Cleese and Booth still felt that they could come up with something new that was good enough, and different enough, to make a noticeable mark.

The idea could not be developed much further until after Cleese had completed filming a movie – *Monty Python and the Holy Grail* (shot in Scotland, through wind, rain and snow, at the start of 1974) – and pondered on some possibilities while indulging in his new-found passion for lightly chilled white Burgundies. Once the shoot was over and he was reunited with Booth back in London, however, the notion of a sitcom was all that he, like she, had in mind. The challenge was increasingly exciting, and the project was definitely on.

Their particular brand of sitcom, they agreed, would assimilate the form of the farce. 'I've always had a tremendous love of farce,' Cleese later explained, 'because what I like to do more than anything else is to really laugh. The essence of farce is almost always that some kind of taboo has been transgressed and the protagonist has to cover up. So he does one lie to cover up the first. As he seems to get caught out in that lie, he has to switch to a slightly different lie and then to a third until you just get bogged down in worse and worse degrees of lying.'[71]

The work of Feydeau, the classic *farceur par excellence*, was the most obvious inspiration, because of the exceptionally springy logic of his intricately choreographed plots; always aware of the

44

need to make the comedy credible, he took care to create believable characters, placed in realistic situations, before allowing – via a web of interconnections that were triggered like tripwires – the chaos to commence. 'While I am organising those lunacies which will unleash hilarity in the audience,' the playwright explained with a coolness that was bound to strike a chord with Cleese, 'I am not myself amused by them, but rather maintain the calm, serious demeanour of a chemist preparing a medicine. Into my little pill I introduce a gramme of *imbroglio*, a gramme of libertinage, a gramme of observation. I then mix these elements together, to the best of my ability, and can predict almost exactly the effect they will produce.'[72] In Feydeau's *A Flea In Her Ear*, for example, each character is given a good, credible reason to begin his or her inexorable descent into delirium: a suspicious wife discovers something that appears to cast doubt on her husband's fidelity; desperate to catch him, she responds by arranging for a friend to fabricate a letter from an admirer inviting him to a seductive-sounding assignation; the husband, flattered but actually faithful, donates the letter to a suitably lascivious man who secretly craves the chance to cuckold him; he, in turn, boasts by showing the letter to another hot-blooded male friend, who immediately recognises the handwriting to be that of his own wife – and then all of the characters converge on a seedy hotel, where identities are confused and intentions mistaken but all of the nonsense makes sense.

It was this kind of carefully paced, cleverly crafted farce that Cleese, and Booth, were now so keen to create: a plausible progression from a reasonably realistic calm to an eminently imaginable comic hell. 'The thing is that everything has to happen in an exaggerated way,' said Cleese. 'So although you may start it quite low key and quite real, it kind of winds up, and people get more and more frantic, trying to keep the frantic feelings in and present some sort of calm façade to someone they have to impress. What I love is the intensity and the emotion because with that comes more frantic behaviour, more energy and the possibility of huge laughs.'[73] This was what Cleese and Booth's new sitcom would seek to convey.

Their first task was to decide on the driving force of their comical fiction. 'Connie is good on character,' Cleese would say, 'so we looked for a good character to base [the sitcom] on.'[74] It did not take them long to recall the extraordinary real-life character of the dreaded hotelier Donald Sinclair. Having already had something of a 'run-out' on screen as the dyspeptic little misanthrope in *Doctor At Large*, it was clear that there was still plenty of comic mileage in the figure of the eccentric Sinclair – particularly when paired with his bossy and sharp-tongued wife, Betty. Renaming them 'Basil' and 'Sybil' (the choice was inspired by a conversation with a mutual friend of the co-writers, the movie editor Julian Doyle, who had recently mentioned an odd elderly middle-class couple bearing those archaic-sounding names, who were still serving as sub-scription collectors for a branch of the Communist Party of Great Britain in Tufnell Park and Camden Town[75]), Cleese and Booth started to assume control over the two characters, revising them so as to maximise their comedic potential. Basil's explosiveness, for example, was nudged up a notch or three ('Connie and I have always had a thing about people who can't suppress their rage – which neither of us can,' Cleese would acknowledge. 'There was a certain part of me in Basil and a certain part of my father, and I suppose a certain part of Connie, too'[76]) and Sybil's sarcasm was invested with a far sharper style of wit.

46

Imitation gave way to creation, and the characters began to breathe, think, feel and interact. With a full six weeks (as opposed to the far more usual two) devoted to the shaping of each script, the two co-writers (sitting side-by-side at a desk in an upstairs room, with Booth scribbling on a notepad and Cleese poised over a typewriter) had the time to explore and examine each figure, finding more things, from draft to draft, to make them easier to believe in, care about and enjoy. The sense of excitement and adventure was, as a consequence, intense. It all seemed so right. It all seemed so real.

The character of Basil, in particular, could quite conceivably have been relocated to an office, a school, a shop, a bank, a political party or a restaurant, amongst a wide range of other possibilities, because, as Cleese would later say, 'Everybody knows somebody who acts like Basil Fawlty when they're under pressure.'[77] The original idea of the hotel, however, still seemed like an inspired choice as a context for the comedy, not only because it kept the central character more or less rooted to the spot, but also because it made it so much easier to keep each episode fairly fresh and relatively surprising: 'You can have almost anyone you want walk in,' said Cleese, 'and you don't have to try and find an explanation.'[78] It also offered something that all good sitcoms required: familiarity. 'If you're in a hotel,' Cleese explained, 'everyone knows what it's like to walk up to a front desk, everyone knows what it's like if someone's casual or rude or overattentive. Everyone's ordered meals in restaurants, everyone's come out the door of their room and wondered where the bathroom is – this sort of thing. Everybody knows what's going on, you don't have to set anything up, you don't have to explain anything.'[79]

The decision to keep Basil's hotel, like Sinclair's hotel, based in Torquay was mainly due to what the town said to Cleese about the provincial English milieu of his youth that still seemed to persist. 'I grew up in a place that was like a small version of Torquay,' he would later explain. 'I grew up in Weston-super-Mare, and I knew that slightly sleepy, rather polite, slightly respectable seaside atmosphere.'[80] The typical kind of English people who lived in such places, Cleese observed, seemed imprisoned within their own shared sense of propriety: '[T]hey can't say, "I'm sorry, this is foolish, not good enough," or, "I bought this pair of shoes and want you to replace it." Because they can't do these simple acts of self-assertion, they tend to develop on the surface a kind of brittle politeness and underneath a lot of seething rage. And I think that that was one of the reasons why they could identify with Basil, also find him funny and, at the same time, quite like him.'[81]

Donald Sinclair's frantic antics at the Gleneagles in Torquay provided the two writers with an immediate repository of incidents upon which certain scenes and even whole episodes could be built, but then other memories of poor service came into play – such as the stay at the hotel in Oxford when, following a fairly boozy evening spent at Merton College, John Cleese's scheduled nine o'clock alarm call came three-and-a-half hours early, at 5.30 a.m., followed – just as he was drifting back off to sleep – by a second call to apologise for the first; and the occasion at another establishment when, following several un- wanted interruptions, Cleese put a 'DO NOT DISTURB' sign on his door, stripped down to his underpants and finally started to relax – only to be interrupted five minutes later by a puzzled-looking young bellhop, who pointed at the sign and asked, 'Is this *supposed* to be out here?'; and the visit to the hotel in St Andrews where, on a night when all six floors of the establishment happened to be empty, Cleese and a colleague were asked aggressively, 'Have ye *booked?*' Then further memories arose of other square pegs rammed into other round holes – such as the BBC programme planner who stormed out of a conference at Broadcasting House muttering, 'If we didn't have to do all these bloody *programmes* all the time we could really run this place *properly!*'[82] It also helped that Connie Booth, drawing on her waitressing days in New York, could contribute so many funny and eye-opening anecdotes of dealing with rude, over-demanding and downright irrational customers as well as bumbling and boorish employers.

A crafty reconnaissance trip to Torquay, however, proved an unexpected disappointment: when Cleese arrived back at the Gleneagles, primed and ready to resume his spying on the dreaded Sinclairs, he was disappointed to discover that the couple had recently sold up and departed to Florida, leaving the hotel in the hands of a new owner who was, alas, 'kind and efficient' and 'the opposite of Basil'.[83] The visit did not turn out to be entirely without reward: the amiable successor to the Sinclairs, Pat Phillips, sat down and told Cleese several funny and evocative tales about his own experiences at this and other establishments, including an anecdote or two about a rather incompetent Spanish waiter with whom he had worked (and often clashed) while managing another hotel in Shropshire.

Back at Connie Booth's base in London, thoughts of various cool and calming members of staff inspired the emergence of the chambermaid Polly – an invaluable confidante for Basil, as well adjusted as he is neurotic, and a kind of 'straight-woman' for everyone else. Similarly, stories of numerous bumbling waiters suggested the need for someone like Manuel – part cause and part effect of the comical anarchy. The character was made a foreigner, Cleese would later explain, mainly because that was simply what most of them, in those days, seemed to be: 'If you went into most [British] restaurants at that time – the 1970s – you were very, very lucky if you got what you'd ordered, because almost none of the waiters could either understand or speak English. Now, that was not *their* fault – this is very important – it was the fault of the owners who were saving money.'[84] Back in the summer of 1970, for example, when Cleese and the other Pythons had been staying in Torquay, there had been an Hungarian waiter called Alex Novak, working just up the road from the Gleneagles at another hotel called The Links, whom the comedians had witnessed making routine errors, misunderstanding basic orders and mispronouncing such words as 'architect' so as to sound like 'heart attack'.[85] It was much the same when Cleese dined out in London: sooner or later the act of ordering evolved into a tiresome game of charades. Cleese went on to make Manuel Spanish 'because most of them seemed to me to be from Spain',[86] and he and Booth gave him such a pleasant disposition to purify all of the comedy: 'If he was sullen, or didn't want to be helpful, or sabotage Basil, it wouldn't be funny. It's the fact that he's desperately trying to help, and still messing up, that makes it funny.'[87]

Memories of several eccentric old semi-permanent guests – merged with the much more specific memory by John Cleese of his old Latin tutor at prep school, Captain Lancaster (whose over-excited readings from *Three Men in a Boat* had made his youthful audience shake with silent laughter) – gave rise to the Old Worldly, newspaper-needy, cricket-loving Major Gowen, as well as to a couple of elderly little spinsters named Miss Tibbs and Miss Gatsby (who were more sharply drawn and substantial versions of the peripheral characters Cleese had included for the 'hotel' episode he had written earlier for *Doctor At Large*).

Each reminiscence formed another precious fragment of the

fictional world of Fawlty. The creation of the various inhabi-
tants, however, commenced on lines distinctly gendered. John
Cleese concentrated on developing the male characters, while
Connie Booth busied herself with the female characters, then
each edited the other. 'I'd sometimes suggest lines for Sybil,'
Cleese would say, 'and Connie would say, "Oh no, no, a
woman would never say that." ' Once all of the basic personae
had been established, the division of labour grew much more
flexible: 'Gradually,' said Cleese, 'Connie started to write more
Basil and I wrote more Sybil, and we co-operated more and
more on all the characters.'[88] The process, though hard work,
proved a pleasure: 'Sometimes,' Cleese would recall, 'we just
laughed until the tears ran down our cheeks.'[89]

The sitcom was now being written. The next step would see
it being cast.

3

A Higher Class of Clientele

I should never have let you write that advert.
Fancy putting 'No riff-raff'!

Not all great sitcoms reach the screen with most of their key first choices still present and comedically correct. *Dad's Army*, for example, tried and failed to persuade first Thorley Walters and then Jon Pertwee to play the character of the pompous Captain Mainwaring before settling, very wisely, upon Arthur Lowe to bring him to life (and Corporal Jones could have been played by Jack Haig or David Jason before Clive Dunn finally signed on the dotted line).[1] Similarly, Warren Mitchell was only given the opportunity to make the part of Alf Garnett in *Till Death Us Do Part* his own after Peter Sellers, Leo McKern and Lionel Jeffries had dropped out of contention (and the sublimely subtle comic actor Dandy Nichols only took on the role of Alf's long-suffering wife, Else, after Gretchen Franklyn, who had played the character in the pilot episode, dropped out before the first full series was filmed).[2] *Fawlty Towers*, however, was one of the more fortunate few, because all but one of those who were asked would say: 'Yes'.

Commissioned officially on 23 January 1975,[3] the first person to commit himself to the new show was not actually a performer at all, but rather a top-class producer/director: John Howard Davies. A former child actor (playing, amongst other roles, the juvenile lead in David Lean's classic 1948 adaptation of Charles Dickens' *Oliver Twist* and the eponymous young hero in the 1951 version of *Tom Brown's Schooldays*), Davies already had an impressive track record as a programme-maker that, as far as comedy shows were concerned, encompassed everything from the conventional sitcom *All Gas and Gaiters* to the strikingly unconventional *Monty Python's Flying Circus*,[4] and was thoroughly trusted by John Cleese (who regarded him as 'a very, very good judge of comedy'[5]). From the moment that he first took home a sample script of the new show to read, he felt that *Fawlty Towers* was going to be something very special indeed. 'I fell out of bed laughing,' he said, 'and was subsequently banned from reading the script at home. It was just so good.'[6]

Once Davies had agreed to oversee the project, the actual casting of each part could commence. Like any other experienced producer, he had access to a good range of trusted contacts, as well as to an unofficial repertory of trusted talents, so he was confident of coming up with several shrewd and practicable suggestions. He was also keen to collaborate with Cleese and Booth, sounding them out to assess their general preferences and then keeping them briefed about each subsequent stage of the casting process.

It was, ironically, the role of Basil Fawlty himself that turned out to pose the most obvious, and immediate, problem for casting. The problem had to do with the height of the man upon whom the character had been modelled. 'In the best traditions of English comedy,' John Cleese would recall, '[Donald Sinclair] was extremely small and his wife was extremely large and she ran him and he ran the hotel.'[7] This little man/big woman dynamic worked so well that, when Cleese first came to fictionalise the relationship for the episode of *Doctor At Large*, the roles were cast accordingly, with the five-foot-eleven-inch Eunice Black playing opposite the diminutive Timothy Bateson, who was barely a fraction above five foot six. When it came to casting *Fawlty Towers*, however, the ratio had to be reversed, because (although the role had been envisaged originally for 'someone like Denholm Elliott'[8]) the six-foot-five-inch John Cleese now wanted to play Basil himself, so Sybil was obliged to shrink.

The person chosen to play her, initially, was the suitably petite Bridget Turner, who was appearing at the time on stage in the West End of London, playing opposite Tom Courtenay as his wife, Ruth, in the original production of Alan Ayckbourn's comic trilogy *The Norman Conquests*. An accomplished graduate (in a company that also included Ian McKellen) of Coventry's Belgrade Theatre in the early 1960s, the critics had described her as 'grimly censorious' in her current role of a brisk career woman enduring an exasperating marriage to a lascivious assistant librarian,[9] and she struck the watching Cleese, Booth and Davies as an actor who was more than capable of intimidating poor Basil. When the offer to play Sybil was made, however, she replied that, having read the pilot script, she did not find the material very funny ('She didn't understand it,' Davies would later reveal. 'She said she thought it was "an apple pie script"'[10]), and therefore passed on the chance to take part.

A number of other actors were then, briefly, considered – only, for one reason or another, to end up being crossed off Davies's original shortlist of fifteen possible Sybils. 'I can't actually remember all of their names now,' he would later say, 'but I did give each one some consideration, without going so far as to send them a script or make them an offer. Then, however, I came to one – quite some way down the list actually – who, when I thought about it again, struck me as though she would really be a very good idea indeed.'[11]

The second person to actually be offered the role, therefore, was Prunella Scales, an extremely versatile and intelligent performer who was not only the right height – five foot three and a half inches – but also the right type: attractive and elegant, but with an ability to slip up and down the social ladder without any sign of strain or stress. Born Prunella Margaret Rumney Illingworth in Sutton Abinger, Surrey, in 1932, she had been an actor since 1951 (taking her mother Catherine's maiden name of Scales for the stage), and her career had encompassed work in theatre, movies, radio and television, appearing in everything from Greek tragedy to French farce, as well as children's drama series (appearing as Martha in the BBC's 1960 adaptation of *The Secret Garden*), soaps (as the bus conductress Eileen Hughes in *Coronation Street* during 1962) and sitcoms (co-starring with Richard Briers in *Marriage Lines*, the very popular show about the ups and downs experienced by a young husband and wife, for five series between 1963 and 1966). It was John Howard Davies – a long-time admirer of her performances – who first suggested her for the role of Sybil (believing that she would be perfect to play a woman who, as he put it, 'could make love and paint her fingernails at the same time'[12]), and, although neither John Cleese nor Connie Booth knew her personally, both writers knew and liked her work and were therefore encouragingly quick to concur.

Davies duly made contact and sent Scales a sample script, and then arranged for her to visit Cleese at his flat in Hyde Park Gardens, where he was recovering in bed from a bad cold. 'Did you like the scripts?' he croaked. 'I think they're brilliant,' she replied. 'Any questions?' he asked. She nodded and said, 'Well, yes: why did they get married?' Half laughing and half groaning, he wrapped a pillow around his head and replied, 'Oh God, I was afraid you'd ask me that.'[13] Although the answer was not forthcoming, she still agreed, happily, to play the part. She already had her own ideas about Sybil.

Having asked herself the usual key questions – 'Who is this person? Where do they come from? Who are their parents?' – and found a voice that seemed to suit – 'I've found that if you get the accent right and the speech patterns, you very often find things underneath the surface' – Scales felt that she was on the way to understanding this person.[14] 'I don't know how [Cleese and Booth] had seen Sybil,' she would later say, 'but I think it was my idea that she was a cut below [Basil] socially – not very well educated, but ambitious, and very careful about her speech. What she had fallen for was Basil's "poshness", and he had fallen for her because she was attractive in a blowsy kind of way.'[15] A more detailed background story was very soon dreamed up: 'I had this fantasy that her parents had been in catering – they'd run a small hotel in Eastbourne or somewhere like that on the South Coast – and so Sybil had grown up in that sort of environment. She probably met Basil when he went for a drink in a local pub where she was doing bar duty, and they'd seen each other and somehow something had clicked. He had his demob money, you know, and all of these fantastic ideas about running his own hotel; she knew the business from the inside, and liked the sound of his plans, so she went along with it all. Then, some time later, all kinds of things started going wrong . . .'[16] As for why the relationship evolved in the peculiar way that it did, Scales worked hard until she arrived at an explanation that at least made some sort of sense to her: 'I think that Sybil's trouble was that, having married out of her class and been fooled by Fawlty's flannel, she has realised, too late, that she has been landed with an upper-class twit for a husband. Whereupon the rot sets in, because he has all these posh and potty ideas about how to run a hotel, and she feels she has a great deal more practical experience and know-how. But behind all of Sybil's apparent disenchantment with Basil, there is still some – just enough – real affection for him, and that is probably what makes her stay.'[17]

Having put together a past for Sybil, Scales also pieced together a particular 'look'. In came the elaborate vortex-style hair, the mildly extravagant make-up and the chichi clothes: 'I think that was probably my idea, yes. I think Sybil saw herself as a "stylish" woman with "sophisticated" hairdos. And she was the type who would have done it all herself – she wouldn't have gone anywhere "fancy". She would have taught herself how to do it – or so she thought. And Basil, of course, didn't really care – he didn't pay any attention to this. He wanted to have his wonderful hotel, of course, but I don't think he had any special ideas about her and her presentation. So she was left to get on with it – and she did.'[18] As for Sybil's extraordinary rattling, gurgling, cackling laugh, Scales summoned it up from a vague theatrical memory: 'I can't really remember, but I think it may have been someone I'd heard laughing in an audience some-where. It just struck me as right for this character.'[19]

Neither Cleese nor Booth, initially, had seen Sybil as being quite like this creature, but, as they stood back and watched Scales start working her way into the part, they warmed to such a thoughtful and vivid reinterpretation. '[W]e were a little du-bious after the first day's rehearsal – it wasn't what we were expecting,' Cleese later confirmed. 'We wondered if it was working. By the second day we realised that the choices Pru was making were very good and probably worked better than what we had in mind. I can't remember now what we *did* have in mind.'[20]

With the two central characters now cast, attention turned to the selection of the supporting players. Connie Booth had already earmarked the role of Polly Sherman – the part-time philosophy student and chambermaid/waitress – for herself, so, in this case, no real decision was needed. Young, sensible and efficient, the character was conceived as a kind of symbol of stability in an otherwise unstable world, as well as something of a confidante to the embattled Basil ('the Horatio,' Cleese would say, 'to my Hamlet'[21]), and Booth thus knew exactly how best to play her. She also knew, as a writer, how valuable the character would be as a catalyst for exposition, soliciting and receiving information that would assist the viewer in appreciating each new situation ('What are you doing?' 'Where are you going?' 'What should we do?') and tying together the various threads of the plot ('But Mr Fawlty . . .'). Having Booth play Polly, therefore, made perfect sense on every level.

Casting the role of the comically incompetent Spanish waiter, Manuel, was, as it turned out, almost as straightforward. John Cleese agreed with John Howard Davies that there was only one choice for the top of the list: none other than an actor called Andrew Sachs.

Born in Berlin in 1930 (but, following threats to the safety of his Jewish father, brought up in West Hampstead from 1938[22]), Sachs had a fine record as a very clever, and physically adept, character actor. Starting out in the early 1950s as a humble assistant stage manager in Worthing Rep – where one of the juvenile leads, briefly, was none other than Prunella Scales –

followed by a stint as stage manager of the Liverpool Playhouse, Sachs had gone on to win many admirers within the industry for his smart and reliable contributions to a fairly wide range of productions, including small-screen Brian Rix farces (*Dial RIX*, BBC 1962), crime series (*The Six Proud Walkers*, BBC 1962) and one-off radio plays (some of which he wrote himself[23]), as well as his work as a mellifluous narrator of documentaries on such sober subjects as the influence on political theory of Karl Marx[24] and (somewhat aptly as things would turn out) the history of the Peninsular War.[25] He had first worked with John Cleese on several of the earliest business training films produced and distributed by the comedian's own company, Video Arts, and, it seems, a certain sure rapport had quickly been struck.

Cleese had then been to see him on the stage during the summer of 1973, acting opposite Alec Guinness in Alan Bennett's *Habeas Corpus*, and had loved every subtle but telling little thing that he did: '[H]e just made me laugh till it hurt. I realised how good he was at physical comedy.'[26] A small role was found for him (a shaggy-sideburned Russian musician called Zhuchkov) the following year in Cleese and Booth's short movie *Romance with a Double Bass*, and, then, at the start of 1975, soon after he had begun appearing in a new West End production of *No Sex Please, We're British*, he was asked to play the part of Manuel.

Sachs, when the invitation came, was enthusiastic but just a little uneasy. 'I love the idea, thank you, John,' he said, 'but could you make him a *German* waiter? Because I'm not sure I can do a Spanish accent.'[27] Cleese agreed to think about it for a brief moment, thought about it, briefly, and then declined. The character was supposed to be inefficient, incompetent and insecure, he reasoned, so a German accent was completely inappropriate. Cleese then reaffirmed his faith in Sachs, insisted that he would make a brilliant Spanish waiter and urged him to go ahead and accept. 'So I buckled down to it,' said Sachs, 'mugged up the accent on the way to the studio, as it were, and we got on with it.'[28]

The one small revision that he requested was a little more facial hair. 'I'd always done "disguise" things,' he later explained, 'because I never liked to "reveal" myself, at that time, very much, and I thought the ideal would be a moustache: "I'll ask the producer if I can have a moustache." I thought he'd never let me, because John was wearing a moustache – they won't have *two* moustaches in the same show. [But] I asked John Howard Davies and he said, "Yes, all right." '[29] Manuel was still Spanish, but now he was also moustachioed.

Many actors other than Andrew Sachs might have been more concerned about securing some hidden padding rather than acquiring any surplus hair, because it was obvious, from the most cursory glance at the scripts, that Manuel would soon be smacked, kicked, poked and punched on what seemed like a distressingly regular basis. Sachs, however, remained supremely unperturbed. A fine technician, and timer, of physical routines, he saw the prospect of such outrageous attacks as invaluable opportunities for him to shine: 'If you get a big man and a small man, and the big man hits the small man, the small man's going to get the sympathy, so I thought: "That's *good!*" '[30] The show was taking shape: another first choice was safely in place.

The performer John Howard Davies chose – again, more or less immediately – to play the role of the hotel's most prominent resident guest, the eccentric old buffer Major Gowen, was a veteran character actor by the name of Ballard Berkeley. Born Ballard Blascheck on 6 August 1904 in Margate, Kent (the third son of Joseph Edward Maximilian Blascheck, a London-born 'society entertainer' and manager of Hungarian extraction, and Beatrice Latchford Pewtress, a singer originally from Melbourne, Australia), Berkeley (as he had 'Anglicized' himself for the stage) had been in show business for the best part of fifty years. An old friend and one-time flatmate of Cary Grant[31] – back in the early, pre-Hollywood vaudeville days when the performer was still known as Archie Leach – Berkeley had gone on to make his debut on the West End stage in 1928 (in a comedy called *The Devil's Host*) and had worked in movies since the start of the 1930s, appearing in such productions as Noël Coward's *In Which We Serve* (1942), Alberto Cavalcanti's *They Made Me a Fugitive* (1947) and Alfred Hitchcock's *Stage Fright* (1950), as well as playing innumerable doctors, detectives, bureaucrats and aristocrats on television in episodes of such high-profile shows as the sitcom *Here's Harry* (1961),[32] classic detective dramas *Maigret* (1963)[33] and *Sherlock Holmes* (1965),[34] and the long-running police series *Dixon of Dock Green*.[35]

Choosing Berkeley to essay the show's most endearing supporting player was, therefore, eminently sensible: he fitted the bill to the proverbial (G and) 'T'. Respectful of tradition (he was the enthusiastic archivist of the theatre world's oldest club for actors, The Green Room) and mildly eccentric (like quite a few other superstitious actors, he refused ever to appear on stage wearing anything that was coloured any shade of green), he was still marked by the memories of a world at war. (When, for example, there was a direct hit on London's Café de Paris during the Blitz, Berkeley, who was serving at the time as a special constable, arrived to find a harrowing scene in the underground ballroom, with the popular bandleader Ken 'Snakehips' Johnson decapitated and rows of elegantly dressed people still sitting at their tables without a mark on them, but stone dead.[36]) He had also played various military officers, judges and toffs throughout much of his long career – all the way from the engineer-commander of *In Which We Serve* to the comical colonel in the 1971 West End production of William Douglas-Home's play *The Jockey Club Stakes* – so a character like Major Gowen was easy for him to command.

The Major, John Cleese would say, was the character he and Connie Booth came to love the most, and both of them would come to adore Ballard Berkeley, too: 'I was hugely fond of him. He was a wonderful fellow. [. . .] Like me, he was an insane cricket fan, and when I'd be in the rehearsal room playing a scene with Sybil, I'd glance over Sybil's shoulder and I'd suddenly see Ballard doing this [*holds up five fingers on one hand and one on the other*], which meant that there were six Australian wickets down. I just loved that man.'[37] With Berkeley on board, therefore, the ideal cast seemed more or less complete.

All that was left was the task of finding the right people to play the hotel's resident pair of old ladies: Miss Gatsby and Miss Tibbs. Once again, it did not take long to track the two of them down: Renée Roberts and Gilly Flower.[38] Both were very experienced character actors: Roberts was a veteran of both the stage (where she had worked for more than fifty years in plays, concerts and revues) and the wireless (making her debut as a soubrette on a show called *Cabaret Kittens* back in 1927[39]), and had also appeared on television in everything from *Play for Today* to *Doctor Who*,[40] while Flower had been performing steadily on the stage since 1920, when she played the part of a Peter Pan-like spirit in Algernon Blackwood's fantasy for children *Through the Crack*, and, as far as her occasional work on the small screen was concerned, had contributed a couple of cameo performances to two recent series of *Steptoe and Son*.[41] Both actors, coincidentally, had appeared together in an episode of the 1974 Ronnie Corbett sitcom *The Prince of Denmark*.[42] Once these two performers had agreed to appear, therefore, it was time for the production process to move on to the next stage.

Contracts were dispatched, signed and collected during May 1975, with payments being scaled in terms both of the importance of the role and the prominence of the performer. John Cleese (in addition to the £500 that he and Connie Booth earned for writing the shows) was set to receive the sum of £500 for playing Basil; initially, Prunella Scales was offered £400 for the series; Andrew Sachs was allotted £140; and Connie Booth £130[43] – but, following the usual set of calls back and forth between agents and the BBC, it seems that these figures were nudged up slightly higher. Ballard Berkeley, Renée Roberts and Gilly Flower had to settle for rather less, although they knew, if the show proved successful, that they would also be guaranteed the odd modest but still very welcome repeat fee. None of them, however, had been drawn to the project primarily for the money (which was just as well). What all of them were excited by was the prospect of being part of something that promised so much. This could, they all felt, turn out to be very, very, special.

The next step was for everyone to meet up, get to know one another and start work on rehearsing the scripts. A brand-new show was about to be brought to life.

FIRST VISIT

Look, if you think I'm going to fawn to some of the yobbos we get in here . . .

4

Bon Appetit?

Can't you see that I'm busy?

It was the summer of 1975, and *Fawlty Towers* was taking shape at an increasingly rapid pace. The situation had been established, the characters created, the scripts drafted (and, on several occasions, redrafted) and the cast assembled. Now the programmes themselves had to be made.

Strange though it now seems, however, not everyone at the BBC was convinced that the show would – or should – ever reach the screen. Several producers who had gained a glimpse of a script had pronounced themselves distinctly underwhelmed by the quality of its contents ('Oh, dear,' one of them had been overheard lamenting about John Cleese in the BBC bar, 'why did he ever leave *Monty Python*?'[1]), and one executive had gone so far as to distribute a memo complaining: 'This is a very boring situation and the script has nothing but very clichéd characters. I cannot see anything but a disaster if we go ahead with it.'[2] Fortunately, the BBC, in those days, contained a far greater number of experienced and influential people for whom tolerance and trust counted for more than cursory readings and knee-jerk reactions, so the series went ahead as planned.

There was much still to be done. The situation, for example, had to be made physical, in the sense that the actual hotel environment needed to be built and brought into view; the comedy also required further refinement, with an intensive period of rehearsal; and the technical aspects of the production had to be assessed and arranged.

Rendering the hotel known as Fawlty Towers tangible and visible was, as it turned out, a relatively straightforward affair. Now assigned the fictional address of '16 Elwood Road' in Torquay,[3] the parts that needed to be seen were soon being crafted for the cameras. 'What actually happened,' John Howard Davies would say, 'was that John had made a plan of the hotel. But it was completely and utterly useless. So I then did a plan that I thought *would* work in a studio before an audience.' This plan of the interior – a basic set comprising a small office to the left, a reception area in the middle, a dining room to the right, a kitchen behind that and then a lounge – was given by Davies to his designer, Peter Kindred. Kindred (a BBC employee since 1964 who was previously responsible for the look of such productions as the 1967 adaptations of *Wuthering Heights* and *Treasure Island*, as well as, during the early 1970s, episodes of *Softly, Softly: Task Force* and *Whatever Happened to the Likely Lads?*) proceeded to discuss the layout with Davies, and, within a short period of time, the set was built for use mainly in Studio 8 (the traditional home of the sitcom) or sometimes Studio 4 or 6 ('It would vary,' Davies later recalled[4]) at the BBC's Television Centre.

Kindred had to work on what was, even for the mid-1970s, an extremely modest budget (the whole production, recalled John Howard Davies, would end up ranking 'as one of the cheapest comedies that we ever made'[5]), but, by using all of the penny-pinching tricks that he had picked up from working on numerous other BBC productions, he found a way to create something that, once suitably blocked and bolstered, would look and – usually – work like the shell of a functioning hotel (although nothing was going to stand up entirely convincingly to action that would involve, for example, Basil banging a waiter's head repeatedly against a supposedly freshly bricked-up wall. During those brief occasions, it was hoped, the viewer's belief would stay suspended while the set was seen to shake). Kindred also managed to incorporate one particular addition requested by Davies: 'A little staircase, outside the rooms "upstairs", that went up and then down again. I'd actually seen one like that a year or so earlier when I'd stayed in the Scotia Hotel in Edinburgh, and I'd rather liked it because it was nonsense – so it seemed perfect for a hotel like Fawlty Towers.'[6] It also proved invaluable for making the 'upstairs' part of the set – which was obviously really on the same level as everything else on the studio floor – look more like a proper upstairs area, with Basil, Polly and Manuel often to be seen running up and down this strange little four-step hillock.

Davies had thought to make sure that all of the walls (and especially those around the lobby) were higher than the norm, because otherwise the six-foot-five-inch John Cleese, when standing in the foreground, would force the cameras to point so far up that they would reveal the absence of a ceiling. Some other problems, however, proved, given the shortage of time, frustratingly irresolvable. The backcloth that was glimpsed whenever anyone entered the lobby, for example, 'never worked satisfactorily,' Davies recalled, 'because it was just too close to the front door. So it never looked real and we had to "white it out" with as much light as possible in the unlikely event that Torquay would actually be sunny.'[7]

Any exterior shots – to be filmed over a five-day period several weeks before the recording of the actual shows – were located mainly at the Wooburn Grange Country Club (which would double for the fictional establishment) in Bourne End, Wooburn Green, a few miles southeast of High Wycombe in Buckinghamshire. John Howard Davies chose the location in part because – being midway between his home and the BBC's TV Centre – it was strategically convenient, but also, more pertinently, because, when he first saw it, the look of the establishment was evocative of the right sort of seriously run-down provincial charm: there were 'ladies in scuffed stilettos and Alsatian dogs round the dustbins, and it smelt of rancid beer, and so, in a sense, it seemed like just about the perfect place.'[8] The hotel sign – planted temporarily nearby – was then rearranged by Davies's production assistant, Iain McLean (a keen crossword puzzler and very adept at anagrams), so as to be shot in a series of fittingly faulty ways (variations would include 'Fawlty Towers' with the 'l', the 'w' or the 's' either missing or hanging down at an angle; 'Warty Towels'; 'Watery Fowls'; 'Flay Otters'; 'Fatty Owls'; 'Flowery Twats'; and 'Farty Towels'[9]) – the idea being to make it seem like a regular and all-too-believable prank by a disaffected paper boy, as well as serve as a comical signature for the start of each new episode.

The odd one or two other fleeting exterior scenes – involving certain quick visits to shops, brief glimpses of car journeys and frantic collections from local restaurants – were mostly shot in and around the streets near the BBC's Victoria Road rehearsal rooms in North Acton, a shooting process that was far more difficult than it might now sound, because each insert had to anticipate the tone and timing (and weather) of an episode that had not yet been recorded. As there would not be any time, or money, to re-film any of these sequences, the odd continuity error – such as the road that suddenly goes from bone dry to rain-drenched, and the misshapen figure in the distance passing for a character who was not yet cast – was almost inevitable, but most of the pegs ended up being slotted fairly snugly in the right-shaped holes.

Some theme music, to accompany the opening and closing credits, was the next thing to be commissioned. Dennis Wilson, who had previously been responsible for scoring the music used in such shows as *Marriage Lines*, *Till Death Us Do Part* and *Rising Damp*, was the man chosen to compose it, and then John Howard Davies hired the very well-respected Aeolian Quartet to perform it. 'I tried to persuade [them] to play it very badly,' he would recall, 'but they were unable to do so.'[10] The completed piece, nonetheless, conveyed an appropriate tone of affected refinement and strained-for respectability – a sort of aural equivalent of warm medium sherry – that Basil would surely have adored.

As far as the scripts were concerned, however, there was more fine-tuning to be done, because neither Booth nor Cleese would ever feel that they were really, truly, 'ready'. Acknowledging the presence of an exceptionally strong 'perfectionist streak', Cleese later said: 'I got terribly wound up over things. Writing *Fawlty Towers* meant going over everything again and again until we got it right.'[11] Usually running to around 135 pages (about twice the length of an average sitcom script in those days) and full of precise instructions, there was still always something in the most recent 'final' draft that, in the eyes of the two co-writers, could and should be further improved. 'You wouldn't believe the technical detail to which [we] worked,' Cleese would recall. 'During the course of a week, I would decide that during someone else's speech, I should look at him three times. And that the first look would be done one way, and the second another, and the third yet another. It was that technical. And you keep doing it until it feels right in your gut.'[12]

When it came to the similarly arduous business of bringing the scripts to life inside the BBC's rehearsal rooms, the atmosphere, mercifully, was unusually benign. 'It was a very happy group,' John Cleese would say, 'because everybody was pleased with what they had to do. Nobody was trying to build their part up.'[13] Andrew Sachs agreed: 'Everyone's suggestions were welcomed. No one was pushing any ego around. John, indisputably, was the leader, but he was a very good father of the family. He was, and is, a very caring, generous man, and Connie was equally warm. Sometimes, just occasionally, the two of them would disagree about something and have a bit of a spat and start shouting at each other, but, in my experience, Connie could never keep it up for very long – she'd always start giggling pretty soon and then it was all over. It was quite charming, actually.'[14] John Howard Davies would also praise Booth for her contribution during this period, remarking that, apart from being 'delightfully intelligent': '[She] was very much part of the package. Her understanding of structure and scripts was absolutely vital. And she acted, especially in the first series, as a very good yardstick, stopping [the rest of] us going too far and bringing a sensibility, a rationale, a logic to everything.'[15]

The rehearsals were therefore calm and methodical but also extraordinarily thorough. 'John was *extremely* rigorous,' Prunella Scales would confirm, 'and he used every second of that limited time to ensure that every little thing was absolutely right'.[16] The cast would have Mondays off (apart from Andrew Sachs, who was still appearing in the West End every day except Sundays),

then come in on Tuesday mornings and run through their lines
('We had a lot of fun at the read-through stage,' John Howard
Davies remembered, 'just getting everyone together round a
table'[17]), while Cleese and Booth worked on yet another minor
revision and listened to any other particular query or suggestion.
'By the time that we arrived for rehearsals on Wednesday,'
recalled Scales, 'John expected us to have learned every word.
He would get extremely irritated if we hadn't, so often we
would have been up all night memorising them. It was a very,
very, tough schedule. And as the week wore on we'd rehearse
every movement, every detail, over and over again. John, quite
rightly, is a perfectionist and he therefore took a lot of pleas-
ing.'[18] Cleese himself was quick to agree: 'I act in the thing only
to keep someone else from screwing up the script. I'd be
happiest if someone would invent a machine to plug my head
into a videotape machine.'[19]

It was, nonetheless, a genuinely collaborative, and mutually
supportive, process: 'It felt to me very much like a team effort,'
Cleese would recall, 'because we all listened to each other a great
deal. If I was doing a scene with Pru, then Connie and Andrew
would just sit there watching, and after a time one of them might
make a suggestion or say that they think something isn't quite
working. Now because Connie and I had written and then
rewritten the scripts, there wasn't an enormous amount of
[further] script rewriting – they were more or less right most
of the time. But how we did them was very much a co-operative
thing with lots of suggestions coming in.'[20] Prunella Scales, for
example, could always be relied on to devise a clever little
sequence with a prop, or a change to the rhythm of her lines,
that seemed to add colour and pace to a scene (such as when
Sybil sits in bed and moves her hands around a circuit consisting

of a box of Black Magic chocolates, a copy of *Woman's Own* magazine and a little red telephone book, while issuing a succession of orders to Basil[21]), and Andrew Sachs was very adept at developing little visual gags that made a funny physical moment even better (such as Manuel's look of mournful fatalism as he stands perfectly still and allows Basil to announce: 'This . . . Basil. This . . . smack on head'[22]). No one ever let up; the rehearsal room buzzed with effort and invention from the start all the way to the finish.

Each working week would end with an anxious Cleese still feeling that the team had had 'two too few days to get it slick', but the weekend was when all of the hard graft would really have to count. Saturday saw the final phase of fine-tuning, and then, early on Sunday morning, the team reassembled for a camera rehearsal, followed in the afternoon by a 'stagger-through' (when, as John Howard Davies put it, the team would 'try absolutely everything to see if it worked'[23]) and a proper dress rehearsal. The actual recording, in front of a studio audience of about 250 people ('warmed up' by a Hampshire-based comic called Dave Armour), took place in the evening, shortly after 8.00 p.m. By about 9.30 or 10 o'clock at night, the show was, at last, 'in the can' and ready for editing.

The process of editing would then take a day or so more to complete, with the pace sometimes slowing to one minute of footage per hour. It was an intense and elaborate task, not only because John Cleese was so keen to see that everything was 'absolutely spot on', but also because the technical style of the production was, by the standards of the time, exceptionally complex. Following in the footsteps of such progressive pro-ducer/directors as Duncan Wood (who pioneered the use of videotape recording and editing on *Hancock's Half-Hour* in the

late 1950s, and then, in the 1960s on *Steptoe and Son*, pushed up
the pace of the popular sitcom by increasing the number of shots
per half-hour from about 150 to 270[24]), John Howard Davies
was working hard to make the show as brisk and as bright as he
possibly could. 'My own particular fixation in those days,' he
would recall, 'was that comedy, if you assume you're showing it
to a bright and adept audience, can't be fast enough, so I
approached it with that principle in mind. It's all got to move
along at an unrealistic pace, as the pace gives the whole thing a
tremendous amount of energy and shape.'[25] Each episode,
therefore, now contained as many as 400 different camera shots,
which meant that there was, on average, a cut every four seconds
– about twice as often as other sitcoms of the time.

It was, as a consequence, an extraordinarily painstaking
process, but the result was deemed to be worth all the time
and effort. 'There was a great satisfaction with the end product,'
Cleese would say, 'after spending twenty hours editing each
show with the director, a real satisfaction there.'[26]

The first episode to be recorded, entitled, 'A Touch of Class',
was filmed one Sunday at the end of August in 1975. The plot
concerned Basil's latest snobbish bid, via a furtive advertisement
in *Country Life*, to 'build up a higher class of clientele' and 'turn
away some of the riff-raff'. Sybil's response is to inform him that
the ad is a waste of money, as the only thing that should matter is
that all of their rooms are occupied and all of the guests pay their
bills. She then instructs her husband to end his obsession with
airs and graces, delay typing out the lunch menu and get on
instead with hanging up a picture that she wishes to see out on
display ('Thank you, dear,' he mutters. 'Thank you so much. I
don't know where I'd be without you. In the land of the living,
probably'). Still depressed by the hotel's current standard of

clientele ('I mean, have you *seen* the people in room six? They've never even sat on *chairs* before. They are the commonest, vulgarest, most horrible, nasty . . .'), his day worsens still further when a scruffy-looking young 'cockney git' called Danny Brown arrives to book a room; although Basil attempts to convince this latest intruder that nothing at present is free, Sybil intervenes, much to his horror, to send yet another common creature up the stairs and into an available bed.

Basil's dark mood is only brightened when the next person to visit turns out to be, of all things, one of his longed-for English toffs, and, better still, not just any old English toff, but rather a proper posh peer of the realm: a gentleman by the name of Lord Melbury. Basil is ecstatic, grinning, fawning and forelock-tugging as he gratefully agrees to place a case of 'valuables' in his safe, arranges for 'his lordship' to take up residency in the most sumptuous room in the hotel, and then scuttles around hither and thither fussing over his very own VIP, demanding that another party surrenders the best-placed table for a spot of lunch ('Come *on!*'), offering him 'a little aperitif . . . as our guest' and agreeing to cash what Melbury calls 'a small cheque' for a large-sounding sum of money ('Oh!' gasps Basil, with a mixture of horror, panic and gratitude. 'Please! Oh, *ha, ha!* Oh, tremendous!') – while repeatedly brushing aside another guest's increasingly plaintive request for 'a gin and orange, a lemon squash and a Scotch and water, *please!*'

His snobbish reverie is shattered when Polly informs him and Sybil that she has just learnt that 'his lordship' is in reality nothing more than a common conman, who, to add insult to injury, is under surveillance by someone from the CID posing at the hotel as the 'cockney git', Danny Brown. Desperate not to believe the news he has been given, Basil tries in vain to stop

Sybil from unlocking the safe and removing his precious VIP's case full of treasures. Brushing her husband aside, Sybil then opens the case and, with an ill-disguised sense of triumph, reveals to Basil the so-called 'valuables' that rest within: two very ordinary old house bricks. Stunned, he lifts one up, stares at it quizzically, and then shakes it by his right ear (as if he hopes it might turn into a reassuringly expensive imported cigar), then, still puzzled, he takes out the other one, stares at it in the same way and then gives it a quick sniff. Finally, after another bemused stare at both, he clinks them together – once, twice – then, clenching a fist, he looks down and emits a low growl like that of a wounded beast.

When Melbury returns, Basil, straining to contain his rage, greets him with a fearsome rictus grin: 'Well, how *are* you, Lord Melbury? 'Ow are yer then?' He reaches out and pinches the startled rascal's left cheek. 'All right, mate? 'Ow's me old mucker?' Basil then smacks him on both cheeks, Eric More-cambe-style, and squeezes his ears. 'Any *valuables* to deposit?' he inquires. 'Any . . . bricks?' Melbury, realising that he has been rumbled, races off, leaving Basil screaming after him: 'You *BASTARD!*'

What makes this sad experience even sadder, for Basil, is that the incident takes place in the presence of two new arrivals: Sir Richard and Lady Morris – a pair of *bona fide* VIPs who have come on the strength of the ad placed in *Country Life*. Horrified at the sight of a hotel manager smacking, swearing at and, ultimately, kicking an existing guest, the couple makes a hasty retreat, pursued by a pathetic Basil Fawlty: '*Please* stay – you'll *like* it here!' Sir Richard, however, is in no mood to listen, declaring, before driving back off to some safe posh place, that he has never known a worse hotel in his life. Basil then stands alone in the rain, at the bottom of the six damp steps to his hotel, and shouts after them: 'You SNOBS! You stupid, stuck-up, toffee-nosed, half-witted, upper-class piles of . . . *PUS!!'*

Back inside, he not only seems like a broken man. He also seems like a man who has been broken many times before, but somehow still keeps going. 'Well,' he sighs, 'I'd better put the picture up.' After thanking both Polly ('Well done') and Manuel ('Oh . . . *Olé!'*) for their part in chasing the fake Lord Melbury off the premises and into the arms of the law, he sighs once again, picks up the hated painting, prepares to hang it on the wall – and is then visited by the next fresh hell in the form of an exceptionally frustrated guest: 'A GIN AND ORANGE, A LEMON SQUASH AND A SCOTCH AND WATER – *PLEASE!'*

As an opening story, 'A Touch of Class' was relatively simple, compared to what other episodes the team had in store, but it was, nonetheless, eminently effective in the way that it set the neurotically farcical tone, fixed the requisite degree of believability and established each key characterisation. As far, for example, as the farce was concerned, it was all very 'English': no sexual activity, but plenty of class tension and the kind of conflict that is driven by a spiralling sense of confusion (a brittle man made pliable by his own prejudices is deceived and then reprieved, only to snatch another demoralising defeat from the jaws of a minor victory). Well-paced and nicely acted, it eased the audience into Basil's ineluctably Fawlty world.

That this world seemed broadly believable was thanks in part to the programme-makers' admirably close attention to detail. Countless tiny touches contributed to the overall picture of a ruffled form of provincial reality. Basil's stripy old school tie, for example, was kept at least a couple of inches too short for the hoped-for distinguished effect. Michael Gwynn, who played Lord Melbury, had his otherwise fairly straight hair shaped at the back so that it splashed out into greasy curls just over the collar – 'Nobody has a haircut like that,' declared John Howard Davies gleefully, 'except the English aristocracy!' Terence Conoley, who was playing another, rather more modest-looking, guest called Mr Wareing, was made to wear an unpleasant pair of sour-cream-coloured socks that seemed, as Davies put it, 'so English and so country-house-Torquay-ish'. It was also decided to populate the dining room mostly with non-actors rather than risk having the distraction of camera-hungry extras, so the tables were taken by, among others, the respective wives of the show's vision mixer and production assistant.

It was against this reassuringly vivid backdrop that the main characters were then established with ease. Basil, of course, dominated the entire episode, revealing one after another of his various flaws, foibles and fantasies as each scene gave way to the next (and, as Cleese was aged just thirty-five at the time and Basil was meant to be in his mid-forties, an extra layer of make-up lent him the right kind of 'lived-in' look), while Sybil clarified the nature of her personality via a series of brusquely precise interventions, and the pair of them only needed a few clipped and chilly interactions to reveal much about the state of their marriage:

> BASIL: Hello, dear. *[Kisses Sybil on the cheek]*
> SYBIL: What are you doing?
> BASIL: I'm kissing you, dear.
> SYBIL: Well, don't.

Similarly, Polly was given a couple of brief but telling scenes to show both her cool-headed and quietly witty ability to look after herself (when, for example, a guest who is ordering a lamb casserole attempts to flirt by asking her if the dish 'comes with a smile', she replies briskly, 'It comes with sprouts or carrots'; when the guest tries again, 'Oh, a smile's extra, is it?', she responds with the calm put-down, 'You'll get one if you eat up all your sprouts'), as well as her more compassionate capacity to act as a confidante ('Don't mention it to my wife,' Basil begs her as he sends her on another furtive errand). The dotty personality of Major Gowen, too, was introduced with deft economy, first via his selective summary of the contents of his daily newspaper – conservative politics: 'Ah, more strikes . . . dustmen . . . Post Office . . .'; and apolitical cricket: 'Ah! D'Oliveira made a hundred!' – and then via a distinctly E. L. Wisty-style take on the latest television – 'I've just been watching one of those nature films,' he announces as he cradles a drink at the bar. 'Did you know that a female gibbon gestates for *seven* months?'

As for the character of Manuel, his misfit status was made abundantly evident straight from the opening scene:

MANUEL: *Qué?*
BASIL: There is too much butter . . . on . . . those . . . trays.
MANUEL: No, no, *Sẽnor!*
BASIL: What?
MANUEL: Not 'on-those-trays'. No, sir – '*uno, dos, tres*'. Uno . . . *dos . . . tres . . .*
BASIL: No, no. *Hay mucho burro alli!*
MANUEL: *Qué?*
BASIL: *Hay . . . mucho . . . burro . . . alli!*
MANUEL: Ah, *mantequilla!*
BASIL: What? *Qué?*
MANUEL: *Mantequilla. Burro* is . . . is . . . *[Brays like a donkey]*
BASIL: *What?*

80

MANUEL: *Burro . . . [Does another donkey impression]*

BASIL: Manuel, *por favor. . .*

MANUEL: *Sí, sí . . .?*

SYBIL: *[Coming back in]* What's the matter, Basil?

BASIL: Nothing, dear, I'm just dealing with it.

MANUEL: *[To Sybil]* He speak good . . . how do you say . . .?

SYBIL: English!

BASIL: *Mantequilla . . . solamente . . . dos. . .*

MANUEL: *Dos?*

'I don't know why you wanted to hire him,' moans Sybil, but Basil, though rattled, remains stubbornly unrepentant: 'Because he's cheap and keen to learn, dear.' Sybil's response – 'It'd be quicker to train a monkey' – ensures, perversely, that Manuel's position, in spite of his chronic incompetence, will remain safe, because Basil could never countenance a sacking that was sanctioned by Sybil.

Every element of this debut episode, therefore, was neatly in place and looking admirably propitious. Behind the scenes, however, there was still a certain amount of anxiety, as, of course, the show had yet to be screened to the nation and not everyone present at the recording had proffered particularly favourable reactions. 'We had no idea how it would turn out,' Prunella Scales would say of the series as a whole, 'but I remember one of the senior producers at the BBC during the dress rehearsal for the first episode, saying, "I don't know what John's thinking of." '[27] The hard work was not yet over.

Soon after the recording had concluded, the post-mortem duly began. Cleese, Booth and John Howard Davies met to discuss their shared misgivings over one character in particular: Polly. 'She, in the pilot episode, was a philosophy student,' Cleese later revealed, 'and we didn't feel that worked as well as an art student, so we re-recorded just a little – maybe four or five minutes – and cut that in to the first episode before it was transmitted to the general public.'[28] With Polly now remodelled as a budding charcoalist (whose sketches currently sell well enough, she says ruefully, 'to keep me in waitressing'), and with a further few tweaks to the editing, the pilot programme was finally deemed ready to meet the public, and critical, gaze. 'I was very pleased with the way it had gone,' Cleese would say of the whole process. 'I felt that we were all right and that we were on to something good.'[29]

Somewhat surprisingly, however, the imminent arrival of this brand-new series seemed barely to register on the journalistic agenda. In stark contrast to the far more competitive and media-savvy marketing style of today's television networks, which trail and trumpet each new offering so strenuously over such a lengthy period that the unfamiliar appears almost overfamiliar by the time that it finally reaches the screen, the BBC in 1975 preferred to leave *Fawlty Towers*, like most of its other debut series, to tiptoe onto television and patiently await discovery. There were no big magazine interviews (apart from one two-page feature in the *Radio Times*, which was somewhat compromised by the fact that the author had not yet seen the show[30]), nor any high-profile advertising campaigns or advance screenings,[31] and even the television pages in most of the national newspapers provided nothing more than the most cursory of references to the show's initial appearance. Tim Ewbank, previewing the day's schedules in the *Daily Mail*, did, to his credit, describe *Fawlty Towers* as the 'most promising' of the evening's few new attractions,[32] and an anonymous writer in *The Observer* declared that it was 'not to be missed by J. C. fans',[33] but that was more or less the highlight of the pre-publicity.

This seems to have suited John Cleese down to the ground, as he gave every appearance at the time of being even more averse to – or at least suspicious of – hyperbole than were his colleagues at the BBC. Invitations to chat shows, for example, were politely turned down, because, as he put it, such appearances struck him as ego trips (and, besides, 'I get nervous and find myself working out anecdotes in advance, which then fail totally'[34]). He even vetoed a proposal to trail the series with an eye-catching *Radio Times* front cover, reasoning that the programmes themselves might not end up justifying such a vote of confidence.[35]

The first episode, therefore, went out on air rather quietly at 9.00 p.m. on Friday 19 September on BBC2. There were only three channels in those days in Britain, and Friday nights were, unofficially, the best and most competitive night of the week as far as comedy was concerned. BBC1, for example, had *Dad's Army* (which at that stage was consistently attracting more than twelve million viewers and was considered to be more or less right at its peak[36]) scheduled at 8.00 p.m., followed by another well-established sitcom, *The Liver Birds*, at 8.30 p.m.; ITV, meanwhile, was showing *Larry Grayson* at 8.30 p.m. and a lavish, hour-long *Stanley Baxter Picture Show* special at 9.00 p.m. Thus faced with the twin daunting challenges of 'follow that' on BBC1 (a completely unfamiliar sitcom having to impress immediately after the screening of two extremely familiar ones) and 'beat that' on ITV (relying on curiosity to lure some viewers away from the unusually high production values of Stanley Baxter's very popular sketch show – which one paper described, rather over-excitedly, as 'one of the major events of the year on television'[37]), the first edition of *Fawlty Towers* ended up faring as well as could have been expected, pulling in a decent enough audience for that time slot on BBC2 (1,868,500 – compared with the 7,726,500 who watched the news on BBC1 and the 11,059,500 who tuned to Stanley Baxter on ITV), but, nonetheless, a relatively modest number of viewers for a show with a real ambition to flourish on mainstream television.[38]

Many of those people who did manage to see the programme were, it seems, encouraged by what they had witnessed. John Cleese's old friend and occasional colleague Michael Palin, for example, watched the opening episode at home with his wife and their dinner guests, and, as he recorded in his diary at the end of the evening, he was 'reduced to tear-streaming laughter on one or two occasions':

> John has used a very straight and conventional Light Entertainment Format in design, casting, film and general subject, but his own creation, Basil Fawlty, rises above this to heights of manic extraordinariness. It all has the Cleese hallmark of careful, thoughtful, well-planned technical excellence and there was hardly a line in the piece or a moment when John wasn't going utterly spare.[39]

Similar opinions, as the days went by and the casual discussions carried on, were passed via word of mouth between ordinary fans of *Monty Python*, British sitcoms and/or John Cleese. No definitive judgments were reached, but, among those who had either seen or heard about the first episode, plenty of people's curiosity had definitely been piqued. The question now was: what comes next?

The Fawlty man cometh:
'Please stay – you'll like it here ...'

John Marwood Cleese: on his way to
becoming something completely
different in the City.

One of these men will soon be an ex-Python: 'I'm fed up with having to turn up at 8 a.m. on Monday morning at Wakefield railway station dressed as a penguin.'

An American friend: 'Only Michael Palin compares with her for funny ideas,' Cleese said of Connie Booth.

awlty prototype: Timothy Bateson as a tetchy hotelier in a 1971 episode of *Doctor at Large*.

Eunice Black as his formidable wife.

'The nice thing about writing *Fawlty*,' said Booth, 'was a man and a woman working together; if they get on it lends a quality you don't get with two men or two women. We laughed at the same things.'

John Howard Davies: producer/director of the first series of *Fawlty Towers*.

idget Turner: the
oman who spurned
e chance to be Sybil.

awlty Towers – actually the Wooburn Grange Country Club in Bourne End, Bucks.

A scene from the very first episode: Basil the snob falling hook,
line and sinker for the scam of a phony aristocrat.

'The Builders': Sybil —undeniably a
woman with spirit – deals with the
Orelly man and Basil.

'The Hotel Inspectors': Mr Hutchinson (Bernard Cribbins) reflects on an erroneous dish.

'Gourmet Night': 'Well, don't say I haven't warned you ...'

'The Germans': 'I'll do the funny walk . . .'

5

A Televisual Feast

Is it possible for me to reserve the BBC Two channel for the duration . . .?

Now that *Fawlty Towers* had made its debut, the series as a whole was well and truly 'alive': it just had to settle, build an audience and thrive. The second episode, to the whole team's relief, would see the show take a giant stride in such a direction.

Entitled 'The Builders', this particular edition could hardly have been any stronger. It began with Basil preparing, reluctantly, to join Sybil and her gang of golfing girlfriends on an excursion to nearby Paignton ('the first weekend we've had off,' Sybil announces excitedly, 'since Audrey had her hysterectomy') while, in their absence, an ornamental garden gnome is delivered and, more importantly, a minor building project is speedily completed. As arrangements have been made for the resident guests to dodge all of the dust and drilling by dining away at a neighbouring establishment – the Gleneagles (a playful name-check for Torquay's former real-life hotel from hell) – Polly is due to supervise the workmen in accordance with Mrs Fawlty's specific instructions (put in a door at the base of the stairs that will lead straight through to the kitchen).

It seems that Basil's original builder of choice for the job – a very competitively priced operator by the name of Mr O'Reilly – has been vetoed by Sybil on the grounds that he is nothing more than a 'cut-price cock-up artist', and Mr Stubbs (who, although he costs a little more, 'does a really professional job and he does it when he says he will') has been hired instead. Basil, however, cannot bring himself to countenance the additional expense (nor, indeed, his wife's supposed pre-eminence), so, just before he follows her meekly out to the car, he takes Polly to one side and, in an anxious whisper, alerts her to a sudden change of plan: it will be Mr O'Reilly's men, after all, who will be making the requested alteration, and, while they are at it, they will also be blocking off the drawing-room door ('So,' Basil confides with relish, 'we can get a bit of privacy away from the plebs'). Polly is shocked, pointing out the fact that Mrs Fawlty has already made it abundantly clear that she is never going to allow anyone at the hotel to use O'Reilly ever again, but Basil brushes her protest aside: 'Look, he's sending his best men – all you have to do is take a quick look when they've finished, all right?'

His ruse soon goes hopelessly awry. An overworked Polly decides that she needs to go upstairs to take a siesta, and, with uncharacteristic rashness, leaves Manuel to man the desk. When O'Reilly's men arrive ('You are Orelly men?'), Manuel, after failing to waken Polly, allows the builders to do as they please – which, for some reason known only to themselves, involves blocking up the *dining*-room door ('This episode,' John Howard Davies would note with a grimace, recalling the shots of strangely pliant walls, 'was when we really discovered how difficult it was to brace sets adequately inside a studio on a one-night sitting . . .'[1]).

Basil then returns ahead of Sybil in order to check that all is well, and is horrified to find that the job has been botched. 'Polly,' he shrieks, 'what have you done to my hotel?' After she points out that, strictly speaking, he is to blame, having hired the outlawed 'Orelly men', he first tries to deny it, then accepts it and starts sobbing in panic and self-pity. Slapped back into sobriety by Polly, he pauses to strangle Sybil's garden gnome and then sets about repairing the damage, calling O'Reilly to demand that he urgently rights his wrongs. Although the Major does his best to reassure Basil that the missing door is 'bound to turn up' sooner or later, he is in no mood to be patient. When O'Reilly himself (played near-perfectly by the Dublin-born David Kelly) finally rolls up full of sweetness and smiles, Basil tries in vain to apprise him of the seriousness of the situation:

O'REILLY: The trouble with you, Mr Fawlty, is that you worry too much. You keep it up like this, and you'll have a stroke before you're fifty. Stone dead you'll be.

BASIL: Suits me.

O'REILLY: Oh! That's a *dreadful* thing to say!

BASIL: Not at all. Get a bit of peace.

O'REILLY: Don't be so morbid! The Good Lord made the world so that we could all enjoy ourselves.

BASIL: Look: my *wife* enjoys herself. *I* worry!

O'REILLY: Well, let me tell you, if the Good Lord had meant us to worry, He would have given us things to worry about!

BASIL: He *has* – my *wife!!* She will be back here in four hours and she can kill a man at ten paces with one blow of her tongue! How am I supposed not to worry?

O'REILLY: *[Calmly]* Just remember, Mr Fawlty, there's always someone worse off than yourself.

BASIL: Is there? Well, I'd like to meet him. I could do with a laugh.

O'REILLY: You'll just have to worry for the both of us. I'm telling you, if the Good Lord—

BASIL: Is mentioned once more, I shall move you closer to Him. Now, *please* . . .

Caught out by Sybil's early return, Basil – the pathetic coward and pathological liar that he is – tries to cast O'Reilly as the saviour of the hour, only there 'to clear up this mess that your Stubbs has made', but Sybil calls his bluff, arguing that, if Stubbs did indeed botch the job, then he should be the one to put it right at no extra expense. An attempt by Polly to pose on the telephone as Stubbs is rumbled, and Sybil explodes.

First, she deals with Basil: 'I am going to make you regret this for the rest of your life,' she tells him, chillingly, before punching and smacking him, hurling a petty-cash tin at him, kicking him and demolishing him with hard words. Then, sporting the painfully naïve and friendly demeanour of a baby seal coming to play with a killer whale, O'Reilly wanders in from the bar:

SYBIL: Why are you smiling, Mr O'Reilly?

O'REILLY: Well, to be perfectly honest, Mrs Fawlty, I like a woman with spirit.

SYBIL: Oh, *do* you? Is *that* what you like?

O'REILLY: I *do*, I *do!*

SYBIL: Oh, good. *[She picks up a golfing umbrella]*

BASIL: Now, Sybil, that's enough . . .

[Sybil uses the umbrella to attempt to slice Basil in two at the waist, then starts beating O'Reilly savagely about the head, neck and arms, shouting: 'Come on then – give us a smile!'*]*

SYBIL: O'Reilly, I have seen more intelligent creatures than you lying on their backs at the bottom of ponds. I have seen better

88

organised creatures than you running round farmyards with their heads cut off. Now collect your things and get out! *[She hits him one last time before striding over to the desk]* I never want to see you or any of your men in my hotel again. *[Starts dialling the phone]* Now, if you'll excuse me, I have to speak to a *professional* builder . . .

Once Sybil has marched off, Basil recovers his composure, catches the battered builder before he can escape and informs him that the two of them are going to complete all of the work themselves. The following morning, the dining-room door is back in place ('Ah!' exclaims the Major cheerfully, 'you've found it!') and everything else appears to have been repaired. Sybil, upon her return, is, for once, palpably perplexed, whereas Basil could not seem any smugger. When Stubbs turns up, she begins to apologise for wasting his time, only for him to point out that a supporting wall is now likely to give way at any moment. Sybil, back on the offensive, looks for Basil to belt, but he is already outside and on his way to introduce the garden gnome, probably quite forcibly, to the hapless Mr O'Reilly.

'The Builders' was one of those bright, busy and very, very funny sitcom episodes that seemed to burn itself immediately on to the popular consciousness, with lines, gestures and exchanges being quoted in countless contexts up and down the country during the days and weeks that followed. Ironically, however, the actual recording had gone so badly, at least from the perspective of John Cleese, that it had left him fearing that the episode was in real danger, when screened, of falling flat:

We performed almost entirely to complete silence. Afterwards I was disturbed and people kept saying, 'No, it was a funny show,' but I moaned, 'What about the audience?' I found out later that a large number of people from the Icelandic Broadcasting Corporation had visited the BBC that day. The BBC, always helpful to shows like mine, thought it would be nice if they put all seventy of them in the front row. They just sat there being very pleasant and charming and Icelandic, and not laughing at all. All we got was a faint whiff of cod coming from the front row which, had we recognised it at the time, might have given us the explanation. And I've got to say it was a pretty tough recording, and it needed quite a lot of editing to tighten it up.[2]

Whatever was done in the editing booth (and it certainly would not have involved adding any 'canned' laughter, because the show never used such a thing) certainly worked, because 'The Builders', as broadcast, won the show many more admirers (it was now competing each week against the news on BBC1 and an hour-long comedy-drama series, called *Beryl's Lot*,[3] on ITV, and the viewing figures were rising up to an average of 2.6 million[4]), and set a high standard for the rest of the series. It was therefore already very clear that the first run of *Fawlty Towers* was going to be something rather special.

The next episode, entitled 'The Wedding Party', was the most impressive so far in terms of the quality of its ensemble acting, as well as, by some distance, the most farcical in terms of its plot. 'It's always struck me,' Cleese would later explain, 'that people who aren't getting enough sex are fascinated by it and those people who get it. More often than not, that frustration takes the form of being very, very cross that other people are getting some. And that's always been Basil's problem.'[5] What followed, therefore, was a sort of tantric trauma for poor Fawlty.

The opening scene, set in the early evening of a sticky summer's day, saw Basil and Sybil in the bar: he serving the Major another drink and searching for fresh supplies of bar

90

nibbles, and she sitting idly by, flirting with a male guest who encourages her raucous laughter (a sound that Basil likens, *sotto voce*, to 'somebody machine-gunning a seal') over the fact that her harassed husband has 'no nuts'. Niggled by Sybil's behaviour ('Did you ever see that film *How To Murder Your Wife?*' he asks the Major. 'Awfully good. I saw it six times') and irritated by her decision to hand birthday boy Manuel the evening off, Basil welcomes the flattering attention of a French female guest named Mrs Peignoir, who rests her hand on his arm, looks up at him warmly and tells him how 'charming' she is finding Torquay.

Sensing that the atmosphere is turning a little too sultry for his liking, he scuttles off in search of those missing nuts. Each scene that follows will see him fight with increasing desperation to keep control of a libido that has lain dormant for so long it is likely to erupt and explode – leaving little more than a tightly knotted tie and a smouldering moustache.

Step one occurs, cruelly, straight after he gets his hands back on his nuts. The hotel's two resident spinsters, Miss Tibbs and Miss Gatsby, fear that the stressed-looking Basil who strides past them across the lobby is suffering from the heat, and he certainly seems unnerved when, as he makes his way back to the bar, he catches sight of an off-duty Polly locked in a steamy embrace with her latest boyfriend ('What kind of a place do you think this is?' he snaps as he breaks the coupling up. 'A *massage* parlour?'). His temperature pops up another notch when he spies two very pert and braless nipples poking out through Polly's top: 'I'm afraid we've abandoned the idea of the topless afternoon teas, so if you wouldn't mind changing before you go in where people may be trying to eat . . .' Once she has gone, he flicks through her sketchbook, shaking his head at the array of supposed erotica, then answers the telephone absent-mindedly: 'Hello, Fawlty Titties?'

Step two takes place when an overtly amorous young un-married couple arrive and claim to have booked a room with a double bed. Basil, already thoroughly rattled, is alarmed by the absence of inhibitions, insisting that he cannot give them a double-bedded room on the grounds that such a move would be against 'the law of England'. The reality is that, unbeknownst to the censorious hotelier, the pair are old friends of Polly's, and are in Torquay to attend the wedding of a mutual friend. The increasingly feverish Basil, however, now fears that the sap is rising fast, and senses sexual double-entendres in every passing remark (such as when someone says that he needs to get some batteries from the chemists: ' "Batteries," eh?' snorts Basil. 'You *disgust* me!').

He is cranked closer still to cracking-point later that night, when he has to get out of bed and open the front door for a tardy and tipsy guest – who turns out to be none other than the flirtatious Mrs Peignoir. As his bad luck would have it, when he bends down to pick up her purse and she topples over on top of him, two more guests – the unmarried couple – choose that very moment to arrive back in the lobby. Confused and profoundly embarrassed, he races back upstairs, where he is 'ambushed' by a drunk and maudlin Manuel, desperate to declare his love and gratitude to the man who gave a poor boy from Barcelona a job in Britain and a home in Torquay.

Things get predictably worse the following morning, when Sybil signs in another pair of guests: Mr and Mrs Lloyd – the mother and stepfather of the unmarried girl. Basil, unaware of this relationship, is astonished when he sees the girl kissing her stepfather. A few minutes later, he is even more startled to see

Polly locked in a warm embrace with the very same man. Then, soon after that, he comes to a halt outside the unmarried couple's door, behind which, if he but knew it, the girl is massaging her boyfriend's bad back while their friend Polly tries on a dress for the upcoming wedding; intrigued by the loud groans of pleasure, Basil slips to one side and hides as his employee rushes out, still fastening the buttons on her waitressing outfit.

He is, by this stage, totally confused, but is still convinced that he has stumbled upon a series of scenes worthy of a Felliniesque erotic event. Everybody, he concludes, must leave the hotel, so he orders Polly to get her hat and coat and instructs the rest of the 'Karma Sutra set' to pack their bags: 'I mean, you *have* had a very, *very*, good time, haven't you! Well, not *here* you don't!'

Then Sybil, upon discovering what her painfully agitated husband has just done, drops the bombshell: the Lloyds are the parents of the girl, and the girl is an old schoolfriend of Polly's, and nothing remotely 'inappropriate' has actually happened. Duly humiliated, he is sent off to make a full and sincere apology: 'I'm so sorry,' he tells them all, 'but my wife has made a mistake.' 'Yes,' one of them mutters. 'I think she probably did!'

Just when the whole sorry saga seems, mercifully, to finally be over, one more excruciating twist occurs. With Sybil away comforting her recently separated friend Audrey, Basil realises that he still has to contend with the increasingly coquettish Mrs Peignoir, who gets him giggling and twitching with nerves when she reveals her intention to sleep *au naturelle* during the coming night. Locking himself inside his own bedroom, he feels safe from her advances. What he has failed to anticipate, however, is the premature return of Sybil, whose knocks on the door he takes to be a sign that his amorous guest is back on the prowl. 'Look, go to your room,' he whispers. The knocking continues. 'Try to control yourself,' he hisses. 'Where do you think you are? Paris?' Still the knocking goes on. 'Shut up, will you, you silly tart!' he screams, losing all control. 'Go *away!* My *wife* will hear us!' Then, from the other side of the door, come the words that he least wants to hear: 'This *is* your wife.' He tries, ludicrously, to rescue the situation – 'Oh!' he moans as she appears. 'What a terrible dream!' – but Sybil postpones the inquisition, because she has heard a burglar downstairs.

Thankful to escape from the expected beating, Basil rushes off, trouserless but still sporting some sensible shoes, waits for the intruder to step out from the shadows and then knocks him out with a frying pan. Crouching down to examine the damage, he realises that he has just crowned poor Manuel – at which point the lights come on and all of the returning wedding guests stand and stare at the infamously fastidious Fawlty, who is now sitting bare-legged on the prostrate back of a helpless Spaniard. '*We've* been,' they announce with an obvious air of superiority, 'to a wedding!'

It was a frenetically funny farce, but the hard physical humour certainly took its toll on Andrew Sachs, who was lucky to hold on to his head in that final scene. 'We'd been practising all week with me hitting him with a saucepan,' John Cleese would remember, 'and I don't know why we didn't get a rubber saucepan. And I was trying to hit Andrew a sort of sliding blow, but just as I started he straightened up, and I caught him a *terrible* one, and I'm afraid he had a headache for about two days.'[6] The sound of metal striking bone reverberated around the studio, and it was quite a surprise that Sachs managed to retain consciousness. 'You know you *hit* me, don't you?' he moaned to Cleese after the recording was over. 'I mean, it was *really* hard! You shouldn't have done that.' Cleese merely replied quizzically:

'What's the *matter* with you, Andrew? We're not doing eight shows a week in the West End. It's once in your life! Now pull yourself together!' 'So,' Sachs would recall with a laugh, 'I complained, but he forgave me!'[7] As hazardous as it sometimes was, Sachs always agreed with Cleese's belief that, with physical comedy, conviction is crucial: 'You've *got* to go for it,' Cleese insisted. 'The moment that the audience sees someone holding back a bit, or not hitting them properly, or not strangling them properly, it's dead. It's dead in the water. So you've got to go for it.'[8] The violence, therefore, was there to stay.

The fourth episode, called 'The Hotel Inspectors', was boosted by a *tour de force* of a guest performance from Bernard Cribbins (an actor with a fine sense of humour who was so exceptionally adept at playing characters with no sense of humour) as 'Mr Hutchinson' – a spectacularly fastidious and pedantic little man with an Hitlerian moustache, tense sweaty hair and a torturously antiquated manner of speaking who could quite easily bore for the whole of Britain. He arrives at the reception desk one morning and summons Basil, who has been left to deal with the guests while his wife ('my little nest of vipers') gossips on the telephone, once again, to her best friend Audrey. 'I'm so sorry to have kept you waiting,' he says insincerely. 'I had no idea my wife was so busy.' It only takes one brief sentence by way of a reply to signal the presence of an unforgettable irritant: 'Fear not, kind sir, it matters not one whit.'

Hutchinson proceeds to ask Basil to book him 'some hired vehicle' (as he prefers not to use the telephone himself owing to 'the risk of infection'); then he demands a specially drawn diagram detailing 'the optimum route' to a certain destination, and then departs for lunch, declaring pompously: 'If anybody wants me, I'll be in the lounge.' Basil is angry and bemused: 'Anyone in particular?' he mutters. 'I mean, Henry Kissinger? Or just anyone with a big net?'

Just as Basil launches into his latest tirade against the 'cretins' who pass for guests these days ('I don't know what it is about this place . . . I mean, some of the people we get here . . .'), Sybil finally puts down the telephone and reveals that, according to Audrey, who has been talking to their mutual friend Bill Morton (an in-joke: it was name of the show's vision mixer), there are some hotel inspectors in town. Basil, clearly alarmed, is eager to seek out more information, but Sybil, as calm as ever, assures him that all that is required is 'a little more courtesy'. Basil is unconvinced, but, before he can dial up any Deep Throats, Mr Hutchinson is back from the lounge, ding-ding-dinging the service bell and ready with a fresh request: 'Now listen . . . there is a documentary on BBC Two this evening about Squawking Bird, the leader of the Blackfoot Indians in the late Eighteen-sixties. Now this starts at eight forty-five and goes on for approximately three-quarters of an hour . . .' Basil just glares at him, stunned by his dull absurdity, but the guest drones doggedly on: '. . . Now, is it possible for me to reserve the BBC Two channel for the duration of this televisual feast?'

Basil cannot hide his irritation – 'Why don't you talk properly?' – and dismisses him sarcastically: 'It is not possible to reserve the BBC Two channel from the commencement of this televisual feast until the moment of the termination of its ending. Thank you so much.'

It is at this moment, however, that Hutchinson, bridling at such brusqueness, points out that, as someone whose 'professional activities' cause him to be in 'constant contact' with the hotel industry, he expects to receive a much better standard of service. Basil, his brain buzzing, takes this to be a revealing little slip, and concludes that Mr Hutchinson must be one of the dreaded inspectors. Snapping straight into full-blown obsequious mode, Basil is suddenly all sweetness and light, guaranteeing the requested televisual treat, and the use of a ping-pong table (albeit one 'not in absolutely mint condition') and offering his guest the special privilege of an early lunch.

Happy to accept such an invitation, Hutchinson sits down, makes his order (a cheese salad, a bottle of ginger beer and a glass of fresh drinking water) and then, predictably enough, proceeds to complain about anything and everything. It does not take long, however, before Sybil intervenes, relishing the chance to inform Basil that the pernickety little man whom he presumes to be a hotel inspector is actually a humble cutlery salesman with a specialist interest in spoons. Furious at this 'deception', Basil strides back into the dining room and 'attends' to this fussy pest of a guest: 'Is there something we can get you, Mr Hutchinson? A tea cosy for your pepper pot, perhaps?' After provoking him as much as is possible without prompting a formal protest, Basil turns his attentions to another diner, the rather stern-looking Mr Walt (James Cossins), whose casual comment that he is 'down here on business with a couple of colleagues' causes a sharp spasm of panic: 'Three . . . *three* of you?' Convinced now that this man is the real hotel inspector, Basil moves quickly to silence the noisy moans and groans now emanating from Mr Hutchinson's nearby table:

BASIL: I'm so glad everything is to your satisfaction.
HUTCHINSON: No it is not! It is absolutely ridiculous! I mean, you are *supposed* to be running a *hotel!*
BASIL: [*Admiring the cheese salad*] My, that *does* look good.

HUTCHINSON: I've had the omelette, a prawn cocktail with a bloody silly name . . .

BASIL: Look at that cheddar. Delicious!

HUTCHINSON: . . . then I had a plate of stew and then the bloody omelette again!

BASIL: Yes, well, can we keep it down a little bit, please?

HUTCHINSON: I mean, all I wanted was a cheese salad. It wasn't as though I'd ordered an *elephant's ear on a bun*, was it?

BASIL: *[Smiling vainly over at Walt]* Thank you, thank you so much.

HUTCHINSON: I mean, the whole thing is absolutely ridiculous!

BASIL: *[Pushing him back in his chair]* Well, I'm glad we've sorted it all out now.

HUTCHINSON: . . . I mean, for a man who's supposed to be running a hotel, your behaviour, *your* behaviour, is totally . . .

[Basil, now desperate to shut the man up, laughs genially at the other guests while, surreptitiously, he places a hand across Hutchinson's mouth and presses the nose with his thumb]

BASIL: Well, I'm glad everything's to your satisfaction now . . .

HUTCHINSON: *[Muffled]* Let me go, let me go . . .

BASIL: Is there anything else *at all* I can get you, sir?

HUTCHINSON: *[Struggling]* Let me go, I can't *breathe!*

BASIL: Ha ha ha ha ha! *[Hissing]* Shut up, then!

HUTCHINSON: *I CAN'T BREATHE!*

BASIL: Mmm, look at that cheese – isn't it lovely?

[Hutchinson struggles for oxygen as Basil tightens his grip and tries to reassure the onlookers]

BASIL: It's all right – he's only choking!

[Hutchinson leaps convulsively; Basil thumps him on the back]

BASIL: Don't worry . . . a bit of cheese went the wrong way.

[More convulsions and thumping, then Basil beams at the others and slips in a quick rabbit-punch; Hutchinson slumps forward with his face buried in his salad]

98

BASIL: Ah, never mind – he's fainted. *[Calls out]* Manuel! *[To Walt]* Poor chap! Bit of cheese!

Having 'dealt' with the bothersome Hutchinson (who is carried out and deposited in the bar), Basil returns to fussing over Mr Walt, but there is more embarrassment still to come. Just as he is affecting regret over his ailing guest ('What a *frightful* shame about that piece of cheese getting stuck in the old windpipe like that'), the man himself returns, like Banquo's ghost, to the scene of his salad-based fate and punches Basil to the floor:

HUTCHINSON: I'm not a violent man, Mr Fawlty.

BASIL: *[Protesting weakly from the floor]* Yes you are.

HUTCHINSON: No I'm not! But when I am insulted and then attacked, I would prefer to rely on my own mettle than call the police.

BASIL: Do you? Do you really . . .?

HUTCHINSON: Yes, I do! Now stand up like a man! Come on!

BASIL: . . . Bit of trouble with the old leg, actually.

HUTCHINSON: *Come on!*

[He picks Basil up. Basil has found a stapler. He shows it to Walt]

BASIL: Look what I've found!

HUTCHINSON: I hope I've made my point.

BASIL: Absolutely! *[To Walt]* I've been looking for that.

HUTCHINSON: I would just like to say that this hotel is extremely inefficient and badly run, and that you are a very rude and discourteous man, Mr Fawlty.

BASIL: *[With manic cheerfulness]* Ah . . . ha ha ha ha.

HUTCHINSON: Did I say something *funny*, Mr Fawlty?

BASIL: . . . Well, sort of *pithy*, I suppose.

HUTCHINSON: Oh really? Well, here's the punch line. *[He elbows Basil in the stomach. Basil doubles up out of sight.]* Now I am going to fetch my belongings and I do not expect to receive a bill!

*[Hutchinson goes off upstairs. Sybil comes in, leans over and looks down
at Basil dispassionately]*
SYBIL: You've handled that, then, have you, Basil?

Once he has pulled himself back up from the floor, Basil tries
desperately to convince Mr Walt that he has just witnessed a
harmless bit of fun between a good sport of an hotelier and a
regular, if rather eccentric, guest, and then promises him a
complimentary meal that evening. When Walt passes on the
offer, revealing that he will soon be moving on, Basil tries to
bribe him, then, realising his mistake ('Oh, what have I done?'),
cracks completely, whining for forgiveness and pleading for a
decent review in the next edition of *The Good Hotel Guide*. A
thoroughly bewildered Mr Walt explains that he has nothing to
do with the hotel industry, and is only in Torquay to sell some
outboard motors.

Basil's relief is immense. Feeling indestructible after escaping
from such a hellish fate, he proceeds to exact his revenge on Mr
Hutchinson, bidding him '*adios*' by placing one custard pie in
the puzzled man's crotch and another one smack in his face,
then, after Manuel has filled his briefcase full of cream, shakes it
thoroughly, places it under Hutchinson's arm and sends the poor
cream-drenched wretch on his way. 'If you ever come back,'
Basil shouts out after him, 'I shall kill you.' Delighted with this
gloriously cathartic exercise, he kisses Manuel on the forehead,
then strides back over to the counter and beams at the new
arrivals: 'Good afternoon, gentlemen. And what can I do for you
three gentlemen?' Another quick look, a pause, and the penny
drops: '*Aaaaagh!!!*'

It was the perfect end to an episode that, right from the start,
had choreographed its comedy with rare precision, locking

Basil's paranoia together with Hutchinson's pedantry in a plot that called for gladiatorial clashes of rival character flaws. Bernard Cribbins, with his deft mixture of aggressiveness and vulnerability, might not have played the part quite as naturalistically as John Howard Davies had originally envisioned (he had wanted to cast a 'straight' actor in the role), but was still remarkably funny as well as very tough (Cribbins later confirmed that those karate chops on his back – executed several additional times for alternative shots – really did hurt: 'Two more takes and I would have been gone!'[9]). Whereas a more subdued and 'smaller' performance would have risked making Basil's attacks on Hutchinson seem more cruel than amusing, Cribbins showed the audience just the right degree of bone-headed bloody-mindedness to make them cheer when his head hit the cheese.

The same could have been said about the performances by the regular members of the supporting cast. Ballard Berkeley, in particular, contributed a wonderfully subtle, precise and disciplined piece of 'background' acting, doing 'nothing' with such conviction that, in contrast to so many actors pitched on the periphery of similar sitcom scenes, the camera never caught him looking the slightest bit self-conscious or robotic. Take, for example, the moments in the dining room leading up to and following Basil's assault on his pest of a guest: Berkeley's Major keeps the viewer focused on the foreground by never straying from his own little sphere of realism, studying the menu avidly, accepting a complimentary torn omelette with absent-minded gratitude and, upon hearing Basil mention a bit of cheese, responds with a dreamy, 'Yes, please!' The most commonly underestimated or overlooked kind of contribution (a watermark of realism), it was, nonetheless, one more reason why such shows flowed so well.

The episode was also notable for its keynote moments of frenzied physical humour. John Howard Davies, especially, was responsible for encouraging such a trend, relishing the chance to show Basil battling to open a stubborn bottle of wine, jabbing Manuel in the backside with a corkscrew, tearing up an erroneous omelette and choking a guest, being attacked by a guest and ending up assaulting a guest with a selection of unordered desserts. Probably the most memorable moment of all, as far as such bits of physical business were concerned, occurred when Basil, tiring of Manuel's chaotic incompetence, picks up a dirty dessertspoon and cracks the hapless waiter hard and flat on the forehead ('You're a waste of space'). 'I'm afraid that was pure John Howard Davies,' the show's director later admitted. 'I remember doing it during the filming of *Tom Brown's Schooldays* [. . .] and we used to play with wooden spoons in just the same fashion. Then some forty years later it came up again.'[10] A stickler for realism in his slapstick, his only regret, he would reflect, was that the various utensils had not been bigger and harder and the countless smacks, kicks and punches even sharper and stronger ('I love a bit of violence!'[11]).

There were plenty of similar incidents, along with frantic farce and biting dialogue, the following week in another glorious half-hour called 'Gourmet Night'. The cruellest episode so far, it kept on allowing Basil a hint of some hope – only to then punish him for his dogged pursuit of a dream.

In a neat little inversion of Henri Bergson's theory that comedy comes from the encrustation of the mechanical on the living (in other words, we laugh when we see a human being behaving in a mechanical way), one of the comic threads running through the episode concerns the encrustation of the living on the machine: Basil is convinced that his car is conspiring against him by acting like a capricious individual. The opening scene, for example, finds Basil in the forecourt, fiddling under the bonnet of the Fawlty vehicle: a clapped-out cherry-red Austin 1100. When he tries – twice – to start it up, it just sits there, not at all bothered. Basil is exasperated: 'Oh, come *on!*' he tells it. 'Is it *so* difficult for you to start? I mean, it's so *basic*. If you don't go, there's very little point in having you!' He gets out and goes round to the front again, bonnet up, more fiddling, more hope. The horn jams on. He is close to losing his patience: 'Now, just pull yourself together, right? *Make the effort!*'

Manuel interrupts this intimate car-driver spat, because, he claims, the telephone is ringing in reception, and Mrs Fawlty is nowhere to be seen. Basil arrives in reception just in time to see Sybil emerge from the office and answer the telephone, so he takes Manuel over to the desk, points at Sybil, and says, in a very businesslike manner, 'This . . . Basil's wife,' then points at himself, 'This . . . Basil,' then holds up his hand and aims it at his waiter, 'This . . . smack on head.'

Everyone seems to be in good spirits today – except Basil. Polly has just sold a sketch; Sybil has just been given a glass of wine; and Manuel, in spite of his stinging head, is flattered to have found another friend – the hotel's new chef, a burly but rather emotional Greek called Kurt. Basil, on the other hand, is in his usual agitated state, still angry at his car (but determined not to take Sybil's advice and pay good money to get it repaired) and depressed by his continuing failure to find any decent class of guest. His latest idea to improve the situation is an exclusive 'Gourmet Evening', but, when his favourite local restaurateur, André, arrives the following Sunday to advise him on the event, the 'ignorant rabble' dining that night remind him of how great is the challenge ahead. The Major, for example, thinks the top-quality soup tastes 'a bit off' ('Well, it's made with *fresh* mush-rooms, Major'; 'Ah, that would explain it'); then there is the spoilt brat called Ronald, who informs Basil that his chips are 'the wrong shape', the eggs 'look like you just laid them' and the meal as a whole is no better than a 'pig's garbage'; and, to compound the insult, Ronald's mother asks why, instead of the home-made mayonnaise, there is no bottle of 'proper' salad cream on the table. Disgusted to be in the presence of these 'proles', Basil tries to focus on making his one special evening of *haute cuisine* a reality, muttering that 'on the other nights we'll just have a big trough of baked beans and garnish it with a couple of dead dogs'.

When the great day finally arrives, however, Sybil announces that the Cooster family has cancelled at the last minute (SYBIL: 'One of them's ill'; BASIL: 'Well, let's hope it's nothing trivial'), leaving just four people present at the grand opening dinner. Basil tries hard not to let her dampen his spirits ('Never mind,' he snaps, pointing out proudly that three of their four remaining guests are none other than 'Colonel and Mrs Hall, *both* JPs, and Lionel Twitchen, one of Torquay's leading Rotarians'), but she continues to nag and niggle: 'I should never have let you write that advert. Fancy putting "No riff-raff"!'

The arrival of the first two so-called VIPs, Colonel and Mrs Hall, sparks some real excitement ('Right – *this* is what it's all about!'), but things start going horribly wrong more or less immediately. Basil is so bewitched by Colonel Hall's pro-nounced facial twitch that he cannot even remember his own name (but, alas, he does remember to inquire about the health of the colonel's daughter – who is, it turns out, now deceased), and even the normally self-assured Sybil, upon catching sight of the extremely diminutive Mrs Hall, finds herself asking, 'What would you like to drink, Mrs Small?' Things go from bad to worse when the second couple turn up, and Mr Twitchen asks to be introduced to the twitching Colonel Hall – a *faux pas* waiting to happen that panics Basil into executing a quick pretend faint ('Ah, I feel better for that!') followed by a hasty exit.

Entering the kitchen, he is confronted by an even more distressing sight: an inebriated Kurt, dozing on the floor after failing to seduce Manuel. The quick-witted Polly comes to Basil's rescue, advising him to order a quick dish or two from André. He does so, and then, after typing up a new and much shorter menu, invites his puzzled guests to make their selections:

COLONEL HALL: 'Duck with orange' . . . 'Duck with cherries' . . . 'Duck Surprise' . . .

MRS TWITCHEN: What's 'Duck Surprise'?

BASIL: Ah . . . that's duck without oranges or cherries.

COLONEL HALL: I mean, is this all there is – *duck?*

BASIL: Um . . . Ye-es . . . Done, of course, the three extremely different ways.

COLONEL HALL: Well, what do you do if you don't like duck?

BASIL: Well, if you don't like duck . . . er . . . you're rather stuck! *[Laughs awkwardly]*

Back in the kitchen, Basil tries to set up some quick starters, but, stuck with an uncooked mullet, he begs the still-prostrate Kurt to mumble some advice: 'Do we *fry* it?' he asks. 'Just go "uh-huh".' Kurt goes 'uh' and is sick all over the fish. ('I was made to cut that shot,' John Howard Davies would later reveal, adding that 'we even had the obligatory carrots in the fake vomit.'[12])

There is still more agony in store for Basil. After managing – just – to get his chronically unreliable car to splutter all the way to André's and back, the freshly cooked duck ends up being knocked to the floor and trodden on by Manuel, so, while Polly, Manuel and Sybil struggle to 'entertain' the now-starving guests with show tunes, strummed guitars and 'humorous' anecdotes, Basil races back to André's for second helpings. In his haste, however, he picks up the wrong serving dish, hurries back inside his car and then, as the motor begins to misbehave for the umpteenth time ('That bloody car!' recalled John Howard Davies, noting that it was almost as bad as it seemed. 'It never travelled at more than twenty-eight miles an hour in its entire life. It's hardly surprising what happened to it!'[13]), he rages at the apparent betrayal:

> Come on, *start*, will you? Start, you vicious *bastard!* Come *on!* Oh, my *God!* I'm warning you – if you don't start . . . I'll count to three: One . . . two . . . *three!* Right! That's it! *[Jumps out of the car and addresses the vehicle]* You've tried it on just once too often! Right! That's *it!* Right, don't say I haven't warned you! I've laid it on the line to you *time* and *time* again! Right! Well . . . this is it – I'm going to give you a damn good *thrashing!*

After beating the bonnet repeatedly with a large branch ('It took a very long time,' the director later revealed, 'to find a branch that was right'[14]), he completes the journey back on foot, and enters the dining room in triumph: 'Ladies and gentlemen! So sorry to have kept you waiting!'

Then comes the *coup de grâce*. Sharpening a knife with panache while beaming at his guests, he lifts up the silver cover of the serving dish and looks down at the duck – which is now, inexplicably, a large and ornate pink trifle. He looks at it approvingly, does a quick double-take, and slams the cover back down. Lifting it up again a couple of inches, he peers disbelievingly inside, then looks around the room in search of the absent duck. He checks on the lower shelf of the trolley, and then, out of desperation, he plunges both hands into the trifle and searches for the bird within. Finding nothing, he breaks into a dazed smile, thinks for a moment, then turns to his guests and inquires brightly: 'Well, er . . . who's for trifle?' When one of them asks what has happened to the promised duck, he pauses, then replies reluctantly: 'Duck's off. Sorry.'

As endings go, this one was stunningly apt, eschewing the conventional sitcom sentimentality to leave Basil high, dry and duckless. It was not only apt, however: it was also highly refreshing to find such a popular – and populist – format deprive, repeatedly, its anti-hero of any degree of a reprieve. Decades before the likes of *Seinfeld* and *Curb Your Enthusiasm* were winning praise for having the audacity to keep their comedy completely free from hugs, homilies and compassion, *Fawlty Towers* was already daring to do just that. It was actually evolutionary rather than revolutionary – Galton and Simpson, in moving from Anthony Hancock to Albert and Harold Steptoe, had already driven the sitcom in the direction of a darker and harsher place, and then Johnny Speight, with the bigoted Alf Garnett, added a more stubbornly cynical SatNav – but, emotionally, Cleese and Booth were now heading even further down that dismal road. Whereas even the Steptoes were allowed the odd fleeting victory (such as the episode in which Albert managed to escape from an otherwise fractious family funeral with an expensive heirloom hidden under his bowler hat[15]), Basil Fawlty seemed a truly, purely, tragic sitcom character, destined never to escape from being hit by the daily wave of humiliation.

The point was made even clearer by the closing episode of the series. Entitled 'The Germans', it supplied us – via a temporarily short-circuited super-ego — with an unforgettable glimpse of what demons were straining to run riot inside Basil's benighted brain.

The show opened with Sybil in hospital on the eve of surgery on an ingrowing toenail. Basil listens impatiently to her last few instructions (collect some 'stuff' from a local shop; remind Chef to scrape the mould off the cheddar; and put the moose head up on the wall in the lobby), before pointing out that, given the upcoming fire drill and the imminent arrival of a party of guests from Germany, he already has more than enough things to do ('I thought slavery had been abolished'). Back on his own at the hotel, however, Basil is irritated to find that he is still under Sybil's surveillance, with frequent telephone calls from her sickbed interrupting his efforts to get the mangy-looking moose up on display ('I was just *doing* it, you stupid woman!'). Matters are not helped by the Major, who, on his way to the bar, overhears the news about the Germans. '*Germans?* Coming *here?*' he exclaims. 'I don't much care for *Germans!*' Clearly in no mood to forgive and forget, he makes his views known in no uncertain terms — 'Bunch of *Krauts!* That's what they are. *All* of 'em. *Bad eggs!*' — before heading off in search of 'a fruit juice . . . or something' ('Drunken old sod,' mutters Basil shortly before enduring yet another interruption from Sybil and then a sudden bang on the head from the moose).

The following morning, Basil is back in reception, determined to stamp his authority upon the new day. The moose head is finally up, and the fire drill is about to commence. Everything appears, for once, to be going exactly to plan.

Unfortunately, however, Sybil calls once again to remind him that she has placed the key to the fire alarm in the safe; what she fails to remind him is that opening the safe will set off the burglar alarm. Chaos breaks out in the lobby as the guests start heading for the exit:

BASIL: Look! What's the matter with you all? It's perfectly simple. We have the fire *drill* when I ring the fire *bell*. *That* wasn't the *fire* bell. Right?

MAN: Well, how are we supposed to *know* that wasn't the fire bell?

BASIL: Because it doesn't *sound* like the fire bell!

ALL: It did!

BASIL: It *didn't!*

ALL: It *did!*

BASIL: No it *didn't.* The fire bell is different . . . it's a semi-tone higher.

WOMAN: A *semi-tone?*

BASIL: At least. Anyway, the fire drill doesn't start till twelve o'clock.

MAN: It *is* twelve o'clock.

BASIL: Well . . . it is *now*, but that's because we've been standing around *arguing* about it!

'I don't know why we bother,' he grumbles, as the guests start ambling back out of the hotel. 'We should let you all burn!'

Manuel, meanwhile, has somehow contrived to set the chip pan alight in the kitchen, so, singed and smoking, he rushes out into the lobby shouting, '*Is fire! Is fire! Is fire!*' Jumping to the wrong conclusion, Basil pushes him back into the kitchen, locking the door as he explains, 'Is no fire! It only bell!' Ignoring his smouldering waiter's screams (which deserved to sound convincing, seeing as the chemicals used to make Sachs's jacket smoke were burning one of his arms so badly – turning it plum red in colour – he would end up receiving £700 in damages from the BBC), Basil calls the guests back inside and tries to attend to the next task, until, after some unwelcome prompting from his guests ('Right, right, I'll deal with it, thank you so much for poking your nose in!'), he finally lets poor Manuel back out, glimpses the flames inside and finally realises what is actually happening. 'Sorry to disturb you all like this,' he tells the returning guests awkwardly. 'The point is . . . er . . . can I put it this way: "Fire"?' He starts barking at them, like a dog to some sheep, to hurry them all back out: '*F-f-f-f-f-f-fire!!!*'

Now that he really does need to ring the alarm, however, he cannot find the key, so he shakes his fist at the ceiling and screams bitterly, 'Oh thank you, God! Thank you so *bloody* much!' Polly, as calm and cool-headed as usual, tells him to trigger the alarm by smashing the glass, but he injures his hand trying, then misses with a typewriter before finally breaking through with the telephone. Racing off to pick up the fire extinguisher, he heads over to the kitchen door and, as he struggles to read the instructions, invites Manuel to pull the nozzle open, then points it towards the smoke and flames – and succeeds only in spraying himself in the face with the foam. Temporarily blinded, he leaps straight up in the air, hits Manuel's frying pan and, concussed, crashes to the floor unconscious.

The next time that he opens his eyes, he is in hospital with a turban-like bandage on his head. 'Well, thank you for coming to see me,' says Sybil, sardonically. It soon becomes clear that the bump on the head has stunned Basil's internal censor, because he now says whatever slips into his head ('My god, you're ugly, aren't you!' he tells Sister). Although the doctor comes into the room and urges Basil to go back to sleep and get plenty of rest, one eye is soon back open and glancing furtively around the room. He is obviously up to something.

Back at the hotel, Polly is busy helping the guests from Germany to settle in when Basil suddenly returns, with his head heavily bandaged and a hospital smock still visible beneath his jacket. 'You OK?' asks a bemused Manuel. 'Fine, thank you, dear,' replies Basil absent-mindedly. 'You go and have a lie-down.' Then it is his turn to be puzzled when, as he resumes his position behind the desk, one of the guests comes up and says, '*Sprechen Sie Deutsch?*' Seeing that he is confused, they translate: 'You speak German?' Basil, his concussed head finally processing the information, smiles with relief: 'Oh, *German!* I'm sorry, I thought there was something *wrong* with you!'

The rest of the episode reveals just how much damage and distress a combination of a backward mind and a bruised brain can cause in a confined space. Lapsing into the Little British delusion that shouting in a foreign accent is the same thing as actually speaking in another language, Basil adopts an Adolf Hitler voice to assure the bewildered visitors, who have merely inquired about the possibility of renting a car ('*ein Auto mieten*'), that there is already 'meat hier . . . in ze buildink!!' Polly arrives just in time to prevent any further offence, and, after hearing Basil whisper to her, '*They're Germans. Don't mention the war,*' she rushes off to call the hospital.

Basil, meanwhile, has wandered into the dining room and, believing himself to be on his best behaviour, is attempting to take some orders: 'Oh, *prawn*, that was it. When you said *prawn* I thought you said *war*. Oh, yes. *Oh*, the war! Oh, yes, completely slipped my mind, yes, I'd forgotten all about it. Hitler, Himmler, and all that lot, oh yes, completely forgotten it . . .' It goes from bad to worse: 'I'll just get your *hors d'oeuvres . . . hors d'oeuvres vich must be obeyed at all times vizout question . . .* Sorry! Sorry!' Polly urges him to answer an urgent call from his wife, but he brushes her aside, warning her in another whisper, 'Listen: don't mention the war. I mentioned it once, but I think I got away with it.' Then he returns to his guests:

> BASIL: So that's two egg mayonnaise, a prawn Goebbels, a Hermann Goering and four Colditz salads . . . no, wait a moment, I got a bit confused there, sorry. *[One of the women begins to sob]* I got a bit confused because everyone keeps mentioning the war, so could you . . .
> *[One of the other guests, who is comforting her, glares at Basil]*
> BASIL: What's the matter?
> MAN: It's all right.
> BASIL: Is there something wrong?
> MAN: Will you stop talking about the war?
> BASIL: *Me?* You started it!
> MAN: We did *not* start it!
> BASIL: Yes you did – you invaded Poland!

He tries to lighten the mood by attempting a joke featuring a man in a bomber over Berlin, then, realising that something far more impressive is now required, he proceeds to place a finger across his upper lip and does his Führer party piece, goose-stepping his way out of the room and then back in again. Much to his amazement, not even this has done the trick:

> MAN: *Stop it!!*
> BASIL: I'm trying to cheer her up, you stupid Kraut!
> MAN: It's not funny for her.
> BASIL: Not *funny?* You're *joking!*
> MAN: Not funny for her, for us, not for any German people!
> BASIL: You have absolutely *no* sense of humour, do you?
> MAN: THIS IS NOT FUNNY!
> BASIL: *WHO WON THE BLOODY WAR, ANYWAY?*

The end comes, mercifully, when Basil spies his doctor sneaking up on him armed with a hypodermic needle. Chased through the lobby, he pauses under the mounted moose and, believing that he has given the doctor the slip, slaps his hands together in triumph – and the moose crashes down again on his head.

Structurally, the episode was, as John Howard Davies remarked, 'two shows in one': the first half was about the failure of communication, and the second about the failure of diplomatic repression. John Cleese agreed, and, like Davies, would end up preferring the former to the latter: 'I think the first half of [the episode] is written beautifully,' he said. 'I've always been fascinated by people trying to communicate and not being able to [. . .]. I don't know why I find it so funny, but I always do. The fact that [Basil's] trying to explain to his guests that it is not the fire alarm but the burglar alarm is just an opportunity for that sort of comedy. I love the moment where Basil says, "I don't know why we bother anyway . . . we should let you all burn." I love that line.' The second half, in contrast, left him feeling dissatisfied: 'I never think [it's] as well written as all that. There are several things in it that I think are wrong.'[16]

'Wrong' is probably too strong a word to describe any aspect of what was still a riveting sequence of scenes, but the pace was, perhaps, a little too forced after the brief lull that followed the fire-drill debacle, cranking the show back up to its second frenzied peak; while both halves had the potential to be expanded into their own respective full-length episode, there was something awkward about the way that they were integrated here together. The ending (which had been improvised just after lunch on the day that the show was due to be shot) was arguably another minor flaw, seeming quite slight and cartoon-like after the intensity of the previous few minutes ('It wasn't entirely satisfactory,' admitted John Howard Davies. 'In fact, looking back, it didn't really work, and was a bloody nuisance, but it *was* a conclusion – and sometimes a conclusion is better than no conclusion, even if it doesn't quite function as it should do'[17]).

One element that probably caused a slight worry at the time was Basil's maniacally xenophobic rant, which always carried the risk of being misconstrued, just as Johnny Speight's material had been for the infamously bigoted Alf Garnett, by the very people it was meant to mock. These scenes were clearly written, however, with the intention, as Cleese himself would later explain, to show how 'people like Basil are utterly stuck in the past. If you look at the episode, all the people that he was interacting with are much too young to have had anything to do with the Second World War. [Most of us can] let go. Basil can't do that.'[18] It was one more coldly comical insight into the sitcom's extraordinary anti-hero, as well as an inspired inversion of the familiar wartime story – depicting the Germans as the peaceful people, and the British Basil as the disruptive madman, in order to mock the act more than any particular actors.

The material certainly had the desired impact during the actual recording. 'This was the first time [on television] that anybody had made these sorts of jokes,' John Howard Davies reflected. 'There was just a *frisson* of shared embarrassment [among the studio audience] which I think added immeasurably to the pain of the whole thing. It made the laughs that bit more poignant.'[19] The reception when the show was screened was a similar mixture of surprise, slight discomfort and huge amusement, because, as well as being a little unnerving for some viewers at the time, it was also so strikingly well-written and cleverly executed – as well as very, very funny – it was hard not to just sit back and admire and embrace its full comedic force ('So tasteless,' said *Fawlty Towers* fan Martin Scorsese, 'it's hilarious'[20]). The joke, after all, was not on the Germans: it was on Basil – as well as, in a way, on us. From the next morning on, anyone who had seen the show now had a new phrase to sum up the terrible anxiety we all have about trying, and failing, to not say the wrong thing: 'Don't mention the war!'

The episode also brought the whole series to a close with a discreetly neat sense of symmetry. As in the first episode, so too in the last, Basil began by being pestered by Sybil to hang something up in the lobby ('And Basil, please get that picture up – it's been there for a week'; 'And do try and find some time to put the moose's head up – it's been sitting there for two weeks'); and he ended up with the task still waiting to be done (the picture stuck on the floor, and the moose's head stuck on Manuel). What happened between these two beginnings and endings – farcical complications, neurotic outbursts and a demoralising defeat for Basil – was what, by the last of the six episodes, viewers had come to expect, relish and remember.

Fawlty Towers had found its fans. Slowly but surely, it had built up an audience and earned their affection and respect. Some had followed it from the start, while others had arrived late, but all of them, by the end, were in agreement: they wanted more.

6

Papers Arrived Yet, Fawlty?

So . . . it's all right, is it?

It was a strange kind of success. In certain circles, among certain people, *Fawlty Towers* had quickly established itself as a favourite topic of conversation, with scenes analysed, characters interpreted and catchphrases (such as Basil's '*Coh!*'; Sybil's 'Oh, I *know* . . .'; Manuel's '*Qué?*'; and the inevitable 'Don't mention the war!') repeated on countless spontaneous occasions. Innumerable schoolchildren, office workers, undergraduates, politicians, taxi drivers, builders, caterers and even (and in some cases especially) hotel managers, waiters and chambermaids could be overheard referring to it, and laughing about it, from one week to the next. On the printed page, however, the series had left only the faintest of traces.

This was not as mysterious then as it might seem now. There were no preview videotapes available in those days, and even studio preview screenings were very rare, so television critics in the mid-1970s were largely obliged to watch a programme 'live' at home, like any other viewer, and then, like theatre critics, rush to get a response ready to be dictated 'down the line' in time for the next day's second or later edition. New sitcoms, with their unfamiliar contexts and characters, represented a particularly high risk for a reviewer anxious to avoid ending up six weeks later with egg all over his or her face, so, even if the pilot editions were duly watched and evaluated, such shows were usually given time to 'warm up' before anything definitive was actually committed to print.

The subsequent dearth of reviews for *Fawlty Towers* was, therefore, more or less inevitable, as, in addition to these common problems, the show also had the 'misfortune' of being screened on a Friday – and all British national daily newspapers preferred to use their Saturday editions to showcase the weekend schedules rather than recall the previous evening's output; thus, anything shown on a Friday, regardless of its worth, tended to be ignored by the vast majority of the national critics (and, as the arts pages of the Sunday papers went to press on Friday after-noons, anything shown that night stood less chance of a mention than anything in any other slot during the week). To make matters worse still, most of the 'quality' broadsheet papers still regarded television, as a potentially 'proper' cultural subject rather than just an occasional source of distraction or contro-versy, with a certain degree of suspicion, considering most of its output to be evanescent and relatively trivial, and thus what critical TV columns existed were by no means guaranteed a daily, or even a weekly, space alongside those that covered the more established areas of the arts.

Fawlty Towers, as a consequence, was never going to register very strongly on the critical radar, because such a radar barely existed. Oliver Pritchett, however, did, to his credit, manage to review the pilot episode the following Monday in London's *Evening Standard*: he remarked that he had found the plot 'thin and obvious', and suspected that all of the other storylines in the series were similarly destined 'to take second place to the manic performances of John Cleese'. He concluded on a slightly more positive note by declaring that, although the first half-hour had been 'a bit frantic in its pursuit of laughs', he 'would still award it a tentative three stars [out of five] and promise to return.'[1] That, in fact, was more or less that as far as the initial national coverage was concerned, but a few more fleeting comments did pop up on the preview pages at the end of that opening week.

The *Daily Express* was especially enthusiastic, with Douglas Orgill recalling the debut as 'hilarious' and asserting that, although he doubted that the next instalment would be able to 'retain the full impact of the first one', if it turned out to be 'three quarters as good it will suit me.'[2] The *Daily Mirror*, on the other hand, was far from complimentary. According to its previewer – a journalist by the name of Tony Pratt – the opening show had been 'almost a one-man effort' by Cleese and there was 'certainly room for improvement.' Beneath these comments was the following depressing conclusion:

MIRROR VERDICT: *Long John is short on jokes.*[3]

It was a snap judgment that certainly niggled: John Cleese saw the clipping, saved it, and would still be referring to it more than thirty years later.[4]

Another critique that cut deep came from Richard Ingrams, the then-editor of the satirical magazine *Private Eye* and most definitely not an admirer of John Cleese (nor, it seemed, of anyone else associated with the *Monty Python* troupe). Relishing the opportunity to slip in the knife as an occasional TV critic, he proceeded to dismiss the show – not only in print but also in the company of countless of Cleese's comedy contemporaries – as laboured, banal and unfunny.[5] Cleese was so irritated by the gleeful severity of the attacks that he would wait patiently for the chance to exact his revenge (which, eventually, he would via a sly little gag during the second series in an episode entitled 'The Kipper and the Corpse').[6]

The second episode fared no better, in the sense that it came and went without provoking much published comment at all, but there were signs, by the Friday of the third instalment, that the series was beginning to acquire some influential admirers. Tim Ewbank, previewing 'The Wedding Party' in the *Daily Mail*, hailed the show as 'the best of the Friday laughs at present',[7] while the *Guardian*, in a pithy aside, judged it to be 'highly amusing'.[8] Slowly but surely, a few more viewers were being nudged in the right direction.

It would be wrong, however, to suggest that everything now being committed to print was uniformly positive. Indeed, by far the most substantial response so far, by Peter Buckman in the *Listener* magazine on 9 October, was actually fairly damning:

> Unfair though it may be to expect pure genius to drip always from Cleese's pen, he and his wife have given themselves pretty hollow characters to play, and they have some little trouble stretching the thing over half-an-hour. Of the cast, only Prunella Scales, as the proprietor's nagging wife, brings any real depth to her part, and this makes her considerably more sympathetic than the monster she is supposed to be. Cleese, moreover, while being lovably manic, is not exactly a great character actor, and tends to do little more than vary his pitch from *forte* to *fortissimo* in his effort to flog matters along. Most regrettably of all, a large part of the funny business revolves around that venerable stooge, a Spanish waiter with faulty English. While not for a moment accusing Cleese and Booth of racism, jokes about dagos and wops horrified some Americans who were watching with me,

and once this had been pointed out, I began to notice all sorts of racist jibes.[9]

Such a negative reaction, however, was far from typical at the time.

Midway through its run, for instance, the show was being billed by the *Daily Express* as the 'funniest' and 'most essential viewing of the week',[10] and even the previously unimpressed *Daily Mirror* was now advising its readers to 'put [the show] on tonight's menu'.[11] Clive James – probably the most insightful, as well as the wittiest, of a new generation of TV critics – had been 'on holiday' when the sitcom had started, but he managed to note (after the third episode) that the show had 'several times had me retching with laughter' before his 'on holiday' sign reappeared.[12] As a consensus started to take shape, so a growing number of other commentators prepared themselves to commit an opinion to print. Peter Fiddick, for example, reviewed the penultimate episode ('Gourmet Night') in the *Guardian*, praising the show for being 'something out of a new mould', and applauding the cast for their willingness to 'cheerfully embrace a range of comic methods that stretches from Pythonesque funny walks, through split-second slapstick, to comedy of manners'. Prunella Scales was the actor singled out for the warmest praise of all, with Fiddick saying of her performance: '[She is] a smashing actress at any time, [and is] having a ball as Mrs Fawlty, adopting a refined whine somewhere between Henry Cooper and Twiggy, and attacking Cleese at the level she finds him, which is usually just below the nipples.' He also found space to salute the contribution made by the producer/ director, John Howard Davies: 'He's done what must on paper have looked improbable, to find the style of shooting and editing, and the precision, that makes all these complicated jokes work, and with a mounting energy that, now I think of it, is hard to believe.'[13]

The broadcaster Joan Bakewell, writing in the *Listener* the following week, spoke as one of those who had been drawn to the show belatedly after being made curious by all of the positive talk: 'I have only recently caught up with *Fawlty Towers* and come to see what I have been missing. Considering how many different styles of humour it taps, it should fail. And it almost does: we laugh with relief that John Cleese and his cronies continually pull it off. There is rattling repartee, full blown custard pie stuff, funny chases and walks, comic stereotypes and hilarious Laurel and Hardy routines.'[14] There were similarly positive observations, here and there, as the days went by, as well as welcome little asides in the odd diary column. The sitcom's impact remained far from spectacular, but at least it was acquiring a reassuringly positive profile: 'The critics,' as John Cleese would put it, 'began to quite like it.'[15]

By the end of the run, they liked it a lot. On the morning of Friday 24 October, when the series was about to come to a close, there was a considerable amount of admiration expressed for what had been witnessed over the previous few weeks, as well as, it seemed, a fair measure of genuine regret that the run was now on the verge of being over.[16] As Douglas Orgill, one of the show's earliest and most consistently enthusiastic journalistic admirers, remarked as he previewed the final edition: 'What can one say about *Fawlty Towers*, except that the week has to be arranged so that one doesn't *ever* miss it?'[17]

Once it was all over, however, those who had loved the show could not quite fathom how it had not found a higher profile. Being screened on BBC2 had been one obvious explanatory factor – traditionally, many of the same viewers who would quite happily sample a BBC2 show once it had transferred to BBC1 would, for some bizarre reason or other, avoid watching it on the 'minority' channel (possibly fearing that, like the lower-middle-class Leonard Bast being flattened by a bookshelf stuffed with classics in *Howards End*, they might be inadvertently exposed to a snatch of Schönberg or Samuel Beckett). The patchiness of the performance remained, however, a matter for puzzled speculation. There were already plenty of firm and passionate fans around, but there were also a surprising number of people who had never seen the show and knew precious little about it. It was often a matter of feet and inches: on the one side, a Fawlty fanatic, and on the other, someone who barely knew that Fawlty even existed. This stark division between admiration and indifference could lead to some odd moments of disorientation.

Michael Palin, for example, was rather surprised to find, when lunching with his old friend John Cleese at Morton's in Berkeley Square, that 'despite having completed a very funny, widely praised series on the awful way people can be treated in hotels and restaurants, John and I are shown to the smallest table in the room, at which John has great difficulty in actually sitting.'[18] It might, of course, have been a case of spiteful retaliation, but it certainly appeared as though the two comedians had wandered into one of those odd little Fawlty-free zones. On another occasion, in no less grand a dining establishment nearby, Cleese and another friend found themselves being fêted and fussed over like visiting Hollywood stars, with plenty of friendly references to the show and its situations. The sense of how the series had actually fared therefore tended to fluctuate, as a consequence, from one day, or even hour, to the next.

Other members of the cast tended to be too preoccupied with their next projects – and the immediate business of learning dialogue and developing characters – to peruse all of the papers and ponder on the impact of their last show. Prunella Scales, for example, would remark: 'At the time, it all went by far too quickly for you to take much notice. Making one show each week – that was such a very tight, very tough, schedule. So all one could think about was learning the lines, getting them in the right order and then doing the live show on the Sunday night. And, after the series was over, there were other things to do, so there was no real opportunity to sit back and reflect on it all.'[19] Andrew Sachs was similarly distracted: 'I hadn't seen much in the Press. I didn't know, really, what, if anything, the show had been doing in terms of reviews or audience numbers or anything like that. This was my first time as a regular member of a series, so I didn't have anything to compare it to. I certainly felt, from my perspective, that the scripts had been really funny and the shows had gone very well, but as for anyone else, well, no, I wasn't sure. What I did know was what I'd gleaned, quite early on during the filming of the series, from a cameraman on the show. I'd gone over and asked him: "You've worked on a lot of these sitcoms and series, how do you rate this one?" He said, "Oh, this is a good one, this is. Yes, this one's *very* good!" And he knew how these things worked, so that made me feel like this was going to be something quite special.'[20]

John Howard Davies, meanwhile, would profess that he had been confident of the show's success right from the start. '*Fawlty Towers* was one of those rare situation-comedies that attracted an audience from page one,' he recalled. 'It was rather like *Porridge* in that respect. Very few other comedies with which I've been involved were instant successes, but, as far as I was concerned,

Fawlty Towers was one. Those who saw it loved it. As for the reviews, however many, or few, there were – they were irrelevant, in my opinion. I'd directed the first few *Monty Pythons*, and we didn't get any reviews at all for that until about episode three, so it wasn't that unusual, in those days, for reviewers to be a little bit sympathetic, or cautious, and wait for a show to bed in a bit. That's why, later on as an executive, I would refuse to let the reviewers see a programme before it actually went out, because I didn't want them, for whatever reason, to colour the viewer's judgment. I thought it was unfair, and, I suppose, unhelpful.'[21]

The BBC could certainly see that, in spite of the show's relatively low-key start, it now had a potentially huge hit on its hands, and, to its credit, the Corporation wasted no time in scheduling a second run of the entire series at the start of the following year. Beginning on 6 January 1976 – still at 9.00 p.m. and still on BBC2, but now occupying a new slot on Tuesdays – *Fawlty Towers* was screened again, and, this time round, the critical praise was quick, clear and unequivocal. 'A thankfully early re-run for the best comedy of last year,' trumpeted the *Guardian*, 'and one of the funniest ever.'[22] The *Daily Express* agreed, welcoming back the 'superb' first series with the advice to prospective viewers: 'If you didn't see it the first time round, don't miss it now.'[23] Even better news was to come later on in the repeated run, when, in a spectacular (but unacknowledged) *volte-face*, the *Daily Mirror's* Tony Pratt – the man who had dismissed the original screenings with the withering remark, 'Long John is short on jokes' – now urged his readers, 'Don't miss the funniest comedy series of last year,' and, by way of a slyly revised concluding judgment, declared:

VERDICT: *Comedy at genius level.*[24]

★   ★   ★

It seemed like the encomia had been holding back for the arrival of an echo. 'Suddenly, on the repeats,' John Cleese would come to reflect, 'you got the impression something was happening; some kind of groundswell of approval was happening.'[25] The regular audience was certainly growing – more than six million viewers were now tuning in each week to watch *Fawlty Towers* for the first or second time[26] – and so was the profile – the phrase 'Fawltyesque', for example, had started to creep into both the Press and the public's common vocabulary (as had Sybil's 'Oh, I *know*, I *know* . . .,' which, as Clive James noted in his *Observer* column, 'you can hear people copying all the time'[27]), and any instance of real-life bad service now seemed to be likened to life in the fictional hotel.[28] The first of many awards would soon follow – on 14 May 1976, the Royal Television Society honoured John Cleese for his 'Outstanding Creative Achievement'[29] (not for the last time, alas, his co-writer's creative contribution was either overlooked or underrated) – and later on in the same year, most unusually for the television of the era, a second set of repeats was slotted into the peak-time schedules.

Beginning at 8.15 p.m. on Sunday 5 September, but this time on BBC1, the new run confirmed the show's stature as a major mainstream success. More critical praise came from the Press – e.g.: 'Supremely funny';[30] 'Compulsive viewing';[31] 'Not to be missed by connoisseurs of fast comedy';[32] 'TV's funniest sitcom';[33] and 'The funniest show on British television'[34] – as well as the odd journalistic apology – 'I hated it first time round,' acknowledged Peter Buckman in the *Listener*, 'but when it was repeated [. . .] I laughed like a drain.'[35] There would also be more awards, including ones for the performers (Andrew Sachs, for example, was named 'Most Promising Artist' by the Variety Club of Great Britain), the producer/director (John Howard

Davies received a BAFTA) and, of course, for the programme itself (the Broadcasting Press Guild judged it 'Best Comedy').

After three screenings within a year, *Fawlty Towers* had gone from being watched by a mere 1,868,500 people to well over twelve million, and it showed no signs of losing its current appeal. In the days just before the era of home video (which was still about a couple of years or so away),[36] each subsequent TV repeat of the sitcom was looked forward to with keen anticipation and then lapped up like a fairly special treat. Lines were learned, scenes memorised and observations exchanged. The fascination with *Fawlty Towers* thus continued to grow and grow. While fans waited for the second series, they deepened their affection for the first.

THE REGULARS

Hallo, Fawlty Towers, how are you, is nice day . . . oh, YOU again!

7

Basil and Sybil

SYBIL: *You're only single once.*
BASIL: *Twice can be arranged . . .*

Right from the start, the relationship between Mr Fawlty and Mrs Fawlty was one of those things that one had to watch with a grimace and a nervous giggle. A marriage made in Hell and then endured on the English Riviera, it was sadomasochism without either the sex or the pleasure – but still, it seemed, with the nature of a grim addiction.

Who were these two monsters? What on earth had brought them together? What on earth kept them from tearing each other apart?

The first series told audiences precious little about the respective pasts of Basil and Sybil, but it did let slip the odd (and not entirely reliable) little hint along the way. We were told, for example, that Basil had once been involved in some kind of military service abroad,[1] and it was alleged that Sybil had fled from finishing school at a disappointingly premature stage,[2] and, as co-founders of Fawlty Towers, it had taken the pair of them 'twelve years to build this place up'.[3] No truly clear and telling biographical details were forthcoming, however, and the viewer was left to reflect on what clues he or she could glean from the screen.

It was obvious, on the basis of such evidence, that Basil practically demanded long-distance psychoanalysis. One could tell, just by looking at him, that he was, as the Major would have put it, 'a queer fish'. The flat, black, greasy hair did not help; nor did the dark, glassy eyes, the frowning moustache and the stiff-lipped, flat-lining mouth. It was his body, however, that sent out the strongest signal that this was a decidedly faulty human being: tall, thin and uneasily angular, it resembled a symbol oscillating between question and exclamation. When he ran, it was almost diagonally, with his eager feet hurtling forwards and his cautious head holding back, making him seem rather like a fatigued accountant straining to pull back an overexcited young cocker spaniel. When he tried to remain still, the effort appeared immense, with the arms never far from a flap, the shoulders tensed tight enough to snap and the chin flitting up, down and around like a super-sensitive radar. Rather than acting as a window through to the soul, this vessel served instead as an unwitting sick-note to the outside world. Whatever was beating deep within the brain and the heart, it was clearly being held prisoner by the flesh and the bone. The whole thing was not so much a body; it was more a battleground where impulse and habit, and hope and fear, fought each other long and hard and fruitlessly.

From where did this weird creature come? It had to be from some cold and lonely corner of Little England. Basil was almost certainly born in the sober South, quite close to, but not quite in, a prosperous and properly respectable middle-class area. He would thus have been near enough to all of the tweedy nobs and toffs to grow up resenting their air of superiority, while longing for the day when, one way or another, they would accept him within their snooty little club. His own family would not have been 'common', but just frustratingly 'middling' – dutiful, prudent, Pooterish people who (deep down) knew their place but were proud of their modest but hard-earned property and were both pleased and relieved to find that there were now slightly more people on whom they could look down than there were those to whom they still had to look up. Basil, as (presumably) their only child, would have been groomed for something mildly but practicably progressive – some sort of stable and respectable position in society, buttressed by a decent wage and a generous pension – so it is by no means inconceivable that, at a push, a place was funded for him at one of Britain's most minor middle-draw public schools; so great, however, remains the adult Basil's craving for the full regalia of privilege and power, it seems slightly more likely that even this proved a dream too far for the Fawlty family, and he was left to go through the motions at a decent but prosaic provincial grammar school.

Whatever kind of education he did receive would largely fail to brighten a fairly dim sort of native wit. Although, for example, Basil would later claim to have studied and mastered several foreign languages, his adult grasp of 'classical Spanish' left him hopelessly ill-prepared to understand the 'strange dialect' that his waiter Manuel 'seems to have picked up',[4] and the number of clumsy *faux pas* he commits when attempting to understand either French (he mistakes a request for '*café au lait*' for an invitation to echo the exclamation '*olé*'[5]) or German (he confuses, among other things, '*Auto mieten*' for the act of securing some meat[6]) suggests that the extent of his education, in this area at least, has been greatly exaggerated. Indeed, the only bona fide skill with which we can be sure he emerged at the end of his years in formal education was an exceptional capacity for twisting, inverting and/or obscuring inconvenient truths.

What, then, did Basil do after leaving school? We know that he served his obligatory stint on National Service. Once again, however, we cannot be confident about his own account of what actually happened. According to him, he fought on the front line in the Korean War ('I killed four men'), incurring a 'touch of shrapnel'[7] for his troubles that would later give him 'a bit of gyp from the old leg'.[8] According to his predictably unimpressed wife, however, he muddled his way through the hostilities from the relative safety of the kitchen as a lowly member of the Catering Corps, and, if he ever did contrive to claim any lives, it was only as the result of his serious short-comings as a cook ('He poisoned them'[9]).

Upon returning to civilian life, he must have considered a number of ways to claw his way up the social ladder before settling on a career as an hotelier, although joining the rat-race was not quite his only option. Torn between meek subservience to his so-called 'superiors' and a fiercely misanthropic need for self-reliance, it must have been tempting for him to withdraw from the battle and seek out some kind of life lived away from all of the others, some safe and assuaging little sanctuary like that stubborn idealist Thoreau had found in the woods near Walden Pond. Ultimately, however, Basil would have felt unable to resist the challenge of defying the doubters to become the biggest snob of the lot, so he stuck it out among the crowd, hating every minute but driven on by the dream of one day soaring high above the *hoi polloi*.

His ideal England – the England in which he feels he would most freely flourish – is a black-and-white world full of hope and glory and cosy country pubs, run by the likes of Ronald Colman, John Mills and Kenneth More and decorated by such well-bred young ladies as Anna Neagle and Celia Johnson; it is a place in which everyone still wears sensible caps or hats, drives Genevieve-style motor cars, reads Dickens, listens to the Home Service, plays cricket, drinks claret and defers without fuss to the great and the good. Basil was never some kind of proto-Thatcherite, because he was never remotely meritocratic, let alone a fanatic about the free market. He is not against the Establishment as such; he is just against an Establishment that has no place within it for him. In his own mind, one suspects, he is convinced that, if only contemporary England would change for the better, then so, too, would he: all of those tightly tangled nerves would relax and unfurl, all of those angry rants would fade away, and he would at last be free to be the real Basil, the good Basil, and all would be sweetness and light. Until then, as far as this deluded buffoon is concerned, he has no choice but to endure the strain of trying to be a fine man in a faulty world, and keep suffering the slings and arrows of outrageous fortune.

He has been suffering more than ever since he met and married that petite but powerful woman known as Sybil. Bolder, probably brighter and certainly far more earthbound and busi-nesslike than Basil, she must have unnerved him in ways that he did not quite understand. Whereas he would have been spec-tacularly sexually repressed (and possibly still a virgin), she would have been experienced, self-confident and aggressively direct. If he had wanted her, he would surely have been far too scared to dare to date her, whereas if she, for some peculiar reason, had wanted him, she would have set off on that muscular mince of hers and forced him twitching and screaming into her bed.

It is not too difficult to imagine what he saw in her: a slim and short, rather attractive, somewhat vulgar, strikingly vivacious and excitingly ambitious young woman – definitely not a budding Celia Johnson, but, in her own distinctive way, certainly very intriguing. It is more of a challenge to imagine what she could have seen in him: perhaps she regarded him as suitable raw material for her to shape and eventually enslave; perhaps she considered him a promisingly pliable business partner who could fund and help drive her own designs; and perhaps she relished the challenge of seducing such a gauche and hapless young man.

Whatever the real reasons that first drew them together, some sort of romance duly began and the pair of them ended up getting married. What followed was a combination of ambitions that fitted together like fingernails dug deep into each other's flesh: Basil wanted a solid material basis upon which he could build up his social stature, and Sybil wanted a commercial project through which she could pave a steady way to luxury; so they settled on co-owning an hotel. Such an essentially incoherent collaboration promised plenty of marital tension, but, just as it is preferable to persevere with the pain of the nails rather than remove them and risk bleeding to death, the couple elected, however perversely, to help each other's hopes survive and perhaps even thrive.

Both were no doubt excited when the joint project began. Basil would have been thrilled by the thought of becoming an hotelier because it offered him a theatre in which to act out his delusions of grandeur. Sybil would have relished the chance to boss a promising business and benefit from its burgeoning profits. By the time that we, the audience, first see them, however, the bitter sense of disillusionment, on both sides, has well and truly taken root.

Neither is now getting what they need from Fawlty Towers. Basil's ambition to escape from the *hoi polloi*, for example, remains frustratingly unrealised. He still craves class and culture and kudos – he does not particularly want to pay for them, or slave for them, but he definitely still craves them – and yet, twelve years on, he finds himself stuck in the same old rut, still at the beck and call of the common folk (including his wife, who sits around smoking and cackling, reading downmarket magazines and reminiscing about her Uncle Ted and his crates of brown ale[10]). Similarly, Sybil continues to dream of the well-earned life of leisure, while struggling to stop her husband from shattering what hopes she still has of ever making it happen ('This is a hotel, Basil, not a Borstal'[11]). As for their marriage: it has come to seem more like an obsessive and irresolvable war.

Both of them have attempted to seek out some form of serviceable distraction. Basil has tried to busy himself with the odd hobby (he collected coins of the British Empire for a time[12]) while improving his knowledge of fine wines (he now thinks he knows that 'a Bordeaux is one of the clarets'[13]), while Sybil has invested a great deal of time and effort in perfecting the intricate style of her extraordinary coil of hair (a forerunner of Marge Simpson's mountainous beehive), acquired a daringly eclectic range of 'fashionable' clothes, taken to consuming a 'vat of wine'[14] and 'a hundredweight of lime creams',[15] and insisted on getting away on a regular basis to indulge in a gossip and round of golf with the girls. Whenever the two of them are obliged to spend any time together, however, the marriage seems primed to explode.

Whatever romance they once shared is long dead, and, apart from one stray blip of nostalgia from Basil about friendlier times spent together ('Let's go for a walk – we haven't done that for years'[16]) and an inexplicably rash attempt to give her a rare peck on the cheek (SYBIL: 'What are you doing?' BASIL: 'I'm kissing you, dear.' SYBIL: 'Well, don't.' BASIL: 'I just thought it might be nice to . . .'[17]), neither husband nor wife seems inclined to mourn its passing. Sex is still something that, on a certain day at a certain time (with a certain sort of person: 'Only one watt but plenty of volts'[18]), Sybil might fancy – in the same way that, on another occasion, she might fancy a slice of walnut cake, a pot of chocolate mousse or a glass of white port – but she could quite easily go without it, and, as far as any conjugal relations with Basil are concerned, she has almost certainly preferred to go without it for several years. He, meanwhile, probably needs it, but has been so long without it that he fears he would expire should he ever get it again (which explains his mixture of incredulity, gratitude, excitement and blind panic when a French female guest starts being flirtatious[19]). The two of them still share a bedroom, but now they occupy separate beds. He wears sensible striped cotton pyjamas, she wears a lacy mauve negligée with various froufrou embellishments; he edges off to sleep by reading *Jaws*, she sits up smoking, eating chocolates, snorting at glossy magazines and sometimes gossiping to Audrey on the telephone. They seldom speak to each other except when they want to complain.

There is not even one person in this marriage. The only thing that they seem to share is a feeling of mutual indifference, invigorated every now and then by cynical niggles and savage *ad hominem* attacks. Basil refers to Sybil as, among other things, 'the Tyrant Queen';[20] 'a toxic midget';[21] 'my little nest of vipers';[22] a 'stupid great tart';[23] a 'great stupid sabre-toothed tart';[24] a 'half-wit';[25] 'a stupid woman';[26] 'my little piranha fish';[27] a 'golfing puff-adder';[28] and 'a sour old rat'.[29] He also mocks her somewhat economical work-rate ('I wish you'd *help* a bit – you're always . . . refurbishing yourself'[30]), bridles at her bossiness ('I thought slavery had been abolished'[31]), likens her raucous laugh to the sound of 'somebody machine-gunning a seal'[32] and, whenever she sets off alone into town, he mutters after her, by way of a good-luck wish, 'Have a nice day, dear. Don't drive over any mines or anything.'[33] Sybil, in turn, refers to Basil as 'cheap';[34] 'toffee-nosed';[35] and (when she is in a good mood) 'a big bad-tempered tomato'.[36] She also ridicules his managerial skills ('You know what I mean by "working", don't you, dear? I mean getting things done, as opposed to squabbling with the guests'[37]), bemoans the fact that he will 'never, ever, learn',[38] rages about his 'pathetic lies'[39] and complains bitterly: 'The day *you* co-operate you'll be in a wooden box!'[40]

The closest thing that Basil has to a shoulder to cry on is his one relatively competent employee: Polly. Although the Major is always happy to concur with his right-wing complaints about the parlous state of the nation ('It makes you want to cry, doesn't it?'[41]) and his loathing of Labour politicians ('I mean, what is happening to this country? It's *bloody Wilson!*'[42]), and is easy to sway on the subject of his wife (MAJOR: 'She's a fine woman, Mrs Fawlty.' BASIL: 'No, no, I wouldn't say that.' MAJOR: 'No . . . nor would I'[43]), it is only Polly upon whom Basil can rely to cover up his mistakes and, when she deems it appropriate, conspire with him to outwit his wife. Sybil, on the other hand, has a firm friend by the name of Audrey: an unseen but intensely neurotic middle-aged woman whose regular and highly dra- matic bulletins on her desperate marital problems ('Any news? . . . Oh dear, he hasn't? . . . Ooh! I *know* . . . He doesn't deserve you, Audrey, really, he doesn't . . .'[44]) probably make Sybil feel that there is at least one woman worse off than herself.

There is no hope, these days, of any constructive communication between husband and wife, because each has become a puzzle to the other. Basil simply cannot understand why Sybil spends so long gossiping on the telephone (SYBIL: 'Audrey has some news that may interest you.' BASIL: 'Oh really? This'll be good. Let me guess . . . The Mayor wears a toupée? Somebody's got nail varnish on their cats? Am I getting warm?'[45]), nor can he make any sense of her own moans and groans ('Oh dear, what happened? Did you get entangled in the eiderdown again? . . . Not enough cream in your éclair? Hmmm? Or did you have to talk to all your friends for so long that you didn't have time to perm your ears?'[46]) or her maddeningly matter-of-fact mentality (whereas he cannot stop questioning why, say, a label for 'PENS' looks more like 'BENS', she simply says, 'Well, when Ben comes you can give it to him', and then moves calmly on[47]). Sybil, similarly, cannot comprehend why Basil thinks he looks good by wearing fusty flat caps, ill-fitting stripy ties, old-fashioned cravats and jackets that are simultaneously bland and garish ('You wouldn't understand, dear – it's called "style" '[48]), or tries to decorate the hotel with such antique curiosities as a 'nasty' old moose head ('It is not nasty, it is superb'[49]), and she dismisses the classical music that he loves so much as a 'racket' ('*Racket?* That's *Brahms!* Brahms's *Third* Racket!!'[50]).

There is not even any prospect of a consensus when it comes to the question of how best to manage their co-owned hotel. Although Basil sometimes likes to sneer that a sort of cruelly organic division of labour has grown up and is now solidly in place – 'My wife enjoys herself. I worry'[51] – neither of them, in truth, seems to know, or understand, what the other one is doing. Every snappy exchange is like one more dialogue of the deaf:

BASIL: We're losing tone.
SYBIL: We're making money.
BASIL: Yes, yes . . .
SYBIL: Just.
BASIL: Yes, but now we can try to build up a higher class of
   clientele! Turn away some of the riff-raff!
SYBIL: So long as they pay their bills, Basil.
BASIL: Is that all that matters to you, Sybil? Money?[52]

Basil laments the fact that Sybil lacks any aptitude for thinking imaginatively. Sybil laments the fact that Basil lacks even a scrap of common sense. Each, as a consequence, has become the other's biggest irritant.

What, then, continues to hold this odd couple together? In Basil's case, a chronic sense of fear certainly helps. He has come to know, as the years have gone by, that what seemed initially to be a rather enticing kind of feistiness in Sybil is actually, when fully unleashed, a capacity for inflicting a mixture of physical and emotional violence worthy of Boadicea and Dorothy Parker combined ('She can kill a man at ten paces with one blow of her tongue,' he cries[53]). One might surmise, therefore, that Sybil holds on to Basil for the same reason that a cat keeps hold of a mouse by its tail: for the sheer sadistic devilment of it all. This does not, however, really settle the matter, because Basil, as a flawed but always eager schemer, could surely find a way to make a break for it (and return, as he puts it, to 'the land of the living'[54]), and Sybil, as an accomplished but cynical flirt, could almost certainly snare herself another unwitting victim. There must thus be something else, something deeper, to explain why this wretched union goes on.

It might just possibly be down to the one quality that they still have in common: *amour-propre*. They both have so much pride that neither can quite bear to admit – to him- or herself as much as to anyone else – that they have been stupid enough to have made such a massive mistake. Divorce is therefore not an option (so they have no choice but to continue to cohabit in separate beds), and neither is the sale of the hotel (so they have no choice but to continue to co-manage at cross-purposes). They are thus, perversely and profoundly, stuck with each other, because so long as they still have each other, they feel there is no need to admit complete defeat.

Freud would have called it denial. Faust would have called it: 'No deal'. The important thing, however, is that, for Basil and Sybil, it is now the only tolerable option available. They might both be miserable, but they are still driven on by their respective dreams, and they cannot face up to failure. Basil still clings to the hope that he can attract a better class of clientele, and Sybil still clings to the hope that the hotel will eventually be sufficiently profitable to enable her to live an opulent style of life. The future, therefore, looks destined to remain Fawlty for both of them – and therefore funny for everyone else.

That, at least, was the way that it appeared to be on the evidence of what was seen on the television screen. Most of the critics certainly thought so. Kenneth Robinson, for example, observed, with a hint of a nervous twitch, that the trials of Basil and Sybil provided 'only a slightly exaggerated account of the brink of hatred that many marriages survive on.'[55] Clive James was similarly impressed, remarking that the 'humour takes off for the Empyrean from an airstrip firmly constructed in reality. That the wife should possess all the emotional coherence, and the husband be continually falling apart, seems to me not just an elementary role-reversal but a general truth of such power that it is only in comedy you will see it stated.'[56]

The viewers at home agreed. These two characters, as comically horrid though they might well have been, were still quite believable. It seemed that there were an awful lot of misfits still about. Everyone seemed to know a Basil, and more than a few seemed to know a Sybil ('Ooh, I *know* . . .'). – and some even knew of certain marriages that were just as bad, and just as weirdly durable, as that.

Basil and Sybil seemed real. They also seemed odd, and unpleasant, and psychologically unwell – but they still seemed real, and they lived on long after each episode had stopped. It might not have suited either of them – 'We're stuck with it, I suppose,' Basil would groan[57] – but it certainly suited the rest of us.

8

Polly and Manuel

You want to run the place?

Polly and Manuel: the waitress and the waiter. Both of them have good hearts, but only one of them has a decent brain. Polly is the one who can usually be relied on to help clear up the mess; Manuel is the one who can usually be relied on, in spite of his best intentions, to help cause it. Both have a certain role to play within Fawlty Towers: she is the rock; he is the rubble.

The audience soon grew to admire Polly for her fairness and common sense: like Sergeant Wilson had always done with Captain Mainwaring, she tolerated Basil Fawlty's oddity, slyly mocked his pomposity and tried to advise when an action seemed unwise. It also quickly became clear that she helped us to believe in what we were watching, because, as the show's very own internal reality check, her apparent normality stopped all of the lunacy from looking like the norm.

Manuel, on the other hand, was a firm audience favourite right from the start, because of his amiable nature, his puppy-like eagerness to improve and his alarmingly unguarded vulnerability. Each week, as the action progressed, he suffered various kinds of physical and verbal abuse, and sometimes he deserved it and sometimes he did not, but it was always painfully clear that this poor little wretch had only been trying his best to help. We also knew that Manuel was often the spark that lit the Fawlty comedy flame: he only needed to set off on the simplest of tasks to shift the story from order to chaos. He was someone we laughed at, and someone we loved.

It made sense that Polly and Manuel were such good friends. She appreciated his kindness, gentleness and seemingly indomitable *joie de vivre*, while he valued her patience, encouragement and consistently sound advice. He cheered her up, and she did her best to keep him safe and well and in a job. Basil and Sybil might have been a couple of monsters, but these two remained reassuringly human.

How, then, did they, of all people, come to work at a place like Fawlty Towers? It was surely more through bad luck than design.

We do know that Polly Sherman never really wanted to be a waitress. Being a waitress was only meant to be a means to an end. Her problem is that the end still remains frustratingly out of sight.

She has not yet tired, however, of the challenge of pushing on as a struggling young Anglophile. Although most of her childhood was lived out in her native America, she appears – judging by the fact that the only old school friends we see her reunited with are English[1] – to have been in this country for quite a while, and shows no signs of being keen to leave. What she really wants to do is pursue a career here in the field of art, but, although her ongoing studies have so far made her sufficiently proficient to sell the odd little sketch, she still has to rely on her waitressing for a basic wage.

She must have first wandered into Fawlty Towers, about two

years ago, in the hope of finding a calm and friendly place in which to work her way through college. What she found there instead was a bad atmosphere, bad management and bizarre scenes of marital strife. Why, then, did she take on a job in such an unappealing environment? We do not know if she was told the fate of her harassed-sounding predecessor, Elsie, who had recently escaped to start a far calmer kind of life in Canada, but Polly would no doubt have been shrewd enough to have seen that the portents were fairly poor. A dearth of alternatives, however, must have persuaded her to go ahead and accept this job as a slightly glorified dogsbody. Something else, sooner or later, would turn up, she would have thought, so the move made sense as a short-term compromise.

Then, one suspects, her perspective began to change in a strange and unexpected sort of way. She appears, after a time, to have started to acquire a quasi-anthropological fascination about the wild kind of life that lurked inside Fawlty Towers. It was so odd, so eccentric and so incredibly unpredictable that it must have been hard not to stop and stare. She might indeed have felt an irresistible need to wait and see what would happen next.

She certainly seems, by the time that we first see her, to have found a niche there that, while protecting her sanity, allows her to witness much of the madness. Basil's manic antics not only keep her on her toes but also provide her with a rich vein of anecdotes about 'the famous Fawlty' with which to entertain all of her friends.[2] The often indolent Sybil, meanwhile, allows her, by default, plenty of time and space in which to assume a greater share of responsibility and exercise a certain amount of initiative. One way or another, therefore, she has come, strange though it seems, to rather enjoy the adrenaline rush that arrives with each new day inside the hotel.

Polly also now takes considerable comfort, and quite a fair measure of pride, from the knowledge that she is actually getting to be rather good at her job. She has developed what the distinguished sociologist Erving Goffman (who made his name with a study of the workings of a Shetland Islands hotel[3]) defined as 'dramaturgical discipline': namely, a willingness, as part of a team presenting a particular image to the public, to promote what is meant to be on show and protect what needs to remain hidden. Such a person, said Goffman, is someone with sufficient amounts of discretion, *sang-froid* and presence of mind to be able to 'cover up on the spur of the moment for inappropriate behaviour on the part of his team-mates, while all the time maintaining the impression that he is merely playing his part.'[4]

Both Basil and Sybil know, reluctant though each may be to admit it, that in Polly they have an excellent team player and an invaluable member of staff – indeed, hiring her has been one of the few decisions that either has so far called right. Basil, for example, might sometimes snap, snarl and shriek at her (calling her such unpleasant names as a 'poor, innocent, misguided child',[5] a 'silly girl'[6] and a 'cloth-eared bint'[7]), but he knows that, when he needs her, she will do what she can to save him from suffering too much humiliation. She certainly succeeds in stopping him from being robbed by the rogue Lord Melbury, and tries valiantly (if in vain) to rescue him from being battered by his wife over the hiring of Mr O'Reilly ('Bravo, Polly!') and contrives, quite ingeniously, to assuage the noisy rage of a troublesome guest:

HUTCHINSON: You told me to shut up!
POLLY: No, no. He told *me* to shut up.
HUTCHINSON: You what? He said it to *me*.

BASIL: Ah, no, I was *looking* at you, but I was talking to Polly.
[Still looking at Hutchinson] Wasn't I, Polly?

POLLY: *[Looking straight at Hutchinson]* Oh, yes.

BASIL: Ah! Did you notice then . . . that I was looking at you
but talking to her?

HUTCHINSON: What?

POLLY: *[Looking at Basil]* You see? He was looking at you but
talking to me. Wasn't he?

BASIL: *[To Polly]* Wasn't I?

HUTCHINSON: *[Looking back and forth]* W–what?

POLLY: *[Looking at Hutchinson]* So you weren't being rude, were
you, Mr Fawlty?

BASIL: *[To Polly]* Absolutely not. You see?

HUTCHINSON: *[Confused]* Me?

BASIL: *[To Hutchinson]* Yes?

HUTCHINSON: Well, if you say 'shut up' to someone, that's the
one you want to shut up, isn't it?

POLLY: *[To Basil]* Well, not necessarily.

BASIL: *[To Hutchinson]* I'm sorry, were you talking to me?

HUTCHINSON: Yes.

POLLY: *[To Basil]* I beg your pardon?

BASIL: *[To Hutchinson]* Ah! There – you see how easily these
misunderstandings occur?

HUTCHINSON: Er . . . y-yes, I do . . .[8]

Polly is, quite simply, crucial to Basil's fortunes: as a fire-fighter,
co-conspirator, occasional confidante and well-meaning
straight-talker ('Oh, just pull yourself together!'[9]), she keeps
finding ways to stop him from falling all the way down to his
ultimate doom. Although Basil is far too repressed to ever reflect
on how much (and why) he really needs her, he clearly dreads
the thought of her absence: indeed, when he is at his most
stressed and insecure, he actually behaves towards her like a cross

between a stern father and an over-possessive lover, warning her not to 'hob-nob with guests' and doing what he can to drive away anyone who looks like a potential suitor (he addresses one such budding boyfriend, Richard Turner, contemptuously as 'Mr Turnip', and reminds him that he is now in a hotel, not a 'massage parlour'[10]).

Sybil, on the other hand, might not bother to 'waste' any praise on her able waitress, but she knows that, whenever things start threatening to fall far apart, Polly is the one employee who can be relied on to help her cancel the crisis. Sybil is too self-obsessed to want to invest any time or effort in cultivating a bona fide protégée; besides, she would not welcome the prospect of having to contend with a younger version of someone as strong-minded, ambitious and sybaritic as herself. The seemingly aimless and uncomplaining but very industrious Polly, therefore, poses Sybil no real threat, and is just about trustworthy enough to allow her to spend quality time away gossiping with poor Audrey or playing the odd round of golf. Like Basil, therefore, Sybil cannot contemplate letting Polly slip away: she is one of the few functional cogs in the Fawlty machine.

When it comes to her supposedly ancillary career as an artist, however, neither one of her co-employers shows much under-standing of what she hopes to achieve. Basil, the brittle tradi-tionalist, cannot make head nor tail of her experiments with non-representational styles – 'What is *this* supposed to be? . . . I mean, what is the *point* of something like that? . . . It's *irritating!*';[11] 'Do you win a bun if you guess what it is?'[12] 'Yes, very modern. Very socialist.'[13] He seems oblivious to the fact the he has become a sort of muse for her more symbolic types of sketch – 'This is a *junk* yard, isn't it? Why's it got a collar and tie underneath?'[14] – and casts doubt on the value of her technical training ('Three years at college and she doesn't know the time of day'[15]). Sybil, meanwhile, is not so much bemused by as completely indifferent to her employee's off-duty activities, although she is always happy to accept a free drink to celebrate the rare occasion of the sale of a sketch.[16] Manuel, predictably, is the only person inside the hotel who truly appreciates Polly's efforts, and he even spots the satirical symbolism: 'Oh! Is Mr Fawlty!'[17]

Manuel, of course, is as great a source of conflict inside the hotel Fawlty Towers as Polly is a source of consensus. Manuel has what Erving Goffman would have described as an unfortunate and dangerous proclivity for committing 'unmeant gestures or *faux pas*' which 'give the show away by involuntarily disclosing its secrets'.[18] If a door needs to be kept shut, a word kept unsaid or a guest kept contented, Manuel will somehow end up doing the exact opposite. A control freak's worst nightmare, he could sustain the supporters of chaos theory single-handedly.

It needs to be noted, in his defence, that this odd little man has not been a waiter for long. He has, however, been brave – or naïve – enough to come all the way from his native Barcelona, where he left behind a mother, five brothers and four sisters, in order to attempt to make a new life for himself in Britain.[19] An exceptionally sanguine soul, he probably hoped to find an interesting job – ideally one that paid well enough to enable him to send plenty of cash back to his family in Barcelona – and start learning how to master a challenging craft. How he ended up in Torquay, of all places, remains something of a mystery.

It is less of a mystery as to how and why he found employment at Fawlty Towers. He was cheap.

Basil simply could not resist hiring someone who was willing to work such long hours for so small a remuneration. The knowledge that Sybil would have spent far more on a properly qualified professional selected from a reputable specialist agency only added to his personal sense of triumph: the pliable, eager, mild-mannered Manuel would be transformed by him into a perfectly decent, but still indecently cheap, hotel employee – and thus prove the superior wisdom of Basil's Way.

The problem so far, however, has been that Basil has struggled to make his way pay. Manuel, as a waiter, is still stuck at stage one. 'We're training him,' Basil keeps explaining, while straining to contain his rage about having burdened himself with such a Sisyphean task. It hardly helps, of course, that this trainee from Barcelona continues to seem so utterly befuddled by the basics of the English language:

> BASIL: There is too much butter on those trays.
> MANUEL: *Qué?*
> BASIL: There is too much *butter* . . . on . . . those . . . trays.
> MANUEL: No. No, no, *Señor!*
> BASIL: What?
> MANUEL: Not 'on-those-trays'. No, sir – *'uno, dos, tres'. Uno . . .*
> *dos . . . tres.*
> BASIL: No, no! *Hay mucho burro alli!*
> MANUEL: *Qúé?*
> BASIL: *Hay . . . mucho . . . burro . . . alli!*
> MANUEL: Ah, *mantequilla!*
> BASIL: What? *Qué?*
> MANUEL: *Mantequilla. Burro* is . . . is . . . *[Brays like a donkey]*
> BASIL: *What?*
> MANUEL: *Burro* . . . *[Does another donkey impression]*
> BASIL: Manuel, *por favor* . . .
> MANUEL: *Sí, sí . . . ?*[20]

Sybil, of course, believes that such confusions prove the wisdom of Sybil's Way: they should have done the sensible thing and hired a proper professional. Manuel might indeed be cheap and keen to learn, but, she is convinced, he will never be a competent, reliable and recognisably English-speaking waiter, no matter how long Basil huffs and puffs: 'It'd be quicker,' she moans, 'to train a monkey.'[21] If she had her way, therefore, Manuel would be handed his cards and sent straight back to Barcelona – and it is this very fact that compels Basil to protect him. Manuel might be an idiot, but he is Basil's idiot, and that makes Basil, in spite of his many rants and violent attacks, Manuel's best bet against getting the sack. To acknowledge that Manuel is wrong would be to acknowledge that Sybil is right, and that, for Basil, would simply be unbearable.

Fawlty Towers, therefore, finds itself well and truly stuck with a waiter who does not know how to wait. No facet of the job fails to flummox him. He is hopeless, for example, at dealing with diners: 'Today, we have veef, beal or sothahhhes';[22] he is incapable of adapting to changes of routine: '*This* is table *one!* Is *Wednesday!* Room Seven is table *five!*';[23] he is a menace in the kitchen: '*Fire! Fire! Fire! Fire!*';[24] and, when required to deputise for Basil at reception, he struggles to make any sense:

BUILDER: Where's the boss?
MANUEL: Boss is, er . . . Oh – *I* boss!
BUILDER: No, no – where's the *real* boss?
MANUEL: *Qué?*
BUILDER: The . . . the *generalissimo*.
MANUEL: *[Confused]* In Madrid![25]

Polly is doing what she can to coach him, but even she is finding his limp grip on the language a cause for concern:

POLLY: I go upstairs.
MANUEL: *Sí*. Is easy.

153

POLLY: For a little sleep.

MANUEL: Is difficult.

POLLY: For a siesta.

MANUEL: *Siesta?* 'Little sleep'?

POLLY: Yes.

MANUEL: *Ah!* Same in Spanish![26]

There is, every now and again, the tantalising prospect of some slight progress. By the final episode in the first series, for example, we find Manuel feeling sufficiently confident about his firmer grasp of his new language ('"Shut up"? Yes, I understand, yes!'[27]) to start affecting the accent: 'I speak English well. I learn it from a book. *Hhhello*, I am English. *Hhhello*.'[28] Such confidence, however, is shown to be misplaced whenever Basil (who now addresses him sarcastically as 'The Admirable Crichton') attempts to make himself understood:

BASIL: Go and get me a hammer.

MANUEL: *Qué?*

BASIL: Ham-*mer*.

MANUEL: Oh – hammer sandwich!

BASIL: *[Groaning]* Oh, do I have to go through this *every* time? Look: a *HAMMER!*

MANUEL: My *HAMSTER?*

BASIL: *No!* Not your *hamster!* How can I knock a nail in with your hamster? Well, I could *try* . . . no, it doesn't matter, *I'll* get it. You come here and tidy – you know, 'tidy'?

MANUEL: Tidy – *Sí!*

BASIL: I get *hhhammmer* and *hhhit* you on the *hhhead* with it. *Hhhard*.[29]

He would surely be forgiven for wanting to give up the struggle and slope off back to his home in Spain – 'Is no sun, is no good

for me,' he moans self-pityingly at one point. 'I homesick'[30] –
but he is actually much tougher and more determined than he
looks. He has come here to succeed, and, no matter how many
setbacks that he suffers, he still believes that, at some stage, he
will indeed be held up and hailed as a rare and immense success.
He has also been buoyed by the fact that, with his 'cute' and
positive personality, he has found it so easy to make new friends.

Just about everyone seems to like Manuel. Polly not only
supports him, and sometimes sketches him ('That's wonderful,
Manuel, just hold it a second'[31]), but has also accommodated
him within her own little fun-loving social circle. Even Sybil, in
spite of her reservations, has warmed to him sufficiently to award
him the odd somewhat indulgent evening off.[32] The only
problems, in this sense, that he has encountered have occurred
when certain people have come to love him not wisely but too
well, as was definitely the case when he inadvertently inflamed
the passions of the hotel's short-lived gourmet chef, Kurt: 'Now
listen to me, Kurty!' he shouts nervously from the other side of
the kitchen door. 'I come in here but no cuddle. You hear me?
No cuddle!'[33]

Basil, predictably, still affects a far cooler response to his well-
meaning but frequently exasperating employee. He smacks him
on the forehead with a spoon when an order is confused –
'You're a waste of space'[34] – and resorts to a similar gesture
when Sybil's temporary absence provokes unnecessary panic –
'This . . . Basil's wife. This . . . Basil. This . . . smack on head'[35]
– and apologises to everyone, except Sybil, who witnesses the
waiter's incompetence – 'Well, he's hopeless, isn't he?' he
complains bitterly to the latest guest whom Manuel has let
down. 'You might as well ask the cat.'[36] Basil cannot help liking
the fact, however, that Manuel – in contrast to just about

everyone else inside the hotel – comes when he is called and tries his best to do what he is told. Whenever Sybil instructs Basil to do some menial chore, he knows that he can at least attempt to instruct Manuel to do it for him. He also knows that, whenever one of his secret schemes needs executing, Manuel can be relied on to be by his side, like a sort of dozy Sancho Panza to his Don Quixote, ready and willing to do his master's bidding. Interpreting all of the screams, slaps, pokes and punches as mere attempts at being cruel to be kind, he remains completely devoted to the man who was mad enough to hire him: '*Mr Fawlty, I love you, I love you, you so kind, you so good to me, I love you, I love you!*'[37]

He and Polly, therefore, look as though they are set to stay where they are for quite a while. Polly will keep on making the hotel seem like a hotel, and Manuel will keep on making the hotel seem like something very Fawlty. Each, in his or her own peculiar way, seems destined to remain indispensable.

9

The Major and The Minors

Say goodnight to the folks, Gracie . . .

Major Gowen, Miss Gatsby and Miss Tibbs: they are part of the furniture of Fawlty Towers. They might be older and slower-moving than the rest of it at times, but they are still part of the furniture. The Major is based largely in the bar, while the two elderly ladies are more likely to be glimpsed in a cosy corner of the dining room, but all three of them help gild Fawlty Towers with a faint glint of a more elegant Edwardian age.

Major Gowen is, as Basil is always happy to acknowledge, the hotel's 'longest-standing guest'.[1] Now well into his seventies, sporting casually curly eyebrows and a stand-easy moustache, he remains, nonetheless, a straight-backed and smartly dressed old soldier (in a 'uniform' that consists of a blue double-breasted blazer with a crisp white handkerchief lodged in the top pocket; gun-metal woollen slacks; and shiny black leather shoes), and he retains an abiding reliance on fixed routines and favourite rituals. He arrives in the lobby at the same time each morning via his long-striding, slightly splay-footed gait, and, smiling expectantly, always makes the same polite inquiry: 'Papers arrived yet, Fawlty?'

We do not know any precise details about his background, but we do at least know that he spent many years abroad serving in the military, defending first a King and then a Queen and always his beloved Country, before settling into a long and leisurely retirement on the English Riviera. An avid reader of all the broadsheets, he now plods through each page of news and sport, seeking out what items seem to speak of the old world to which he once belonged so proudly. This is the world in which Great Britain still had its great Empire, the class hierarchies held firm, officers and gentlemen did the right thing, ladies knew their place and county cricket actually mattered. This is the world in which Major Gowen still feels most at home.

It no longer exists, of course, except deep inside the old boy's head – so he likes to live in there. He can be alarmed whenever any hint of harsh modernity manages to impinge itself on this antiquated vision ('More strikes! Dustmen!! . . . Post Office!!! . . .'[2]), but tries to compensate by concentrating on what precious few steadfast pleasures are still around – such as first-class county cricket ('Hampshire won!'[3]), single malt whisky, blended whisky, Bombay Sapphire gin, guns and golf, *Test Match Special*, decent English cheese, Gentleman's Relish, well-made nature documentaries and the occasional England Test success ('Ah! D'Oliveira made a hundred!'[4]).

This insulated existence has certainly made him an increasingly unreliable guide to his current environment. While he knows that the hotel is still co-managed by the Fawlty couple, he sometimes confuses Polly with her predecessor, Elsie,[5] and struggles to recognise the identity of the new Spanish waiter, Manuel ('Come here, come on . . . what's your name?'[6]). Such absent-mindedness, however, is offset by his remarkably calm brand of personal pragmatism, which ensures that nothing ever truly shocks the system. When, for example, the 'Orelly' men have done their worst and bricked up the wrong space in the lobby, the Major – in stark contrast to the harassed Basil – stays preternaturally unfazed:

BASIL: Good morning, Major. I'm so sorry, I'm afraid the dining-room door seems to have disappeared.
MAJOR: Oh, yes – so it has! It *used* to be there.
BASIL: Yes, well, I was silly enough to leave the hotel for a few minutes . . .
MAJOR: Yes, well, these things happen, you know. Now, I wonder where it's got to? Don't worry, it's bound to turn up . . . Ooh, er . . . have the newspapers arrived yet?[7]

There are only two subjects that still have any chance of rattling his rusty cage: foreigners and women. Foreigners remind him of all his old foes and former battles, and so, whenever one or more of them turns up within the hotel, he cannot disguise his immense displeasure. The supporting players are bad enough (MAJOR: 'Tell me – are you, by any chance . . . *French*, at all?' VISITOR: 'Yes.' MAJOR: 'Good *Lord!*'[8]), but, when the main protagonists turn up, the eyes bulge, the cheeks burn and the bellowing duly begins: '*Germans?* . . . Coming *here?* . . . Oh, I don't care much for *Germans* . . . Bunch of *Krauts!* That's what they are. *All* of 'em. *Bad eggs!*'[9]

Women represent a far more complicated problem; as a veteran red-blooded bachelor, he still rather likes them, but he has long given up the struggle to understand them. 'Strange creatures, women,' he reflects – noting their tendency to do odd things like slipping off 'to powder her . . . powder her hands . . . or something', as well as the apparent disinclination of some of them to return everything that they borrow ('She's still got my wallet!') – but he has to admit that he much prefers them to foreigners ('*Hate* Germans . . . *love* women'). If pressed for an opinion on the even trickier topic of women who also happen to be foreign (and not just common-or-garden foreign but also German to boot), he will furrow his brow for a moment and think hard before concluding solemnly: 'Good *card* players . . . but, mind, I wouldn't give them the time of day.'[10]

He tends to regard that most frightening of home-grown women, Sybil Fawlty, from a safe but respectful distance, and she, in turn, allows him to negotiate a way past her unscathed – SYBIL: 'Good morning, Major.' MAJOR: 'Er, very well, thank you!'[11] – but he much prefers the more familiar company of her husband. Basil limits himself to the odd mumble of protest when pretending to listen to the rambling anecdotes – 'Well, can't stand around all day . . .'[12] – and acts as a suitable marker to help structure the old buffer's day ('Morning, Fawlty!'; 'Evening, Fawlty!').

The highlight of the Major's day arrives at the start of the evening, when it is finally time to take a tincture or two at the bar. He can hardly hide his excitement as the clock starts ticking down – 'By Jove! Nearly six o'clock, Fawlty!'[13] – but does his best not to seem *too* needy – 'Yes, well, ah, when you're ready. . . . No immediate hurry . . .'[14] Once the shutters go up and the spirits are opened, he waits for his cue – 'The usual?' – and then, affecting a sense of mild surprise, scrutinises his watch, hesitates self-consciously, and then replies as casually as he possibly can: 'Oh, er . . . er . . . oh, why *not* indeed, why *not?*'[15] The little ritual reaches an end after one last polite nod in the direction of sobriety – 'I might have a . . . er . . . fruit juice or . . . something'[16] – when the first tumbler of Scotch is consumed.

Basil might sometimes mutter under his breath that the Major is a 'drunken old sod',[17] but he actually rather likes having such an amiable old soldier around. He is, after all, a resident toff with a title, and so, even though neither the toff nor the title is now in particularly good condition, Basil still feels that the overall effect lends the hotel a bit more class – and that, for him, is all that matters. If the mangy moose head is good enough to be put up on display on a wall in the lobby, then the Major is quite good enough to be left on show in a comfortable leather chair in the bar. He gives the environment, as he himself might have put it, a certain sort of '*Je ne sais quoi*',[18] and it would not seem right without him.

It would not seem quite so right, either, without the hotel's two very elderly and inseparable spinsters, Miss Ursula Angina Gatsby and Miss Abitha Tibbs.[19] Resembling two dried-out survivors from the last party to be held on the *Titanic*, they totter their tiny-footed way hither and thither via lobby and lounge, rarely revealing any specific intention apart from the hope of having a little, sensibly paced, fun.

Both of them are now on the edge of their eighties, and they give off the impression of having been firm friends ever since the earliest days of their childhood – a period, or at least a state of mind, to which they now seem to be fast returning (MISS GATSBY: 'Yes, you know, Abitha: *bubbity-bumble!*' MISS TIBBS: 'Oh: *buzz-buzz-buzz-buzz!*'[20]). They now live a late life of leisure, perhaps after having inherited a decent amount of disposable wealth from a well-placed relation or two, and they just want to relish every idle moment. Retaining great pride in their respective appearances, they change their outfits with huge enthusiasm to suit the mood of each occasion, mixing and matching a wide range of items drawn from a pair of ancient but well-stocked wardrobes, and embellish their various flapper-era fashions with black satin headbands, feather boas and long rope pearl necklaces. All kinds of things seem to cause them, in this quiet environment, some level of excitement: a cooked lunch, an afternoon's excursion into town, the arrival of a new guest and even the odd fire drill have all been known to get them looking exceptionally bright and lively. There is one individual, however, who appears to excite them more than any other: the man they pay so they can stay in the hotel.

For some inscrutable reason, these two ageing ladies come over all flirty and flustered in the presence of none other than Basil Fawlty. He only needs to appear for them to split up and, in a startlingly fast pincer movement, rush up on either side of him, with each one clinging tightly to an arm as, looking up adoringly, they fuss and fawn all over their reluctant friend:

> MISS TIBBS: Are you all right, Mr Fawlty?
> BASIL: What? Yes, *yes*, thank you very much. Are *you* all right?
> MISS GATSBY: Yes, yes.
> BASIL: *[Looking distracted]* Good, good. Well, we're *all* all right, then. *[He rushes off]*
> MISS GATSBY: Must be the heat!
> MISS TIBBS: Yes, and he's getting *taller*, isn't he!
> MISS GATSBY: I don't think he's very *well*, dear − I think we ought to take *care* of him . . .[21]

They are not exactly jealous of Basil's wife, but they do seem to envy the time that Sybil gets to share, however grudgingly, with her agitated spouse:

> MISS TIBBS: Ursula and I think you're a very naughty boy, don't we, Ursula?
> BASIL: *[To himself]* Oh, God . . . *[Trying to sound charming]* Oh, really?

MISS TIBBS: Going away for the weekend and leaving us all
  alone!
MISS GATSBY: *Tch, tch, tch!*
BASIL: Ah, yes . . .
MISS TIBBS: Ah, but we *know* where you're going – the cat's out
  of the bag!
MISS GATSBY: *[Coyly]* You and your *wife!*
BASIL: Well, it's only Paignton.
MISS TIBBS: *[Patting his arm]* Aah! Well, have a *lovely* time. It'll do
  you *good*. You *need* to get away from things.
BASIL: Yes, well, we're going together . . .
MISS GATSBY: And don't you worry about us!
BASIL: Oh. All right.[22]

Like anyone who finds himself, however unlikely, the subject of
an infatuation, Basil finds that he can be extraordinarily cruel to
these two smitten women without diminishing the intensity of
their adoration. On the occasion of the hotel's inaugural
Gourmet Night, for example, he snaps at them as though they
are prisoners rather than guests:

BASIL: You two – you're supposed to be in your rooms!
MISS GATSBY: Oh!
BASIL: You're not allowed down here tonight, remember?
MISS GATSBY: Oh, doesn't it look *pretty!*
MISS TIBBS: What are you cooking?
BASIL: I'll send you up a menu with your bread and cheese.
  Now get out![23]

Each playful phrase from them seems to prompt the rudest of
retorts from him – MISS GATSBY: 'Don't do anything we
wouldn't do!' BASIL: 'Oh. Just a little breathing, surely?'[24] –
but no offence is ever noticed, let alone taken, by these firmest of

Fawlty fans. While he goes on regarding them as little more than a quaint pair of period irritants, they continue to see him as their very own charming heartthrob of an hotelier.

It is not a relationship that ought to work, but, in some exceptionally peculiar way, it does. Basil is far too repressed to accept any praise, but he still needs to have it wash over him, like a tiny wave lapping against a lonely rock. It does not make him feel any better, but, secretly, he hopes that it might help stop him from feeling any worse. They, on the other hand, need to have someone harmless but vaguely important about whom they can care, and he, for better or for worse, is the misfit who happens to fit the bill.

It is a faulty relationship, without any doubt, but then faulty relationships are just the kind that suit a place like Fawlty Towers. There is Basil and Sybil. There are also the criss-crossing interconnections that link one or both of them, in various ways, to Polly, Manuel, the Major, Miss Gatsby and Miss Tibbs. These are the ties that bind these seven characters together. These are the dynamics that make each one of them tick.

After the first six extraordinary episodes, these people seemed real, they seemed distinctive and they seemed worth talking about, thinking about and following. What fans of *Fawlty Towers* therefore wanted to know now was: what on earth are these characters going to do next?

SECOND VISIT

I'll see what I can do . . .

10

Is Difficult

I'm sorry, but this puts us out just as much as it puts you out . . .

It proved a surprisingly long wait for the second series of *Fawlty Towers*. Following the success of the initial outing in the autumn of 1975, the show was widely expected to make a speedy return, but, as one year gave way to another, and then another, and the decade began to run down, there was still no sign of any fresh *Fawlty Towers*.

The demand for more was most definitely there. The BBC had kept on repeating the six existing episodes, and the viewing figures, far from declining, had kept on rising. Scripts of three of the six episodes ('The Builders', 'The Hotel Inspectors' and 'Gourmet Night') appeared in book form at the end of 1977, and (following an initial print run of 150,000 copies[1]) sold exceptionally well. More and more foreign broadcasters (some forty-five different stations in seventeen separate countries during 1977 and 1978[2]) were now screening the sitcom abroad. The actors, in spite of their appearances in countless other roles, continued to be associated closely with the show's characters, and the well-known lines and phrases – such as 'Oh, I *know* . . .' – never seemed to stop being quoted.

Everyone thus seemed to be waiting for a second series of *Fawlty Towers* but, for one reason or another, the second series, time and time again, failed to appear. This prolonged absence was by no means planned; it just seemed to happen. There were distractions, there were disruptions and there was pressure, and each factor would play its part in delaying the show's return.

Distractions, given the calibre of both the two co-writers and the rest of the cast, were more or less inevitable. John Cleese and Connie Booth first sat down together to discuss the second series at the start of October 1976,[3] and it seems that they intended to push ahead (planning not six but seven new episodes[4]), but then came one interruption after another, and the project kept being put back on the shelf *pro tempore*.

Connie Booth, who was keen to develop her acting career, became increasingly busy with her various other commitments, appearing in such high-profile television productions as *The Glittering Prizes* (BBC2, 1976),[5] Jack Rosenthal's *Spaghetti Two-Step* (ITV, 1977),[6] the three-part adaptation of Jack Jones's story about the nineteenth-century Welsh musician Joseph Parry, *Off to Philadelphia in the Morning* (BBC1, 1978),[7] and the Jack Gold-directed play *Thank You Comrades* (BBC2, 1978).[8] She also toured with the Cambridge Theatre Company for seven months during 1977 in a production of *The Glass Menagerie* and, later the same year, took part alongside John Cleese both in the Amnesty International fund-raising event *An Evening Without Sir Bernard Miles* (later screened on ITV, and released in record form, under the new title of *The Mermaid Frolics*[9]) and Joe McGrath's small-screen Sherlock Holmes spoof, *The Strange Case of the End of Civilization As We Know It* (also on ITV).[10]

Cleese, meanwhile, spent part of 1976 in New York, appearing at the City Center in a *Monty Python* stage show. He also took part in two Amnesty theatrical events back in London – *A Poke in the Eye* (1976) as well as *An Evening Without Sir Bernard Miles* (1977) – wrote, appeared in and co-produced a number of new training films for Video Arts, and contributed to several television shows (including a profile for BBC1's *Tonight* programme and a spot on the same channel's weekly book review, *Read All About It*, in 1976;[11] there was also a role alongside Diana Rigg in an edition of BBC2's *Three Piece Suite* in 1977;[12] and, later the same year, a guest spot on ITV's internationally popular *The Muppet Show*).[13] The bulk of his writing time during 1977 was spent working with his fellow *Monty Python* members on their next movie project, and so, once again, his and Booth's sitcom was left not quite in suspense (there were still certain discussions and scripting sessions squeezed in here and there) but certainly stuck on the back burner. At the start of 1978, he lent his support to his ailing *Python* writing partner, Graham Chapman, who was recuperating from a nervous breakdown precipitated by his alcoholism. Cleese then spent some time in Australia filming a couple of lucrative television commercials (for Paul's Ice Cream and Nudge Confectionery), before moving on in September to Monastir, in Tunisia, for three months of shooting *Monty Python's Life of Brian*. Something therefore always seemed to be in the way of a serious and prolonged return to Fawlty.

It was a similar story with the rest of the cast. Prunella Scales, for example, worked more or less incessantly, looking after two young sons while maintaining an eminently successful career: 'One was mercifully busy,' she would recall, 'so, although the talk went on about the second series, there were always plenty of other things for me to do.'[14] On stage, she played six different characters in the Frank Marcus adaptation of the Schnitzler play

Anatol (1976); co-starred alongside John Stride in the marital tragicomedy *It's All Right If I Do It*, and appeared at the Brighton Festival in a Royal Shakespeare Company production of George Bernard Shaw's *Man and Superman* (both in 1977); co-starred the following year with Norman Rossington in the popular comedy *Breezeblock Park*; appeared at the Old Vic opposite her husband, Timothy West, in *The Smith of Smiths*; and starred in the biographical portrait *An Evening with Queen Victoria* and the 'musical entertainment' *The Trial of Queen Caroline* (all in 1978); in movies, she contributed to the Walt Disney adventure *The Littlest Horse Thieves* (1976), Peter Cook and Dudley Moore's comic version of *The Hound of the Baskervilles* and the wartime drama *The Boys from Brazil* (both released in 1978); on radio, she could be heard in Oscar Wilde's *The Importance of Being Earnest* (BBC Radio 3, 1977),[15] Roger Snowdon's *Mistinguett* (BBC Radio 4, 1978)[16] and Pauline Spender's *A Gallant Romantic* (BBC Radio 4, 1978);[17] and she could also be seen on television in *The Golden Trashery of Ogden Nashery* (BBC2, 1976);[18] two series of the Peter Jones sitcom *Mr Big* (BBC1, 1977);[19] Alan Bennett's *Doris and Doreen* (ITV, 1978);[20] and she even popped up as a panellist on a couple of editions of *Call My Bluff* (BBC2, 1977).[21]

Andrew Sachs was similarly busy. He continued appearing on stage in *No Sex, Please, We're British* (1975–6), and also took part in the army comedy *Reluctant Heroes* and the French bourgeois satire *Perrichon's Travels* (both in 1976). He was a regular contributor to the television sketch show *Took and Co* (ITV, 1977),[22] and played a Manuel-style waiter called Guido in a 1978 British movie comedy entitled *What's Up Nurse!* as well as a Spanish hotel manager named Don Carlos Bernardo in the big-screen version of the sitcom *Are You Being Served?* Also in 1978, his fascinating experimental play called *The Revenge* (which featured no words but only sounds) was broadcast by BBC Radio 3,[23] and he appeared in an episode of the ITV sitcom *Rising Damp*,[24] as well as the Peter Sellers movie *The Return of the Pink Panther* (as a mental patient, claiming to be Hercule Poirot, who ridicules the credentials of Clouseau).

The career of Ballard Berkeley, meanwhile, was ticking along very nicely indeed: he was making several guest appearances on television (including two *Mike Yarwood* shows on BBC1 during 1976[25]) as well as maintaining a familiar presence on the stage (such as in William Douglas-Home's 1978 light comedy *The Editor Regrets*). Even the semi-retired Renée Roberts and Gilly Flower continued to accept the odd high-profile engagement, with Roberts appearing in an episode of *The Duchess of Duke Street* (BBC1, 1976),[26] while the slightly more sprightly Flower contributed to single editions of *The Two Ronnies* (BBC1, 1976),[27] Michael Palin and Terry Jones's *Ripping Yarns* (BBC2, 1977)[28] and *The Fall and Rise of Reginald Perrin* (BBC1, 1977).[29]

None of the cast of *Fawlty Towers*, in short, was waiting idly for its return. All of them hoped for such a reunion, but, until word reached them that it was actually going to happen, they made sure that their diaries remained full.

Something else, however, occurred during this period that proved disruptive as well as distracting: the increasingly troubled marriage between John Cleese and Connie Booth finally ended in an uncontested divorce. The pair had been separated, on and off, for just over two years when, in a New York hotel room in the spring of 1976, Booth told Cleese that it was time to come to terms with the fact that their marriage had run its course. She then proceeded to immerse herself in her work. He responded by taking himself off, by way of a change, to Robert Carrier's culinary academy at Hintlesham Hall in Suffolk, where he enrolled in a cookery course while continuing (as did Booth) with his regular sessions of counselling and group therapy back in London.

It took about a couple of months for the British media to find out about the break-up and then bring it to the public's attention. On 2 June 1976, the journalist Paul Callan, writing in the *Daily Mirror*, reported that Cleese ('36') and Booth ('31') were now – sort of – living apart. 'We have decided to separate for an indefinite period of time,' he quoted Connie Booth as saying. 'But we are still living in the same house,' she added, 'although in different sections.' She did her best to explain the logic of the situation: 'I know it sounds rather silly to say we have separated while we are still living under the same roof, but we are staying here now because of our child.' Callan pointed out that the child, Cynthia, was now five years old. As for what would happen to this arrangement in the mid- to long-term, Booth said: 'We will decide in a year's time whether or not to sell the house and go our separate ways.' She then stressed that there was no one else involved – 'We are still very friendly' – and it was confirmed that there were still 'plans for a second series'.[30]

Early in 1977, Cleese moved out of the family home in Woodsford Square, Holland Park (taking one of his and Booth's two treasured Siamese cats with him), and rented a basement apartment in a pretty pink-and-white house half a mile away in Notting Hill Gate while he searched for a suitable new house to buy. A journalist who visited him there a couple of months after he had moved in described the mildly disorientated and some-what forlorn scene: 'There were piles of notes and papers spread out in corners of every room, signs that he'd been moving round the house, working away at his various works, but they were transit spots rather than roots [. . .] On the table was a half-empty bottle of red wine, some liver pâté still in the greaseproof paper, some water biscuits, and beside it, half opened, a copy of Maurice Ashby's biography of King John.'[31] It was a dark time for Cleese, as it was for Booth, but there were still a number of deadlines to meet and several projects to ponder, so, even though life seemed to have stalled, work continued to run. There was always something that needed, fairly urgently, to be done.

In September, the estranged but still amicable couple went with their daughter on a fortnight's vacation to Jamaica, and then, in January the following year, spent a couple more weeks together when the Python team met up in Barbados to discuss the casting and script for their forthcoming *Life of Brian*. Back in Britain, neither Cleese nor Booth seemed in any kind of hurry to formalise the change in the nature of their relationship (although he did move into a huge house in Holland Park that he had recently bought for the knock-down price of £80,000 – about £350,000 by today's values – from the rock star Bryan Ferry[32]), and they continued to collaborate whenever they could on new ideas for *Faulty Towers*.

According to Booth, the group therapy sessions that they still attended together proved invaluable for maintaining their creativity during this period: 'If it hadn't been for group therapy, I don't think we could have worked on the second series. We were able to begin to see each other more objectively.'[33] Cleese claimed to agree, explaining to a journalist at the time: 'I think there's too much togetherness in marriages. And when you discover a sort of independence it's very nice. It sounds cold-blooded, but I think that it works much more than the excessively romantic attitude which we do get pushed at us.'[34] By the summer of 1978, however, both of them felt ready to bow to the inevitable, and so, on 31 August, John Cleese sued for a 'quickie' divorce.[35]

Work on the next series of their sitcom (the intended number of whose episodes had by this stage been reduced from seven to a more conventional – and manageable – six) would survive the end of their marriage, but, as Connie Booth later acknowledged, the process proved far more of a strain on both of them the second time around. So great was their desire to surpass what they had achieved with the previous six scripts that they frequently found themselves plagued by false starts and mental blocks. Promising ideas were explored, developed, written up, revised, revised again and then, reluctantly, scrapped. Other potential scenarios were retained but, after numerous efforts, left frustratingly incomplete. They were accumulating material that was, by most other shows' standards, exceptional, but they wanted something that seemed even better for *Fawlty Towers*. They wanted something spectacular, something stunningly funny, but still, at heart, plausible and true. They had, therefore, to keep criticising themselves, keep questioning their ideas and keep hoping for inspiration. There was nothing for them to do but continue writing, rewriting and re-rewriting. 'This show is very hard,' said Booth. 'John and I went to Monaco with our daughter and nanny to work on some scripts and came back depressed because we couldn't get anything going.'[36]

The greater fame that had come with *Fawlty Towers*, the first time around, had made both writers feel somewhat uncomfortable. They had dreamed up the show back in 1974 in relative isolation and privacy. Now they felt as though they were being watched. Connie Booth had never consciously courted the media spotlight – indeed, its glare would be one of the reasons for her eventual withdrawal from the whole show-business style of life – she just wanted to act and write, so the many knocks on the door, unwanted phone calls and speculative articles in the tabloids disturbed and depressed her. John Cleese, on the other hand, was more resigned to what came with such territory, having grown used to – if not exactly tolerant of – the late-night *Monty Python's* legion of avid fans ('people talked about "supporting" *Python* as though we were a football team'[37]), but even he found the far more intense, widespread and intrusive interest generated by prime-time success difficult to understand or accept. *Python* had earned him the odd wordy profile in the likes of the *Guardian*, *The Times* and the *Daily Telegraph*; *Fawlty Towers* was now bringing him plenty of tittle-tattle from the tabloids – and he hated it. 'I've suddenly become public property,' he complained, a little disingenuously, in 1977. 'If I farted in Regent Street it would make two lines in the *Daily Mirror*.'[38] He had also grown to loathe any lazy links between himself and his Fawlty alter-ego: 'They always say to me, "I suppose there's a lot of Basil in you." Do you imagine they say to Sir Laurence Olivier, "I suppose there's a lot of the Moor in you"?'[39]

The most intimidating form of pressure, however, was felt from the full weight of public expectation. Every fan of *Fawlty Towers* just seemed to assume that the second series would be at least as hilarious, if not more so, as the first. Cleese and Booth, on the other hand, were the two who had to sit down in the cold of each morning, stare at the blank piece of paper and wonder what on earth they could write that would satisfy and delight the broad audience. Conjuring up the first series had been an adventure; bringing to life a second one seemed more like a solemn responsibility.

The key challenge, they knew, was to move things on for the better; the key fear was that, by trying to do so, the immense success of the first series would end up being defiled. It therefore was, as John Cleese would later confirm, an extraordinarily intimidating task:

> The problem we had [. . .] was that the expectation was unreasonably high. Because I realised that people were already remembering the first series as better than it was. Because, if there are three or four things in the first series that are really funny, the audience remembers that as the kind of general standard, rather than the highlights, and they expect the second series to be at the highlight level all the way through. So it was a huge effort to get those scripts as good as I think they finally were.[40]

There were two basic aims for the second set of scripts. One was to make the stories seem less obviously farcical but richer and more realistic ('a little bit more in the area of Alan Ayckbourn,' said Cleese[41]). The other was to make the key characters more complex, intriguing and believable.

Greater realism was achieved not by any major changes to the nature of the narratives, but simply by working harder than ever to make the plotlines unfold in a slightly more subtle manner. While Cleese, in particular, wanted to deal with more challenging themes (because, he said, controversial and even quasi-taboo areas – such as faked disabilities and troublesome corpses – would make the comedy less familiar and a little more dangerous as well as arousing a greater degree of anxious laughter[42]), he and Booth made an effort to lend the action more light and shade,

engaging the emotions as well as the intellect. Like magicians
who had mastered the art of misdirection, they delighted in
finding new ways in each plot to keep the viewers surprised and
excited as well as amused, planting the laughs a little deeper in
the soil.

Each major character, meanwhile, was given a slightly sharper
biographical presence as well as a more elaborate personality.
Basil, for example, was belatedly handed the town of Swanage
for his birthplace,[43] as well as a trace of a vague family tradition
that suggested he had tried and failed to emulate a maternal
great-grandfather by forging a career for himself in the medical
profession. Sybil was given a few similarly odd or evocative
background details, including a voracious appetite for the racy
novels of Harold Robbins (which are dubbed 'pornographic
muzak' by her uncomfortable husband[44]), an untutored fascination for New Age trinkets ('May I ask . . . the sign on the chain,
by the Egyptian fertility symbol – what is that . . .?'[45]), a
growing interest in healthier lifestyles ('I've cut out butter
. . .'[46]) and an eccentric old mother who has become, Sybil
admits, 'a little bit of a trial': 'It's all right when they have the life
force, but mother, well, she's got more of the death force, really.
. . . She's a worrier . . . She has these, well, morbid fears they
are, really . . . Vans is one . . . rats, doorknobs, birds, heights,
open spaces . . . confined spaces . . . it's very difficult getting the
space right for her, really, you know . . . Footballs, bicycles,
cows . . . and she's always on about men following her . . . I
don't know what she thinks they're going to *do* to her . . .
Vomit on her, Basil says . . .'[47]

Some things were left more or less the same. Basil was still as rude
as ever about his guests ('A satisfied customer. We should have him
stuffed'[48]) – and still as oversensitive about any real or imagined

slight (when one metropolitan type is overheard opining that *What's On in Torquay* must be 'one of the world's shortest books', [49] Basil is left apoplectic with indignation). Similarly, Sybil was brought back just as vain and sybaritic as before, always 'refurbishing' herself ('No, no, it's lovely,' she says of a new wig that she has been studying, 'it's just a bit *buttery* with my skin. I think I need something more *topazy*, for my colouring, you know, more *tonal*. . .'[50]) while gossiping to Audrey on the telephone ('I don't know why she stays with him . . .'[51]) and flicking through the latest glossy magazine ('Oh, that's pretty . . .'[52]).

Several relationships, however, were revised to varying extents, and one or two were allowed to evolve. The conspiratorial trio of Polly, Basil and Manuel would, if anything, grow tighter and more daring than ever, with all three of them bound together by the knowledge of where all the bodies are buried. Basil was also given an alternative foil in the form of a new character called Terry, the hotel's cockney chef, whose penchant for telling little white lies, along with the odd great big multicoloured one, probably reminds Fawlty of himself (thus ensuring that he regards the chef with a volatile mixture of resentment and admiration). The arrival of Terry would have a more negative effect on Manuel, who watches with a slight sense of insecurity and envy as this chirpy, cheeky, somewhat cocky cockney muscles into the kitchen and starts calling his dear friend Polly 'Poll'. Miss Gatsby and Miss Tibbs, meanwhile, were still allowed to fuss over and flirt with Basil, but now they were also made to seem more concerned than before about the Major, whose fast-multiplying number of 'senior moments' ('What was the question again?'[53]) are clearly causing them some alarm.

By far the most intriguing developments, however, would relate to the marriage of Basil and Sybil. The exchange of insults would keep on coming (he calling her a 'hideous fire-breathing old dragon',[54] a 'rancorous coiffeured old sow',[55] and an 'enormous savage rodent';[56] and she calling him 'an ageing brilliantined stick insect',[57] while condemning his 'hopeless lily-livered lies'[58] and his 'sledgehammer wit'[59]), but from now on there would also be moments of vulnerability as well as hints about mutual feelings of frustration, insecurity and hurt. Each one now seemed to be testing the other's true feelings instead of just dismissing their respective delusions.

Whereas in the first series, for example, Sybil had appeared to flirt with other men merely as a means of distraction from the dullness of her disappointing husband, she would now do so in order to provoke and then analyse his reaction.

> SYBIL: Tell me, Basil, what is it about the Mediterranean type that antagonises you so? Is it because women find them attractive?
>
> BASIL: Sybil . . .
>
> SYBIL: You seem to think that we girls should be aroused by people like Gladstone and Earl Haig and Baden-Powell . . . don't you . . . ?
>
> BASIL: Well, at least they had a certain dignity. It's hard to imagine Earl Haig wandering around with his shirt open at the waist, covered with identity bracelets.
>
> SYBIL: Well, he didn't mind the medals, did he? The military decorations . . .
>
> BASIL: That's not the point.
>
> SYBIL: I suppose the reason you confuse them with monkeys is that monkeys have *fun* – they know how to *enjoy* themselves. That's what makes them sexy, I suppose . . .[60]

Basil, in turn, would try harder than before to niggle Sybil about other women:

BASIL: You know, dear, that outfit that Mrs Abbott was wearing, you should get yourself something like that.

SYBIL: What, for the gardening, do you mean?

BASIL: Mmm, an attractive woman. How old would you say she was, Sybil?

SYBIL: Forty-eight? . . . Fifty?

BASIL: Oh, *no*, Sybil!

SYBIL: *[Pretending that she is not rattled]* I really don't know, Basil. Perhaps she's twelve.[61]

There would even be one extraordinary occasion when the sight of Sybil, perched almost coquettishly on the edge of Basil's desk, prompts him to place a hand on her slender waist and sound almost wistful about their relationship:

BASIL: Seriously, Sybil, do you remember, when we were first . . . manacled together, we used to laugh quite a lot.

SYBIL: Yes, but not at the same time, Basil.

BASIL: Ah, that's true. That was a warning, wasn't it? Should have spotted that, shouldn't I? *Zhoom!* What was that? 'That was your life, mate.' That was quick – do I get another? 'Sorry, mate, that's your lot.'

SYBIL: *[Anxious to get on with more pressing matters]* Basil.

BASIL: *[To himself]* Back to the world of dreams. *[To Sybil]* Yes, dear?

SYBIL: What are we going to do?

BASIL: Give it another fifteen years?[62]

While Basil would not usually seem any less neurotic nor repressed than in his earlier outings, there would definitely now be something more sensitive and, at times, almost 'needy' about Sybil. She would actually be heard addressing Basil – without the usual spiky irony – as 'darling', and, on the odd occasion, would even deign to ask his advice ('Do you think we should . . . ?'[63]).

The bitterness was still undeniably there – 'You never get it right, do you?' Sybil complains about Basil's snobbish attitude towards their guests. 'You're either crawling all over them licking their boots, or spitting poison at them like some Benzedrine puff-adder!'[64] – and so was the barely suppressed feeling of desperation – 'Coping's easy,' snaps Basil. 'Not puréeing your loved ones – that's the difficult part.'[65] There was now, however, a much more evident sense of regret: 'When I think,' Sybil groans at one point, 'of what I *might* have had . . .'[66] Most of all, Sybil seems to be increasingly niggled by the thought that others might now be even more bemused by their marriage than either she or Basil has been: 'They all think you're peculiar, you know that, don't you? They've all said at one time or another, how on earth did the two of us ever get together. Black magic, my mother says . . .'[67]

Each new script would thus find her sounding as though, beneath all the bile, she actually cares about this marriage. When, for example, she moans about being 'cooped up in this hotel all day', she complains to Basil that 'You never take me out'[68] – whereas, in the first series, she would have been happy to go off and leave the old misanthrope behind. Similarly, when she suspects that he has forgotten an important milestone in their fifteen-year marriage, she behaves as though she is genuinely hurt, rather than just irritated or merely indifferent.

It was this kind of added depth, this kind of extra layer, that made Cleese and Booth feel satisfied with the new scripts that they had written. It had taken so long for the six episodes to come to fruition, and so much had happened behind the scenes, but, at last, the material for the second series was ready. The time had finally come to bring *Fawlty Towers* back to life.

Word went out to the rest of the cast – to Prunella Scales, Andrew Sachs, Ballard Berkeley, Gilly Flower and Renée Roberts – and to all of the relevant parties at the BBC. Healthy pay rises were negotiated (Cleese, for example, was promised £9,000 for his contribution to the series, while Andrew Sachs's fee rose to £350[69]), the contracts were signed and the schedule was settled. It was going to happen. After almost four years of waiting, it was really going to happen.

There was an eerie sense of 'business as usual', as well as a *frisson* of excitement, when the various members of the cast reassembled at the rehearsal rooms in North Acton one dark and chilly winter morning. They had all been here before, they all knew what to do, and they were ready to get straight on with it. According to Andrew Sachs, there was not even any acknowl-edgement that the two co-writers were now no longer a married couple and were living entirely apart: 'John came in at around ten o'clock, then Connie came in five minutes later. I thought she'd been parking the car, but then she went up to him, gave him a kiss and said, "Good morning. Did you sleep well?"'.[70] Everything, and everyone, was focused on the task of reviving *Fawlty Towers*. Nothing else was allowed to matter.

The original team had returned, however, with a new director and producer, because the man who had held both of these positions during the first series, John Howard Davies, had just become BBC TV's new Head of Comedy, and was therefore otherwise engaged. 'We'd had plenty of discussions about doing the second series,' he would recall, 'but John and Connie were going through a divorce and there were all those other distractions, so it had dragged on, and, by the time that everything was finally ready, *I* couldn't do it, unfortunately, because I'd taken up that other post, so, although I obviously retained an interest in the series and would read all of the scripts and suggest one or two changes from time to time, I had to get other people in to actually make it.'[71] Bob Spiers was thus brought in by Davies as his successor as director, and Douglas 'Dougie' Argent was appointed the show's new producer.

A shrewd, good-natured and reassuringly phlegmatic young red-headed Glaswegian, Bob Spiers had joined the BBC in the late 1960s as an assistant floor manager, working on the likes of *Doctor Who* and *Cilla*, before graduating to the role of director, first filming several dance sequences for BBC1's *Seaside Special* (1975) and then overseeing such popular comedy shows as *It Ain't Half Hot, Mum* (one series, 1976), *Dad's Army* (four episodes, 1977), *The Goodies* (one series, 1977) and, most recently, *Are You Being Served?* (one series, 1978). Much more of an instinctive, American-style director than many of his British contemporaries – in the sense that he 'thought with the eyes' rather than relied on routine camera angles and cuts – he was well suited to follow John Howard Davies and preserve the playfully fast-paced spirit of *Fawlty Towers*.

The appointment of Douglas Argent seemed similarly apt. A BBC employee since the start of the 1960s, he had been presiding over television programmes for fifteen years, beginning with Jack Rosenthal and Harry Driver's Preston-based *Comedy Playhouse* pilot, *A Picture of Innocence*, back in 1963, and then continuing with such shows as *Till Death Us Do Part* (seven episodes, 1966–7), *Steptoe and Son* (one series, 1974) and – his most significant personal success – *The Liver Birds* (nine series, 1969–79). When he was asked to join the team responsible for the return of *Fawlty Towers*, he was already busy planning the inevitably troublesome production of Spike Milligan's forthcoming series, *Q8* (1979), but was more than happy to add such an exciting and prestigious project to his workload.

There was one other addition to the old *Fawlty Towers* team. A forty-two-year-old, Brighton-born but East End-raised actor named Brian Hall was brought in to play the part of Terry, the hotel's new chef (who used to work at Dorchester – not The Dorchester but 'in Dorchester – about forty miles away . . .'[72]). A solid but relatively little-recognised performer, Hall had appeared in sixteen episodes of the BBC police drama series *Softly, Softly: Task Force* (1971–2), as well as one episode[73] and the second movie spin-off[74] of another popular police series, ITV's *The Sweeney* (1975), before the surprising but very timely invitation came for him to become a fixture in the Fawlty kitchen. 'I was broke and wondering where the next job was coming from,' Hall would recall. 'Then my wife, Marlene, told me a BBC producer [Douglas Argent] had phoned, wanting me to appear in *Fawlty Towers*. I couldn't believe my luck. [. . .] I rang the producer, who asked if I wanted the job. "Is the Pope Catholic?" I said. "Of course I'd like to do an episode." "Not one," the producer said. "All six." I was speechless.'[75]

Hall had thus set off excitedly to North Acton to meet Cleese, Booth, Bob Spiers and Douglas Argent, still half-expecting to be told that it had all been an unfortunate mistake. 'I'd been asked to act out a scene as the cockney chef,' he later said, 'but I knew nothing of his character and wasn't giving it my best shot. I said to John: "I really want this job, but I haven't much to go on. Can you tell me something about Terry?" Other directors would have given me a ten-minute breakdown of the character, but all Cleese said was: "The police are after him." It was simple, yet brilliant. Those five words told me that the man Cleese wanted was nervous, always looking over his shoulder, and I based my performance on this. I impressed John enough to get the job, but I've always suspected it was something else that convinced him I was right. At one stage I had said to him: "You're very tall, and it's easy for you to intimidate people, because you're always looking down on them. But I can intimidate YOU – even though you're a foot taller than me." "Really," John said, fascinated. "How would you do it?" I stood a few inches from him, stared straight at his chest and started talking. After a few moments, he said: "Yes. I see what you mean. That's the most intimidating thing I've ever experienced." He had a look in his eye that said, "There's something mad about this man – he'll do for us".[76] In fact, Cleese and Booth would come to enjoy Hall's charmingly shifty characterisation so much that, as the series developed, they started adding the odd line or bit of business to increase his time on screen.[77]

With Hall on board, the cast was complete, and the work could really begin. Each rehearsal session was, just like it had been back in 1975, very intense but absolutely invaluable. So keen were Cleese and Booth to ensure that every tiny detail was comically pertinent, and each characterful nuance made proper sense, they listened to all of the opinions that were offered and evaluated each one with genuine care. After spending so long together sitting side by side, bouncing ideas back and forth in the same old lonely room, the two of them relished being part of such a broad and bright ensemble.

'[T]he best bit of this business,' said Cleese at the time, 'is rehearsing. Rehearsing is discovery time; discovery is play. It's like being back at school and having your favourite lesson. You get a great sense of discovery and a great sense of fun.'[78] A number of old trestle tables were arranged so as to pass for the hotel's reception desk, beds or kitchen bench, some poles were placed where the edges of the actual (and now slightly expanded) studio set would be, and the actors plotted and blocked out their movements, tried out the sound and rhythms of their dialogue and began building their performances. Connie Booth kept pushing Cleese to look for new visual ways to make Fawlty seem more alive and surprising: 'She says Basil works best when he's unpredictable.'[79] Cleese, in turn, tried to come to terms as quickly as possible with the greater physical toll that being Basil, after the best part of a four-year break, was now taking on his middle-aged body (having relaxed, relatively speaking, for so long, the neurotic erectness of the character was now proving more draining than ever, and plaguing him with muscular pains in the neck, shoulders and back).

Andrew Sachs – armed, or rather lipped, with a slightly thicker fake moustache – was finding it easier to pick up from where he had left off as Manuel. Scouring the scripts for the character's most intriguing scenes, he started working on each fresh bit of physical business, choreographing every little twist, tumble and fall, as well as sharpening the timing of some complicated and quick-fire verbal exchanges.

Prunella Scales, suitably enthused by the richness of the new material, was similarly eager to resume, and develop, her portrayal of Sybil. 'There *was* more pathos about the relationship,' she would reflect. 'I think that development was quite organic. It seemed to have grown out of what we'd found out about the two of them, Basil and Sybil, during the first series. In that sense, it was another sign of just how well written the scripts actually were. I don't know if I brought anything significant to that change, but, if so: "hooray hooray". And even if not:

"hooray hooray", anyway!'[80] While the creative process, this time around, was probably even more collaborative than during the previous occasion, the pace was, if anything, more rapid than ever. 'What I remember,' Prunella Scales would say, 'is how much pressure there was on all of us to learn the lines. It was just as much of a blur then as it had been the first time in that respect. I don't remember any significant difference between rehearsals for the first and second series. They were both very hard work, and we all stayed up late each Tuesday night to make sure that we knew every single line.'[81]

The recording sessions on Sunday evenings also followed the same pattern as four years before: a camera rehearsal in the morning, followed in the afternoon by a 'stagger-through' and a proper dress rehearsal, and then, at 8.00 p.m. in the evening, the actual filming began. The plan was to record the first two shows on consecutive Sundays, followed by a week-long break to allow everyone to recuperate, then the next two were due to be shot, followed by another week off, and then the final two were scheduled to be completed. One of the few minor changes to the process was that Cleese tended to ask rather more often for certain brief scenes to be shot twice, because, as the director Bob Spiers explained, 'John was quite keen to have a second go at them in front of an audience'[82] (a particularly ominous innovation for Andrew Sachs, who, if Manuel was involved, ended up being smacked or stabbed all over again – but this time on a different, and unexpected, part of his body). Another concern of Cleese's was to ensure that the sound level of the studio audience's laughter was kept low enough in the mix so that he could talk over them and maintain the great pace of each scene. Bob Spiers also featured more two-shots (framing a couple of actors) in order to accentuate the greater richness of certain relationships, particularly when Basil and Sybil were sharing a significant exchange.[83]

A couple of days after each recording, Bob Spiers would take the tapes over to John Cleese's house in Holland Park and the two of them sat down and spent an hour or two during the morning watching what had been filmed (discussing as they did so which parts of each take worked best), and then, after a quick lunch, they went over a few more issues and angles. Spiers would then go back to the editing room and, often toiling well through the next day and on into the night, produce a polished edition of the programme. With the opening episode due to be broadcast about three weeks into the shooting schedule, the pressure was definitely on.

The pre-publicity for the second series of *Fawlty Towers* at the start of 1979 would be far more noticeable than what had been prepared four years previously for the first, but it was still, nonetheless, relatively – and deliberately – understated. There was a front cover picture, along with an interview inside, for the *Radio Times*,[84] and the odd newspaper preview (the most memorable being a brief chat with Cleese by, of all people, Tony Pratt – he of the 'Long John is short on jokes' jibe in 1975 – who now welcomed the show back, without so much as a blush, in the pages of the *Daily Mirror*. 'Only six shows were made,' he declared, 'but they were of such quality that they remain fresh in viewers' minds as monuments to inspired lunacy'[85]), but there was absolutely no danger that the series would be allowed to seem overhyped. Expectations were already so high that all most people really needed were the date, time and channel of the opening episode.

Those basic details were as follows: Monday 19 February,

9.00 p.m., BBC2. The two viewing alternatives, this time around, consisted of the *Nine O'Clock News* on BBC1 and the wartime drama series *Danger UXB* on ITV. It was a fairly decent slot. It promised fans an excellent start to their week. The countdown had thus begun. The waiting was almost over. *Fawlty Towers* was finally coming back.

I I

Freshly Squeezed

Are you all satisfied?

The third Monday in February 1979 arrived, and, at nine o'clock that evening, the familiar theme music began, the sign outside the hotel said 'FAWLTY TOWER' (with the 'L' half hanging off) and then, inside, the action started. *Fawlty Towers* was back on the screen.

The opening episode, entitled 'Communication Problems', drew the viewer in immediately with a scene set in the busy hotel lobby: Sybil and Polly are dealing with guests, Basil is finishing a telephone call and, through the entrance, comes a formidable-looking elderly woman (played with adamantine power by the well-known character actor Joan Sanderson) who, shouting as though she was standing on a cold and lonely Caspar David Friedrich mountain top, announces herself as 'Mrs Alice Richards'. What follows is a classic battle between Basil and one of his most awkward guests, as well as a farcical pursuit of a lucrative bet.

The problem with Mrs Richards, it soon becomes apparent, is that she is deaf – or rather, she prefers to use her relatively impaired hearing as an excuse not to listen to what anyone else is saying.[1] The problem – or at least one of the problems – with Basil, meanwhile, is that he has just received a very tempting tip about a 'nice little filly' called Dragonfly that is running at Exeter in the afternoon, but, as Sybil has banned him for the rest of his life from the pleasure of betting, he fears that he will miss the chance to win himself a comforting sum of money.

Before he can contrive a way to act behind Sybil's back, Mrs Richards summons him to her newly booked room to complain first of all about the inadequate size of its bath (MRS RICHARDS: 'It's not big enough to drown a mouse!' BASIL: *[Muttering]* 'I wish you were a mouse, I'd show you') and then about the substandard view that came with the room:

MRS RICHARDS: When I pay for a view I expect something more interesting than *that*.

BASIL: 'That' is *Torquay*, madam.

MRS RICHARDS: Well, it's not good enough.

BASIL: Well . . . may I ask what you were *hoping* to see out of a Torquay hotel bedroom window? Sydney Opera House perhaps? The Hanging Gardens of Babylon? Herds of wildebeest sweeping majestically . . .

MRS RICHARDS: Don't be silly. I expect to be able to see the sea.

BASIL: You *can* see the sea! It's over there between the land and the sky.

MRS RICHARDS: I'd need a telescope to see that!

BASIL: Well, may I suggest you consider moving to a hotel closer to the sea? Or preferably *in* it?

MRS RICHARDS: Now listen to me: I'm not satisfied, but I have decided to stay here. However, I shall expect a reduction.

BASIL: Why? Because Krakatoa's not erupting at the moment?

MRS RICHARDS: Because the room is cold, the bath is too small, the view is invisible and the radio doesn't work.

BASIL: No, the *radio* works. You don't.
MRS RICHARDS: What?

After even an ear-bleeding blast from the radio fails to stop all of
the what-whatting, Basil cannot resist any longer asking the
patently obvious question:

BASIL: Madam . . . don't think me *rude*, but may I ask . . . do
   you, by any chance, have a . . . hearing aid?
MRS RICHARDS: A *what?*
BASIL: *A HEARING AID!!!*
MRS RICHARDS: Yes, I do have a hearing aid.
BASIL: Would you like me to get it mended?
MRS RICHARDS: *Mended?* It's working perfectly all right!
BASIL: No, it isn't!
MRS RICHARDS: I haven't got it turned on at the moment.
BASIL: Why *not?*
MRS RICHARDS: The battery runs down. Now what sort of
   reduction are you going to give me on this room?

Exasperated, he ends up advising her to speak to his wife, and
then rushes off to dispatch Manuel to the nearest betting shop
('Big secret. Sybil no know . . .').

When the horse wins, the struggle begins to keep the money
– a very handy sum of £75 – a secret from Sybil. Manuel sneaks
the cash to Polly, who then, when the moment is right, slips it to
a highly delighted Basil. Anxious to cover his tracks, he moves
quickly to keep Manuel securely within a crafty ring of silence:
'Please try to understand this before one of us dies,' he pleads.
'You know nothing about the horse.' Then, however, comes
the crisis: Mrs Richards informs Sybil that £85 has been stolen
from a bag hidden under her mattress, and Sybil confides to Basil
that she saw Polly counting a similarly sized sum of money a

short while before. Realising that this must have been his precious winnings, he races off to warn his co-conspirator, and, after a painfully convoluted semaphored struggle, the two of them manage to semi-convince Sybil that Polly won the money on a horse that Basil had tipped to triumph. Sybil, however, is still suspicious: 'If I find out the money on that horse was yours,' she warns her shifty-looking husband, 'you know what I'll do, Basil . . .' Clearly shaken by that thought, he waits until she walks off before calling after her: 'You'll have to sew 'em back on first!'

Now the tension is mounting. Spotting the Major strolling towards the bar for his first snifter of the evening ('Six o'clock, old boy!'), Basil hatches another plan: slip his winnings to the Major for safekeeping until Sybil tires of searching through all of his tweedy pockets ('Understood, old boy — cheers!'). The following morning, when Mrs Richards returns to check if Fawlty has summoned the police, he does his perfunctory best to placate her — 'They're very busy today,' he declares cheerfully. 'There was a lot of bloodshed at the Nell Gwynn tea-rooms last night' — but then the Major arrives at reception, and Basil finds, to his horror, that the old boy appears to have forgotten all about the stash of cash. Then, just as Sybil and Mrs Richards resume the discussion of her supposed theft, the Major suddenly rediscovers the money and, in a tragic case of confusion, hands it straight over to Sybil. 'You see?' she says to Mrs Richards, 'I knew it'd turn up.'

Mrs Richards counts the notes and concludes that she is still £10 short. While Sybil volunteers to search upstairs, Basil tries desperately to convince the troublesome guest that this money is actually his. He calls on the Major to clarify the matter, but gets nowhere ('*What*, old boy?'). He then orders Manuel to step out of the ring of silence and reveal the truth of the matter, but, with heartbreaking inevitability, the waiter only proceeds to clear his throat and announce proudly: 'I forget everything! I know *nothing!*' Sybil returns and orders the shattered Basil to give Mrs Richards £10 from the till, which he duly does by head-butting the top and then handing over the note. Broken all over again, he also offers her the shirt off his back, vows to send Manuel to a vivisectionist and then, head bowed, starts to weep.

Then, however, things get much better before getting even worse. The denouement of this particular episode is one of the most painfully cruel in the whole history of sitcoms.

A vase is delivered for Mrs Richards; it transpires that she bought it the previous day, and had absent-mindedly left behind a spare £95 in the shop. It suddenly dawns on Basil that, at long last, he is about to snatch victory from the jaws of defeat. 'I'm ten pounds up on the deal,' he gasps to Polly. 'Even if I give her ten . . . I'm still ten up! Polly . . . for the first time in my life I'm ahead! I'm *winning!*' When Mrs Richards comes back to reception, Basil relishes the moment, getting her to confirm that the other money is hers while he shows off the current wad of notes in his hand ('*This* is *mine!*'). He hands over £10 to Polly to pass on to the somewhat bemused Mrs Richards, and then, when Sybil reappears, passes off his own cash as the winnings Polly now wishes him to store in his safe. Everything now seems perfect – and then it all goes horribly wrong. Just as he is holding the vase out to Mrs Richards, the Major bursts excitedly back into view, and bellows: 'Fawlty – you *DID* give me that money! You won it on that *horse!*' Sybil then snatches away his money, and he, in trying to snatch it back, drops and smashes the vase. 'That cost seventy-five pounds!' shouts Mrs Richards, and, as poor Basil despairs, Sybil takes great pleasure in counting out the cash.

It was an extraordinary half-hour: cleverly plotted, superbly choreographed, breathtakingly well-paced and thoroughly absorbing – and, of course, exceptionally funny. Firmly in the best tradition of cold-hearted comedy *Schadenfreude* (as Mel Brooks so memorably put it: 'Tragedy is if I cut my finger . . . Comedy is if you walk into an open sewer and die'[2]), it featured more naked pain, suffering and despair than most peak-time dramas dared to cover in twice the time, but it still managed to make one laugh as one gazed deep into all of the darkness. The immediate critical reception, however, was, as both Cleese and Booth had feared, distinctly mixed. Paul Madden, writing in the *Listener*, described the show's return as 'the event of the TV week', but then judged the opening episode to have been 'disappointing'.[3] Several other reviewers chose simply to ignore the programme entirely, giving some readers the impression, rightly or wrongly, that they were damning the show with their silence. It all added up to a mild anticlimax, but it would prove to be extremely short-lived. Praise for the programme soon started pouring in from viewers and critics alike, and the series was widely and sincerely celebrated both inside and out of the entertainment profession.

The actor Siân Phillips, for example, writing as a 'guest previewer' in the *Radio Times*, declared just before the arrival of the second episode that John Cleese and the rest of the programme's 'brilliant company' were 'worth an extra licence fee' on their own.[4] The poet Roger Woddis even penned an ode to the show, the first stanza reading:

> *When night descends on clerk and broker,*
> *And shopgirls hurry home from hell,*
> *When addicts settle down to poker,*

And shadows darken farm and fell,
To lure us from the mediocre
The Fawlties cast their awful spell.[5]

The second episode was called 'The Psychiatrist', and, rather fittingly, John Cleese's own psychiatrist was in the studio audience to watch it being recorded. Full of twitches and winks to some of the more glib reductionisms of the Freudian case books, the show was arguably a little too eager, for once, to signpost its meanings (which threatened at times to reduce a deliciously complex character like Basil to the level of a drily neurotic archetype for an overly simplistic psychiatry course), but, nonetheless, it also boasted several gloriously well-timed and perfectly executed comic moments that charmed as well as amused.

The story opens with Sybil flirting with a young guest called Mr Johnson (who, with his creamy open shirt and tight leather trousers, looks like a large parsnip lodged in a condom), and seemingly delighting in doing so right under the nose of her rattled husband: 'You're only single once,' she says playfully to Mr Johnson (nicely played by Cleese's old friend Nicky Henson[6]). 'Twice can be arranged,' Basil barks out from the bowels of the office. Sybil is in her element, cackling away at the 'easy and amusing' man's jokes while gazing admiringly at the medallions that rest on his bare chest. Basil, on the other hand, is even more tense and testy than usual, squirming and scowling at the sound of each new saucy innuendo; with his braces seemingly tugging his waistband up as far away as possible from the dangerous area of his genitalia, and his sober tie knotted as tightly as a tourniquet around his Adam's apple, even his clothes seem painfully repressed.

Then Dr Abbott and his wife arrive for a brief stay at the hotel. Basil, on hearing that a guest has a title such as 'doctor', suddenly gets excited, spinning round and welcoming another supposed grandee to his nice little establishment: 'We hadn't been told you were a *doctor!* How do you do, *doctor!* Very nice to have you with us, *doctor!*' Then, to his amazement, he discovers that Dr Abbott's wife is also a doctor: 'You're *two* doctors?!' He can hardly believe his luck: 'Charming people,' he says to Sybil after they have set off to their room. 'Professional class. Educated, civilised . . .'

Later on, in the evening, Basil cannot resist fawning over the couple while they attempt to dine, serving them complimentary glasses of cognac and port as he digs out the odd little detail about how posh these two professionals might actually be. She, he discovers, is a paediatrician. This – once he has worked out what it means – meets with Basil's full approval. Her husband then reveals that he is a psychiatrist. Basil, without seeming to miss a beat, says absent-mindedly, 'Very nice too,' and then promptly drinks the doctor's complimentary glass of port ('Cheers! I'll get you another one'). The panic has started.

Sybil, with her sharp but prosaic little brain still buzzing from an earlier chat about fertility symbols and astrology, is simply fascinated to hear more (SYBIL: 'It's a relatively new profession, psychiatry, isn't it?' MRS ABBOTT: 'Well, Freud started about Eighteen eighty.' SYBIL: Yes, but it's only now we're seeing them on the television . . .'), but Basil has clearly taken the news very badly. He slips off into the kitchen, where he warns a puzzled Polly about the supposed hazard ('*Psychiatrist!*'), and then summons Sybil for an unsolicited briefing ('Just keep your distance . . . I mean, remember who you are, all right? Well, just don't tell him about yourself'). Asked to explain what on earth it is that is alarming him, he grows more agitated than ever:

BASIL: If he wants to be a psychiatrist that's his own funeral. They're all as mad as bloody March hares anyway but that's not the point. Look! *Look!!* How does he earn his money? He gets paid for sticking his nose . . . –

SYBIL: Oh, Basil . . .

BASIL: No, I'm going to have my say! – . . . into people's private . . . um . . . details. Well, just speaking for myself, I don't want some total stranger nosing around in my private parts – *details!* That's all I'm saying.

SYBIL: They're here on holiday. They're just here to *enjoy* themselves.

BASIL: He can't.

SYBIL: Can't what?

BASIL: He can't tell me anything about myself that I don't know already. All this psychiatry, it's a load of tummy-rot. You know what they're all obsessed with, don't you?

SYBIL: What?

BASIL: You know what they say it's all about, don't you, mmm? Sex. Everything's connected with sex. *Coh!* What a load of cobblers!

From this point on, of course, he can think of nothing except sex – or rather, he can think of nothing except other people thinking that he can think of nothing except sex. An attractive young Australian woman named Raylene arrives in reception and, when he catches sight of the St Christopher symbol nestling just above her full and well-shaped *poitrine*, he is consumed by self-consciousness: 'Very nice . . . Your thing. I mean, your charms – your *charm!*' He takes her cases up to her room and, while she stands by the bathroom door and stretches her tired arms high above her head, he goes inside to change a bulb, reaches back for the light switch and ends up flicking her left nipple. This, alas, is the very moment that Sybil has chosen to arrive with a stray item of luggage. 'Sybil, *Sybil, SYBIL,* I'm sorry,' he pants after her, 'I didn't know she was there,' but she is utterly unimpressed: 'It's *pathetic,*' she snaps. 'I've read about it, Basil. The "male menopause" it's called. Oh, and one word of advice: if you're going to grope a girl, have the gallantry to stay *in* the room with her while you're doing it, *hmm?*'

Displacing his mind back to the potentially priapic Mr Johnson, he hears the sound of an unknown and unregistered woman laughing inside the louche man's room, so he sets about catching the scoundrel in the act. First, he sneaks into an empty room next door and puts an eager ear to the wall – only for the occupants, the psychiatrist and his wife, to return unexpectedly ('This wall . . .,' he explains unconvincingly, '. . . er, we've had some complaints from downstairs . . . I'm giving it a check . . .'); then he barges in on Mr Johnson with a bottle of champagne, but is frustrated to find that the woman must be hiding; then he sneaks into the darkened room on the other side and heads again for the wall, only to find that, of all people, Raylene is asleep on the bed, and, as she wakes, her screams bring the psychiatrist back on the scene. Finally, and very rashly, he enlists the help of Manuel, taking him outside to hold the ladder while he climbs up to peer into Mr Johnson's room – but chooses the wrong window and, to his horror, finds himself staring straight into the faces of the psychiatrist and his half-undressed wife. Checking the state of the glass – *tap-tap-tap* – before rather nonchalantly leaning back, he falls down to the ground with a loud crash. Manuel's well-intended attempt to explain the situation to an alarmed Sybil – 'I tell him "careful" but he got to see girl!' – backfires spectacularly, and she administers a ferocious smack to Basil before banning him from their bedroom and slamming the door in his face. 'Crazy,' Manuel tut-tuts sympathetically. '*Crazy*. I say to her, "You try to see in girl's room" and *[shrugs]* she go crazy!' Realising what has made the situation look even worse than he thought it would seem, he picks up Manuel, turns him upside down and proceeds to shake him vigorously like an almost-empty bottle of ketchup – an action that is witnessed, inevitably, by the wife of the psychiatrist.

After spending a sleepless night huddled up in the broom cupboard, Basil plots his revenge on the insufferable Mr Johnson. Hearing yet another woman emerging from somewhere near his room across the hall, Basil leaps out brandishing a broom – and finds himself, yet again, in the uncomfortable company of the psychiatrist and his wife ('There's enough material there for an entire conference,' mutters one doctor to the other as they set off down the stairs). Back in the darkness of the broom cupboard, he knocks over a pot and, after picking it back up, is irritated to discover that he now has one hand covered with some kind of sticky black substance. Mr Johnson, meanwhile, opens his door, looks around and whispers to his girlfriend that the coast appears to be clear, but the sound of Raylene emerging from nearby sends them scurrying back inside. Basil, hearing a door close, leaps out and sees a young woman walking away, so he lunges at her – '*Right – that's it!*' – but then is shocked to see that he has just assaulted none other than poor Raylene again, and, worse still, has now left an incriminating black handprint on her right breast. Raylene's scream brings Sybil racing out into the hallway, where, surveying the sorry scene, she notes Basil's black hand, and Raylene's black breast, and then Basil, realising how it all must look, tries to cover up the black breast with his black hand ('Sorry – I got confused!').

The ending, once again, is sheer agony for Basil. He enters Raylene's room to apologise, but, as he glimpses her disappearing into the bathroom to change her top, moves to slip back out – just as someone knocks on the door. 'Come in,' says the now dressed-again Raylene, and Sybil leans in to apologise for her husband's undeniably peculiar behaviour: 'He's going through rather a disturbed time,' she says with a strained smile. Raylene assures her that no real offence has been taken, but, just at that moment, Sybil spots a stray, almost penile-like little finger holding the wardrobe door shut from the inside. 'Basil?' she asks, knocking hard enough to cause a bruise. 'Hello, dear,' he says cheerily as the doors come open. 'Just checking the doors . . .' *[tap-tap-tap]*.

Furious, she marches off, raging at her husband's cowardly antics, but Basil insists that, this time, she must stop and let him finally prove what has really been going on: 'Stand there and watch!' He then knocks on Mr Johnson's door and announces that he knows that someone else is lurking inside – 'a female person, perhaps a lady, you know – an opposite person of the contradictory gender.' Johnson calmly replies that Basil is absolutely right: the woman in question is Mrs Johnson, his mother. 'Oh, I see,' smirks Basil. 'This bit of crumpet's your old mummy, is she? Oh, this is rich. Old mother Johnson popped up for a quickie, did she?' He calls for her to come out, and she does – and she is clearly Mr Johnson's elderly mother. 'How do you do,' says a stunned Basil. 'Are you enjoying yourself?' The door shuts. Sybil departs. He then stands alone in the hallway, grimaces, squats down, wraps his arms tightly over his sunken head and hops in dark despair – just as the psychiatrist and his wife return to their room.

Two episodes into the run, and the series was already, in terms both of ratings and reviews, a clear success. There was still the odd critical qualification (the *Daily Telegraph*'s Sean Day-Lewis, for example, while stressing that *Fawlty Towers* 'remains the funniest and best-crafted home-grown formula around' – complained vaguely that its 'limitations are more obvious this time'[7]), but, in general, the responses were getting progressively warmer (and Michael Palin responded to the latest 'marvellously constructed' episode by recording in his diary: 'It's so good it makes me want to give up'[8]). Most people had stopped comparing the new shows with their selective memories of the earlier ones, and were now just enjoying the episodes on their own terms.

Those who did still harbour any doubts would surely have let them go after watching the third instalment, which was entitled 'Waldorf Salad'. Here was arguably the best effort so far: not quite as emotionally draining as the first show, and not as obviously manipulative as the second, but a fine realisation of a very, very funny idea. It was the kind of polished gem of an episode that one just sat back and laughed one's way through from start to finish.

It featured an American. An aggressive, irascible, intolerant and very, very impatient American. The American in question is a man called Mr Hamilton. Right from the start, Basil does not like him.

As Mr Hamilton – who has just marched into reception – proceeds to complain about the journey, the left-side traffic conventions, the weather and practically everything else, Basil glances at the Englishwoman near him and grimaces: 'I'm sorry about this.' The American carries on, moaning about this, that and the other. 'See what I mean?' Basil mutters to the woman conspiratorially. 'Rub-*bish*.' The woman responds calmly by gesturing at the American: 'May I introduce my husband?' She, Basil now realises, is Mrs Hamilton. He rubs his nose anxiously while he thinks of how to camouflage this latest *faux pas*, then smiles politely at Mr Hamilton, looks around and moans, 'The rubbish we get in here!' He picks up a piece of paper ostentatiously – 'Look at that!' – screws it up and shows it to Sybil: 'More rubbish, dear!'

The Hamiltons, however, are hungry, and, as luck would have it, this is a particularly bad time to be hungry at Fawlty Towers. Diners have been complaining all day about the inadequate service, but Basil, with that horrible old English fatalism, has just brushed them off by blaming the foreign Manuel: 'He's hopeless, isn't he? You think I don't know? I mean, you only have to *eat* here. We have to *live* with it. I had to pay his fare all the way from *Barcelona*. But you can't get the staff, you see. It's a nightmare!' The situation looks even less promising for the Hamiltons because, as Basil tries to explain, they have arrived after nine o'clock at night, and 'the chef does actually stop at nine.' Mr Hamilton is rattled: 'Why does your chef stop at nine – has he got something terminal?' As he is in no mood to be messed with, he pulls out some notes: 'How much of this Mickey Mouse money do you need to keep the chef on for half an hour? One . . . two . . . twenty pounds, huh? Is that enough?' Basil looks at the lovely notes and cannot resist: 'I'll see what I can do.'

Terry the chef is rushing off for his latest karate lesson ('My karate means a lot to me'), so Basil resolves, unwisely, to go it alone. First, he offers to get the late-dining couple some drinks: 'Two screwdrivers,' barks Mr Hamilton. 'I understand,' says Basil, 'and you'll . . . leave the drinks?' Although he succeeds in persuading them to abandon the DIY and settle instead for a vodka and orange, he still ends up failing to please. The orange juice, Mrs Hamilton complains, is not fresh. Basil is bemused: he has only just opened the bottle. Once it is explained that 'freshly squeezed', rather than 'freshly unscrewed', orange juice is required, he scuttles off again, brings back the right drinks and then attempts to discover what the two of them want to eat:

MR HAMILTON: Could you make me a Waldorf salad?

BASIL: Oh, er . . . a . . . *Wall* . . . ?

MR HAMILTON: Waldorf salad.

BASIL: Well . . . I *think* we're just out of Waldorfs.

MR HAMILTON: *[To his wife]* I don't believe this!

MRS HAMILTON: It's not very well known here, Harry.

BASIL: Yes, er, may I recommend tonight the . . .

MR HAMILTON: Now look, I'm sure your chef knows how to fix me a Waldorf salad, huh?

BASIL: Well, I wouldn't be *too* sure . . .

MR HAMILTON: Well, he's a *chef*, isn't he?

BASIL: Yes, yes, you wouldn't prefer . . .

MR HAMILTON: *[Losing his patience]* Well, find out, will you? Just go out there and see if he knows how to fix me a Waldorf salad!

Now Basil is trapped. He goes off to the kitchen, waits a moment and then returns: 'He's not *absolutely* positive,' he reports. 'He's almost got it. It's lettuce and tomatoes, walled in with . . . ?' Mr Hamilton snaps back: 'No, no, no! It's celery, apples, walnuts, grapes!' His wife completes the list: 'In a mayonnaise sauce.' Basil still tries to convert them to the simpler pleasures of pâté or grapefruit ('It's halved . . . with a cherry in the . . . centre . . .'), but to no avail: both of them want their Waldorf salads, and then to follow, they add ominously, they want a couple of *filets mignons* ('Steaks!' shouts Mr Hamilton, leaving nothing to chance. 'Done rare! Not out of a bottle!'). There is even more trouble for Basil once he gets back into the kitchen, because Sybil has found out about his foolish scam, knows that he is clueless about any kind of cuisine ('What is a "waldorf" anyway?' he asks her. 'A walnut that's gone off?') and is ready to launch herself into damage limitation mode ('I'll find everything – just go and get a bottle of Volnay!').

Sybil's mistake is to explain to Basil that the salad gets its name from the Waldorf Hotel in New York. Armed with this knowledge, the low-watt light bulb goes on inside his head, he shoots straight back out into the dining room and attempts to sell the Hamiltons the idea of a 'Ritz salad': 'It's a traditional old English . . . thing. It's apples, grapefruit and potatoes . . . in a mayonnaise sauce.' When they decline the offer, he rambles on with a convoluted excuse that succeeds only in making Mr Hamilton erupt with rage, ordering Basil to march back into the kitchen and tell the chef in no uncertain terms that 'if he doesn't get on the ball you're going to bust his ass!' Basil is not too sure about the 'ass' bit, but he can see that Hamilton means business, so he does as he is told and disappears back into the kitchen. Unfortunately for him, Sybil has just emerged directly from there with two plates of perfectly well-prepared Waldorf salad, so, after loudly berating the imaginary chef for failing to come up with these very dishes, he reacts furiously when he returns and finds all of the ingredients present and correct. Ignoring the fact that Mr Hamilton is at last close to being content, Basil snatches his salad and sets off back to the kitchen to go through the whole sorry charade all over again. Sybil stops his nonsense this time by winding him with a well-placed punch, and it seems as though a semblance of calm normality has been restored, but Basil is soon back with what he is deluded enough to think will sound like a written *mea culpa* from the chef ('If only I'd listened to Mr Fawlty,' he reads self-consciously, 'none of this fiasco would have happened . . .').

The sudden sight of smoke coming from the kitchen signals the final nail in the coffin of his con: the steaks are now on fire. He rushes off to the kitchen and resumes his frenzied one-man dialogue, but by this time Mr Hamilton has rumbled him, and walks in on the pitiful scene. 'May I introduce Terry . . .' says Basil, gesturing at a gaping space. Basil then does his best to do a 'spontaneous' double-take: 'Where did he go?' Hamilton is chillingly contemptuous: 'Maybe he went to get something to eat.'

The Hamiltons have had enough. Mr Hamilton announces that they are leaving, and, as a parting shot, declares: 'This place is the crummiest, shoddiest, worst-run hotel in the whole of Western Europe!' Basil draws the line at that, insisting that his hotel has had 'thousands of satisfied customers'. Mr Hamilton calls his bluff: 'Let's ask them, huh?' Basil jumps in and badgers a few of his current clientele into saying 'Yes, we're satisfied,' but, just as he begins his gloating victor's speech, a lone voice pipes up: 'I'm not satisfied.' Another guest then chimes in: 'No, we're not satisfied.' Before Basil can dismiss these dissidents, Mr Hamilton insists that he stays still and quiet while everyone else has their say, threatening that he will 'bust your ass' if there is any attempt at retaliation ('Everything's *bottoms*, isn't it,' mutters Basil bitterly). Suddenly, the complaints start mounting up, and Basil surveys the guests and feels utterly betrayed:

This . . . is . . . typical. Absolutely . . . typical. Of the kind of *ARSE* I have to put up with from you people. You ponce in here expecting to be waited on hand and foot, well, I'm trying to run a *hotel* here! Have you any idea of how much there is to do? Do you *ever* think of that? *Of course not!* You're all too busy sticking your noses into every corner, poking around for things to complain about, aren't you? Well, let me tell you something: this is *exactly* how Nazi Germany started! A lot of layabouts with nothing better to do than to cause trouble. Well, I've had fifteen years of pandering to the likes of you and I've had enough. I've *had* it! Come on: pack your bags and *get out!*

Upon finding that Mr Hamilton – who appears to be, if anything, even more petty and vindictive than him – is arranging to book taxis for everyone exiting the hotel, Basil snaps completely, hurrying all of the guests away ('Come on, out: *RAUS! RAUS! RAUS!*'), and then explaining to his startled wife that it is a case of 'either they go or I go'. One look at her blank expression convinces him to change tack: 'Well, goodbye, dear. It's been an interesting fifteen years but all good things must come to an end . . .'

He sets off out of his own hotel, goes down the steps, rubs his hands and walks a few paces away, but then reflects on the fact that it is raining heavily, he has no change of clothes and has nowhere to go – so he spins around and swans back into reception: 'A room, please,' he asks of Sybil. 'Number twelve is free, I think. Now, I'd like breakfast in bed at half-past ten in the morning, please. That's eggs, bacon, sausage and tomato, with a Waldorf salad, all washed down with lashings of hot screwdriver . . .'

Few other sitcom episodes had seemed so audaciously un-adorned and sharply focused as this. A man orders a Waldorf salad, and then waits – and waits – for said Waldorf salad to arrive: in comparison to the richly elaborate farce of the previous instalment, this edition appeared positively minimalist. Rather like a Hitchcock suspense movie, we were made privy to the deception right from the start, and then left to watch the man responsible for it gradually fall apart under the strain of the mounting pressure. Another reason why 'Waldorf Salad', like the earlier 'Communication Problems', was so involving as well as entertaining was that Basil was now being handed such spectacularly unpleasant opponents; seeing him struggle against a fog-horned solipsist like Mrs Richards or a brash and boorish materialist like Mr Hamilton, one found it harder to denounce his dogged duplicity (whereas the troublesome guests he encountered in the first series, such as Mr Hutchinson the spoon salesman, were merely misfits, these new ones seemed more like monsters). The hotelier is not in the right, but neither are some of his customers; he might still be a monster himself, but, to a certain extent, he now seemed more like our monster, and, with a furtive blush of embarrassment, we would sometimes catch ourselves willing the rotter to win.

It was clever comic quality such as this that helped make the show more popular than ever. Midway into its run, this second series of *Fawlty Towers* – which was now being watched by about eleven million viewers each week[9] – seemed to have been firmly confirmed as a national institution. It was not just getting exceptionally positive reviews. It was also getting long and warmly admiring essays. Jack Waterman, for example, reflected in the *Listener* on the enduring appeal of the sitcom (noting that it seemed 'to have been around, if not quite as long as *Coronation Street*, certainly for a long time', thanks to repeats whose number 'is probably evidence that it scores a long way above most ideas for "situation comedy" '), and he saluted the high standard of both the production and the performances (*'Fawlty Towers* excels visually, with no small debt to the achievement of disaster effects, be it a bottle of wine arcing through the dining room, a duck being shattered on the kitchen floor, or the fleeting glimpse of Fawlty's aghast face fading off the top of a ladder. The acting is brilliant') and he also praised the peculiar power of the show's anti-hero:

> As far as the comedy is concerned, [Basil] could well represent the missing bit of Aristotle: the mirror image in farce of the tragic hero who, through inborn faults, encompasses ruin and disaster for all. Our emotions are then purged, not with pity, but with laughter, by the device of comeuppance which overtakes this manic, envenomed, juggernaut version of Mr Pooter just as surely as the original Mr Pooter was able to write in his diary: 'Made exit with dignity, but tripped over mat.'[10]

The next edition of the show – called 'The Kipper and the Corpse' – explored another taboo topic by using a real-life anecdote as its base. John Cleese had asked a friend of his at the old Langan's restaurant – a caterer by the name of Andrew Leeman who had trained at London's Savoy Hotel – what was the worst problem with which hoteliers had to contend, and Leeman ('without a moment's thought') had said: 'Dealing with guests that had died.' It was not uncommon, he went on, that a large hotel would have to spirit away about ten or twelve dead bodies each year: 'The old dears knew the Savoy would always treat them really well, so they would check in with a bottle of pills, take them in the night, and in the morning the Savoy staff would walk in, pick up the phone and say, "We've got another one." Then the problem was getting the stiffs into the service elevator without alarming the other guests.'[11] Inspired by this insight, Cleese worked with Booth on an appropriate plot, and named one of the characters after his candid friend at Langan's.

The story revolved around a businessman called Mr Leeman, who books a room for the night after telling his three colleagues that he is not feeling particularly well. The pasty-faced little man (played in an understated and disciplined way by a former acrobat named Derek Royle – 'We had to find a really good actor,' said the director Bob Spiers, 'who was prepared to be carried around [and sometimes dropped] for most of the episode'[12]) is clearly ailing as he heads off towards the stairs, but that does not stop Basil from complaining to Sybil that the poor old soul did not bother to say those two little words, 'good night' ('It's not the Gettysburg Address!'). Basil gets even more resentful when Leeman returns to reception to ask if he can book himself some breakfast – some kippers – to be served in bed: 'Is it your legs?' Basil inquires sarcastically.[13] 'Most of our guests manage to struggle down in the morning.' After inviting Leeman to choose between breakfast trays made out of rosewood, mahogany or teak, Basil shouts out after him: 'You go along and have a really good night's sleep, then. I'm hoping to get a couple of hours later on myself, but I'll be up in good time to serve you your breakfast in bed. If you can remember to sleep with your mouth open you won't even have to wake up. I'll just drop in small pieces of lightly buttered kipper when you're breathing in the right direction, if that doesn't put you out!'

The following morning in the dining room, various other guests are sitting down to breakfast: the lugubrious Dr Price (played by the ever-reliable, hangdog-faced Geoffrey Palmer) has ordered some sausages and a cup of coffee, while the posh elderly lady Mrs Chase (Mavis Pugh) has requested eggs for herself and a plate of thinly sliced sausages, a bowl of tepid water and a plump cushion for her pampered pooch ('He's a little Chitzu'). In the kitchen, Basil is being reassured by both Sybil and Terry the chef that the kippers are still perfectly edible even though they are clearly past their sell-by date ('That's just to cover themselves,' says Sybil). Basil remains unconvinced ('Poisoning is still an offence in this country, you know, Sybil'), but, reluctantly, he agrees to take the fish up to Mr Leeman. Although the guest appears to be sitting up awake and ready to start reading his newspaper, Basil cannot get so much as a muttered 'Thank you' from him ('Un-be-lievable,' he moans to himself as he sets off back down the corridor. 'Not a single bloody word!'). Polly rushes past him towards the stairs: 'Forgot the milk,' she explains, heading in the direction of the room occupied by Mr Leeman. 'Well, don't get talking to him,' sneers Basil. 'You'll never get away.'

Moments later, however, the news gets back to the kitchen that Polly has discovered Mr Leeman stone-dead in his bed. Basil, thinking that this must have been a case of expiry-by-expired-kippers, races to the room and, while Sybil seeks out Dr Price, hides the plate, holds the fish and proceeds to panic. Polly, spotting that the kippers have remained uneaten, points out that the dead guest must have expired long before the breakfast tray arrived – thus prompting a hugely relieved Basil to dance a celebratory jig ('Oh, *thank* you, God! Oh, isn't it *wonderful?* I'm so happy! *Hooray!*') until the sudden presence of Dr Price scares him into slipping the kippers inside the front of his pullover and affecting a respectful sense of regret ('Sad, isn't it? *Tch, tch, tch* . . .'). Once the time of death is confirmed as about ten hours ago, the no-nonsense Sybil tells Basil to move the deceased into the downstairs office to await the arrival of an undertaker.

Covering the corpse quickly with a bed sheet and a handful of bath towels, Basil teams up with Manuel and Polly to transport it as discreetly as possible to its temporary destination. No sooner do they sneak outside the room, however, than Miss Tibbs turns up to catch sight of the body and starts screaming hysterically '*Murder! MURDER!*' – thus panicking Polly into slapping her unconscious. 'Oh, spiffing!' moans Basil, staring at the supine septuagenarian. 'Absolutely *spiffing!* Well done: two dead, twenty-five to go!' Another close call follows soon after – when two more guests arrive inconveniently on the scene, one of Mr Leeman's limp arms is almost spotted and Miss Tibbs wakes up wailing in a wardrobe – before they finally deposit the deceased in the appointed place downstairs.

Normal service appears set to resume when, hearing a shriek come from the office, Basil and Sybil arrive to find Mr Leeman slumped in a chair and, once again, Miss Tibbs flat out on the floor. 'What did you put him *there* for?' Sybil exclaims. 'Well,' says Basil, 'he wouldn't fit in the safe and all the drawers were full.' Reluctantly ('Our guests . . .' he grumbles. 'They give us trouble even when they're dead'), he gets Manuel to help him relocate Leeman to the kitchen. Held up halfway there by a distraught Mrs Chase, who is convinced that her beloved Chitzu has just been poisoned by poorly prepared pork, they finally make it through the lobby and into the kitchen, where Dr Price's burnt sausages are filling the room with smoke. The starving doctor investigates and, horrified at the insalubrious sight, immediately orders Basil and Manuel to take the corpse back out of the kitchen, so they dump it in a laundry basket and leave it in the hall while a fresh set of sausages are put in the pan for Dr Price.

Returning to the laundry basket, Basil and Manuel are interrupted again: this time by three people who announce that they have come to 'collect' Mr Leeman. Mistaking them for undercover undertakers, Basil says, *sotto voce*, that he is in the basket. 'What's he doing in the basket?' one of them asks. 'Well,' says Basil with a slight chuckle, 'not much!' Seeing that they do not believe him, he opens the lid and looks inside: 'Oh my God – he's gone!' Polly arrives just in time: fresh laundry, she realises, has just been delivered. She, Basil and Manuel race out of the hotel, stop the van just in time and return with the other basket.

'There seems to be some kind of misunderstanding . . .' says one of the visitors. They are there, he explains, to take their colleague Mr Leeman into town for a meeting. The penny drops. 'Oh, I see,' cries Basil awkwardly. 'M-Mr *Leeman!*' Polly picks up the cue: 'We thought you said . . . the *linen!*' Sybil then arrives to break the news to Leeman's friends, while Leeman's corpse is carried back upstairs – first into a room where a lonely looking guest called 'Mr Ingrams' (Cleese's long-awaited revenge, served corpse-cold, on Richard Ingrams for his mean critique of the first series[14]) appears to be in the process of inflating a rubber woman ('*Sorry!*'), then into another occupied bedroom, then back downstairs again into the kitchen where Dr Price is still cooking his sausages, then back out into the lobby where Manuel collapses with exhaustion and crawls inside the vacant laundry basket. Basil, hearing Leeman's saddened colleagues coming back out from the office, has no time to do anything other than prop the corpse up beneath the hat stand and then hover nervously in front of it. One of the departing visitors remembers, alas, that he needs to retrieve his hat. 'I'll have it sent on,' says Basil a little too forcefully, but the man is adamant that he wants to take it now. There is only one thing for it, Basil realises, so he says: 'Polly, will you get Manuel out of the basket, please?' Manuel, very grudgingly, gets out of the basket and, with help from Polly, presents the man with his hat.

The crisis seems, at last, to be over. Then Miss Tibbs reappears: 'Mr Fawlty,' she says solemnly, 'I want a word with you in your office!' Then Mrs Chase reappears with another report on her poorly Chitzu: 'My baby's dying!' Then Dr Price reappears: 'I've just cooked these sausages myself and they're off!' Basil then does what he does best – he passes the buck: 'Ladies and gentlemen, there have been a lot of cock-ups this morning, you all deserve an explanation, and I'm happy to say that . . . my wife will give it to you. Thank you. Thank you so much!' With that, he sneaks into the laundry basket and is carried out to the van, with the fading sound of Sybil shouting after him: '*Basil! Basil!! Basil!!!*'

Once again, *Fawlty Towers* had found a logical, believable and remorselessly funny way to deal, on prime-time mainstream TV, with a topic as potentially dark and delicate as death. The magical trick was for the comedy to hold up the fact of the death, and then focus more on Basil's stunningly selfish reaction to that death. The discomforting plausibility of his huge relief, and even pleasure, upon discovering that, tragic though it was, it was not *his* fault ('Oh *joy!*'), worked as well on the audience as Frankie Howerd pointing accusingly at someone whose mind is dirty enough to make them laugh at a double-entendre. There were thus no real complaints following its transmission; there was just a strong sense of admiration and respect, and the critical plaudits continued (with, for example, the columnist and playwright Keith Waterhouse hailing Basil as 'one of the great comic characters of our time'.[15]). The only question was, once again, 'How can they possibly top that?'

Viewers would have to wait longer than expected for the arrival of the penultimate episode in the series, which was entitled 'The Anniversary', because of a bout of industrial action (1979 was one of the worst years for strikes and other disruptions in the history of British television – ITV, for example, would be off the air for ten whole weeks from August to October because of a dispute with a union over pay[16]). Scheduled originally for 19 March, the show was replaced by a repeat ('Gourmet Night') and only reached the screen the following week. The delay, however, turned out, as far as the production team was concerned, to be a blessing in disguise. The 'great joy' that came with making this particular episode, John Cleese would reveal, was due to the fact that the team had a little longer than usual to rehearse it: 'We got about five days into rehearsal and [then] a splendid thing happened: a BBC executive got into an argument with a rigger – someone who puts the lights up – and eventually punched him [N.B.: It was actually the other way round].[17] And the unions went on strike, and we couldn't record the programme on the ordinary day. It was postponed, and they settled the strike, and everything was put off a week. [. . .] And we had all this time to rehearse it, and it was really, really good, because everyone was able to get familiar with the show and then bring little things to it. So I think it's one of the very best episodes.'[18]

'The Anniversary' was indeed a very polished episode of the show. It was also quite unusual, in the sense that it shone a light on those areas of the Fawlty marriage that were normally left to languish deep in the darkest shadows. Sybil's more vulnerable and emotional side – which had been hinted at in recent editions – now came out for all to see; Basil's fear of his wife was leavened with a soupçon of sentimentality; and the pair of them were actually shown to have a small network of mutual friends (including one who dared to address them affectionately as 'Bas' and 'Syb').

The farcical melodrama focused on the fact that the Fawltys are about to celebrate their fifteenth year together as a married couple, and Sybil fears that, like last year, Basil has completely overlooked the significance of the date. While she therefore wanders about the hotel looking uncharacteristically melancholic, sighing repeatedly, slapping violently shut a succession of menu covers as though they contained men's slumbering genitalia (another clever little touch from Prunella Scales, who was always unusually smart and subtle with props), and generally dropping plenty of heavy hints about memory and forgetfulness, Basil seems unusually chipper, as well as blissfully oblivious to all of her clues. Once she has moved on in a huff, however, he allows himself a moment of smug self-satisfaction ('Do I detect the smell of burnt martyr?') and then reveals to Polly what he is really up to: 'I forgot last year and I got flayed alive for it, so we've got some friends arriving in about ten minutes for a surprise drinks party, Manuel's making a special paella for tonight, got some champagne . . . but don't tell her I've remembered yet . . . let's let her have a bit of a *fume*.'

Polly, meanwhile, has concerns of her own about a second-hand car that she is desperate to buy. Having asked Basil several times before for a hundred-pound loan, she explains to him anxiously that the deadline for offers runs out at the end of the week. Basil, however, mutters vaguely about 'the cash-flow situation vis-à-vis the frozen assets' and, once again, refuses to give her any decision until after all the anniversary events. Failing to appreciate Polly's predicament is his first error of the day. His second comes hot on its heels, when a clearly emotional Sybil, having tired of trying to nudge her husband subtly into recognising their special date, summons him to the office for one last attempt:

SYBIL: Do you know what day it is today, Basil?

BASIL: *[Still relishing the ruse]* Um . . . it's the . . . sixteenth today, dear.

SYBIL: It's the seventeenth, Basil.

BASIL: No, no, it's the sixteenth today, dear.

SYBIL: *[Quietly furious]* It's the *seven*teenth, Basil.

BASIL: Well, we'll soon settle this, dear. *[He goes out to the reception desk and consults a newspaper. She follows him.]* Oh, yes, you are right. The seventeenth of April. Well, well, well . . .

SYBIL: Does that *stir* any memories in you, Basil?

BASIL: Memories? *[He pretends to get an idea]* Agincourt?

SYBIL: . . . What?

BASIL: Anniversary of the Battle of Agincourt? *[Sybil slaps him on the cheek, walks back into the office and slams the door. He is clearly very amused.]* Trafalgar? Crécy? Poitiers?? Yom Kippur???

Still congratulating himself on daring to tease someone as formidable as Sybil, he begins to placate Terry – who wants to know why he is not the one who will be preparing the paella tonight – when Manuel breaks in with some startling news: 'Mrs Fawlty – she go!' Horrified, he races out of the hotel, only to see his wife drive off before he can catch her and explain. This departure is then followed by the arrival of the first couple of friends for the surprise party.

It has all gone disastrously wrong. Welcoming Alice (Una Stubbs) and husband Roger (played by Ken Campbell – a last-minute replacement for Julian Holloway, who, because of the delay due to industrial action, had been obliged to move on to his next engagement), Basil acts on Polly's typically quick-witted advice and announces that Sybil is ill. Roger – a bit of a 'card' with a comb-over – takes this news in his stride, delighting himself by making a laboured pun out of 'Syb' and 'ill', but Alice is more concerned, and has to be prevented forcibly by Basil from heading up the stairs to check on the health of her friend ('She's very swollen up,' he explains urgently, adding for good measure that 'she's lost her voice' and is 'having a bit of a sleep'). Herding the pair into the bar, he gets them some gin and tonics while Roger – who is obviously not quite as stupid as he seems – whispers to Alice that he suspects the Fawltys have actually had a bit of a row.

The pressure is cranked up further when the next pair of friends comes in: the robust-looking Virginia (Pat Keen) and the mousy pipe man Arthur (Robert Arnold). Virginia happens to be a nurse, so, when she volunteers to go up and examine Sybil, Basil has to act fast and, thanks to yet another priceless cue from Polly, declares that a doctor has already been and diagnosed his poor wife's condition as 'not completely serious but slightly serious'. The challenges, however, keep on coming: two more guests, smart Kitty (Denyse Alexander) and sober Reg (Roger Hume), turn up and announce that they have just seen Sybil driving around in town. Straining his initiative to the limit, Basil insists that this sighting was actually of someone else: namely, 'that woman who looks slightly like Sybil'. The real Sybil, he repeats, is the one with the puffed-up face and legs, without a voice, who is fast asleep upstairs.

Virginia the nurse remains unconvinced ('There's something very peculiar about this . . .'), and Roger the wag cannot resist joking how even more peculiar it is that the ailing Sybil has found the time and energy to slip out and drive around town, so Basil, snapping with self-righteous indignation, rashly changes tack and tells all the doubters: 'I'll just pop upstairs and ask her to stop dying and then you can all come up and identify her!'

Leaving them standing awkwardly about in the bar, he rushes out into the lobby, grabs Polly ('Would you give me a hand?') and drags her up the stairs with him. When it transpires that he actually wants her to put on one of Sybil's swirly wigs, get into bed and pretend to be the poorly Mrs Fawlty, she reacts angrily, and, even though he threatens to ensure that she'll 'never waitress in Torquay again', she is adamant that, on this occasion, she will not comply: 'I help out at reception, I clean the rooms, I deal with tradesmen, I mend the switchboard, I change the fuses, and if you think my duties now include impersonating members of your family, you have got one more screw loose than I thought. I'm *not* doing it. Do you understand?' Basil, ever the craven con man, tries miming a heart attack, but Polly, hearing the first knock at the door, spots her chance and says: 'A hundred for the car.' Basil has no choice but to accept her terms and, with the room kept in near darkness, the ludicrous deception goes ahead.

'*Happy Anniversary!*' the crowd of them all cry, bumping into each other as they try to feel their way forward through the Stygian gloom of the room. Basil limits them to a quick wave from a safe distance, but then, hearing a car drive up outside, peers through a crack in the curtains and sees the worst sight possible: Sybil coming back. '*Aaaagh!*' he screams. 'I've just remembered something downstairs,' he tells the startled crowd. 'Y-You stay here and have a chat with Polly – *SYBIL!*' Back down in the lobby, Basil arrives just as his wife walks in. Sad and subdued, Sybil (who is not only superbly well played here, as always, by Prunella Scales, but also very sensitively filmed by the director Bob Spiers), seems unnervingly bereft of her usual feisty powers. 'I came back for my clubs, Basil – I'm not stopping,' she says coolly, expecting him to break down and beg her to stay.

'Oh, aren't you?' he replies, sounding distracted and looking decidedly shifty. 'Okay.' Sybil is astonished and obviously very hurt at such a callously casual snub: 'You don't even *want* me to, do you!' She rushes off, crying as she goes. 'Cheerio, dear,' he calls out to her, then he races straight back up the stairs. He reaches the bedroom just as Polly punches nurse Virginia to prevent her from feeling her glands. 'She *hit* me, Basil!' cries the tearful Virginia. 'She lashed out!' Basil dashes over to Polly and gives her a slap: '*Don't!* Don't hit our friends! I know you're not feeling a hundred per cent, but *control* yourself!' The startled visitors beat a hasty retreat to the door.

Sybil, meanwhile, is outside in the forecourt being comforted by her best friend Audrey (the character's first and only on-screen appearance) as she sits and sobs in her car: 'They're all the same, dear,' Audrey assures her. 'They're all the same, dear, believe me!' Agreeing to get away from it all with a nice game of golf, Sybil suddenly remembers that she has still got to retrieve her clubs from inside the hotel, so she sets off towards the entrance. Arriving in the lobby just as her old friends are about to leave, there is a stunned silence, and time seems to stand still: she stares at them; they stare at her; she stares at Basil; and Basil stares at her. 'How . . . extra-ordinary,' he says at last, very slowly. 'We were just *talking* about you!' He offers her his hand: 'Basil Fawlty. We met once . . . at a fête . . .' She is too bemused to speak, but lets him take her arm and guide her past the guests and off into the kitchen: 'Let me show you where it is . . .' Calmly negotiating a way round Manuel and Terry, who are on the floor fighting each other over their rival paellas, Basil puts her inside a cupboard, saying, 'I'll explain everything in a moment, dear.' Returning to the lobby, he sees off all of their profoundly confused friends, then turns to Polly and says: 'Piece of cake.'

There follows a nervous glance over in the direction of the kitchen: 'Now comes the tricky bit . . .'

Aptly described by one critic as 'agonisingly funny',[19] it was certainly the most 'Ayckbourn-like' episode so far, and, therefore, it was just what Cleese and Booth had wanted: an ensemble comedy of excruciating social embarrassment and increasingly fast-paced farce, but also with one or two surprisingly insightful moments about an emotionally dysfunctional relationship. Far from signalling the imminent end of the Fawlty fiction, it actually suggested that so much more, potentially, was still ahead.

The second series was due to come to the end of its illustrious run on Monday 2 April 1979, with an episode entitled 'Basil the Rat'. Thanks, however, to a further bout of industrial action, the show was again postponed (with a repeat of the US sitcom *Rhoda* being shown in its place). Then a new set of schedules began, and, remarkably, it would be six whole months before the last episode of *Fawlty Towers* finally reached the screen.

The team had only just completed the initial read-through of the script when news of the delay came through. 'As it turned out,' the director Bob Spiers would recall, 'I think it worked brilliantly to our advantage, because after we had read through, and I'd analysed just what was involved in this episode in terms of special effects, and rats running around all over the place, and just the number of scenes that we had to do, it had finally become, in my opinion, totally and completely impossible to do this show with [the normal] one day in the studio. So I think we just had to finally say the game was up, that this was just too complex to achieve in one hit, and we needed to pre-record certain bits.'[20] The delay, therefore, allowed Spiers to negotiate some crucial changes with the powers-that-be: 'Very grudgingly, they agreed to allow me two days in the studio, and some pre-record time to do the special effects pieces.'[21] The episode was then recorded twice, American-style, before two separate studio audiences, and then, using mainly the second perform-ance as the basis of the master tape, the finished show was edited and made ready for broadcast.

Finally shown on BBC2 at 9.00 p.m. on Thursday 25 October, the episode featured another splendid set of guest performers (especially the wonderfully subtle John Quarmby as the dourly dutiful 'Mr Carnegie'), and yet another darkly audacious comic scenario. There had been disability, sex and death to disturb Basil in previous episodes, as well as a distress-ingly un-English outbreak of plain speaking. Now, for his sins, he would have to fight off nightmarish thoughts of poison, pestilence and plague.

The action began when Basil, fresh from another nagging from Sybil, wanders into the kitchen and finds that there is a bland-looking middle-aged man kneeling down by the opened fridge and peering closely at a large plate of meat. 'Shall I get you the wine list?' Basil inquires. The man looks up: 'Mr Fawlty?' Basil is oozing sarcasm: ' "Mister"? Oh, please, call me "waiter". Look, I'll go and get a chair and then you can really tuck in – there's some stuff in the bin you might like, you know, potato peelings, cold rice pudding, that sort of thing. Not exactly *haute cuisine*, but it'll certainly help to fill you up.' Sybil comes in, so Basil checks the stranger's name and then affects an introduction: 'Mr Carnegie, the scavenger gourmet.'

It turns out, much to Basil's sudden distress, that Mr Carnegie the scavenger gourmet is actually from the Public Health Department, here for the six-monthly check-up, and he is far from happy with Fawlty Towers. Revealing that it is falling short of the required health and hygiene standards, he warns Basil that, unless a very long list of improvements are speedily acted upon and achieved, the hotel will be recommended to the council for closure. Ominously, Carnegie promises to return the following day to assess what basic changes have been made.

Basil is terrified. 'We are in trouble,' he tells Terry the chef, whose cavalier reaction plunges him into an even worse panic (TERRY: 'The better the kitchen, the filthier it is. Have you ever read George Orwell's experiences at Maxim's in Paris?' BASIL: 'No, do you have a copy? I'll read it out in court!'). Sybil, however, is made of sterner stuff when it comes to these kinds of catering crises, and she is already busy implementing changes and generally getting the hotel into a far more presentable state. Her immediate orders for Basil are for him to find Manuel and get him to remove a couple of dead pigeons from the water tank.

Grudgingly accepting this mission ('Yes, my little commandant'), Basil tracks down Manuel in his bedroom, where, after struggling to make him understand about the pigeons ('This is not a proposition from Wittgenstein, *listen . . .*'), something else gives him more cause for concern: a large rat idly scratching itself inside a cage on Manuel's bedside cabinet. Astonished, he asks Manuel what he is doing with a rat in his room, but the little waiter brushes the question aside: 'Is my hamster.' Basil is incredulous: 'Of course it's a *rat!* You have rats in Spain, don't you? Or did Franco have them all shot?' Manuel continues to insist that the creature is actually a hamster, explaining: 'I say to man in shop, "Is rat!" He say, "No, no, is special kind of hamster. Is Filigree Siberian hamster." Only one in shop. He make special price – only five pound!' Basil has heard enough, and, much to Manuel's horror, proceeds to carry the cage out of the room.

Back downstairs, Sybil insists on pointing out all of the calamitous things that would have happened had the health inspector discovered this unconventional pet on the premises. 'Can't we get you on *Mastermind*, Sybil?' moans Basil. ' "Next contestant, Sybil Fawlty from Torquay. Special subject: The Bleeding Obvious".' The question of what to do next is complicated when a greatly agitated Manuel arrives to plead for a pardon for his pet. 'Perhaps,' says Sybil *sotto voce* to Basil, 'it would be simplest to have him put to S-L-E-E-P.' Basil, glancing at Manuel, requests a quick clarification: 'Who – him or the rat? We might get a discount if we had 'em both done.' Manuel, meanwhile, cannot make sense of the whispers he has overheard: ' "*Spleep*"??' Polly, however, intervenes to reveal that she has found a friend nearby who will provide a nice new home for the rat, so she and Manuel set off while Basil and Sybil are left to breathe a huge sigh of relief.

One disaster has been averted, so everybody resumes working hard to get things ready for the imminent return of 'old snoopy-drawers' Carnegie. In the kitchen, Terry is replacing the cooker filters, Polly is cleaning the tiled walls and Sybil is just about to put the hotel's cat out of harm's way (this cat, incidentally, proved far more troublesome to the cast than the placid rat: 'I think the trainer had forgotten to bring the trained one and just picked one off the street,' Bob Spiers later joked[22]). Progress is clearly being made at a breathless pace, even though one member of staff continues to lag well behind. Manuel eventually returns, apparently heartbroken, with a black armband on mournful display ('We didn't win the war by getting depressed you know,' says Basil by way of encouragement), but Polly soon whispers to him some acting advice – 'Much too much – just a *little* bit sad' – and, immediately, he brightens up. His subsequent furtive request to Terry for some slices of fillet steak confirms our suspicions: Polly has conspired to let him keep his beloved rat in an outhouse at the back of the hotel (sneaking there a little later with some food and water, Manuel claps his hands, looks around and, very sweetly, calls out: 'Basil . . .').

There turns out, however, to be another problem: Basil the rat has escaped. Manuel races off to tell Polly. The Major, meanwhile, has picked up the papers and is just about to settle down for his usual leisurely read and drink in the bar. Glancing up, however, he is startled to spy a rat squatting on the next table. 'Stay where you are, old chap,' he whispers excitedly, and tiptoes off to get his gun. When Basil arrives in the bar, he is alarmed to find the Major patrolling the area with a rifle. '*Vermin*,' he mutters. 'We haven't got any, this week, Major,' Basil sighs. 'No Germans staying this week.' But the Major is not for turning: 'He was sitting *there*, on that table, eating the *nuts* if you please!' Basil fears the worst ('He's really gone this time'), and then something even worse than *that* occurs. '*What* did you say it was?' he double-checks. 'Vermin,' says the Major. 'A dirty *rat!*' Suddenly, horribly, it all becomes clear to Basil.

Leaving the Major on guard in the bar, he marches into the kitchen, where, he can now see, even Terry is in on Manuel's rat conspiracy. Moving on into the lounge, he finds Polly half-hidden under a table, calling out his name and promising him cheese. 'Here I am,' he says, sadly. Polly leaps back up. Basil eats her chunk of cheese and then catches her before she can escape: 'He's called "Basil", is he? Don't play dumb with me – I *trusted* you!' Dismissing her uncharacteristically pathetic excuses – 'He must have escaped, Mr Fawlty, and . . . come back,' she splutters. 'They "home" ' – he demands some swift and effective action: 'Let's have a little Basil hunt, shall we? And then we'll deal with the sackings later on!'

Back in the kitchen, he takes out a veal fillet from the fridge, sprinkles it with rat poison and places it on the floor. Shortly after, Mr Carnegie arrives at reception and announces that he is in a hurry to start checking on what changes have so far been effected. The sudden sound from the bar of two shots from the Major's gun startles Carnegie, forcing Basil to think quickly – 'Bloody television exploding again!' – but not convincingly enough to stop the inspector from inspecting. With the Major clearly only too eager to start explaining ('He was sniffing around here just now!'), Basil resorts to desperate measures and knees the poor old boy in the groin. Mr Carnegie is close to accepting that it has all been a stray starling-related misunderstanding when Manuel, who has heard the shots, comes running towards reception and inquires anxiously as to the well-being or otherwise of Basil. Now Sybil, as well as Carnegie, is puzzled, so, before Manuel has quite finished identifying Basil as his rat, Polly jumps in to explain that the chef's pet name for his ratatouille is 'Basil', as he likes to put a great deal of that particular herb inside. Now Manuel is really alarmed: 'He put *Basil* in the ratatouille? *Aaaaaghhh!!!*' Sybil then smoothes things over as best she can – 'He's from Barcelona' – and takes the dazed Mr Carnegie away as quickly as she can on his tour.

In the kitchen, Terry reassures Manuel that he hasn't 'made any bleedin' ratatouille', but the waiter is straight off in search of the rodent, knocking all of the veal fillets on the floor as he pushes past Polly. Terry picks them back up and puts them on top of the fridge, but, when Basil reappears and finds the cat nibbling on one of the slices, he grabs it, slips the fillet on a high shelf and shuts the animal safely outside. Having then washed his hands dutifully, he spots that his rat bait has disappeared, so asks Terry what he has done with that particular bit of veal. 'Got 'em all up, Mr Fawlty,' says Terry calmly, handing two plates to Polly for the dining-room. Basil, upon discovering what has actually happened, sprints off and retrieves the dishes just before the diners can eat them. 'Sorry,' he says awkwardly. 'Ah . . . veal's off – sorry.' One of the perplexed diners (played by Melody Lang – the wife of Andrew Sachs) points out that the dishes clearly already contain veal, but Basil explains: 'No, no, er, this is, er, veal substitute. Er, we're giving it a try . . . and it's a bit of a disappointment, I'm afraid. In fact, it's no substitute at all.'

It is a narrow escape, but by this time Mr Carnegie, accompanied by Sybil, has moved on to inspect the kitchen. Basil, arriving to pick up a bottle of Beaujolais, pauses to listen as Carnegie says encouragingly positive things ('Well, it would appear that this kitchen is now in a satisfactory condition . . .') – then he spots the packet of rat poison that he left on the top of the fridge. Instinctively, he drops the bottle and snatches the packet ('*Sorry!*' he cries with a forced smile as Carnegie glances round. 'It slipped'). The positive comments continue, so Basil slips the poison out of the door and picks up another bottle of Beaujolais, but he cannot resist staying to witness the end of the appraisal. 'It's ten to one, I'd like to take lunch here if I may,' Carnegie says. Basil smiles in the background with a mixture of pride and profound relief. Carnegie continues: 'I couldn't help noticing you had some veal over there.' Another bottle of Beaujolais bites the dust. '*Veal?*' croaks Basil. Sybil confirms, in her innocence, that they do indeed have some good-quality Dutch veal available. Basil (echoing Reg Cleese's cosmopolitan take on cut-price types of meat) butts in to claim that, in fact, the veal on offer is actually Norwegian, and 'not the absolute apex

quite honestly,' adding that, 'I don't think it's a winner, frankly –
more of a veal substitute. It's got a lot of air pockets in it, that sort
of thing.' The flannel fails to work: Mr Carnegie is determined
to eat some veal – even if it is Norwegian veal.

While Carnegie and Sybil move on to reception, and the
prospect of a poisoned health inspector is plaguing his mind,
Basil is persuaded by Terry to pop outside and check on the
health of the cat that nibbled on one of the fillets: 'If the cat is all
right . . . that means that slice is all right!' Finding that the cat is
alive and seemingly fine, Terry sets to work trimming the fillet
and preparing it for the peckish Carnegie's plate. Once the
health inspector has had his veal placed on his table, Basil staggers
out the back, opens the door, holds a hand over his pounding
heart and allows himself a deep and hugely relieved sigh. Then
he catches sight of the choking cat. He flies back through the
kitchen, straight into the dining-room and snatches away Mr
Carnegie's veal a split-second before the first bite is taken ('Sorry
– ah . . . not hot enough – *aaaggh!!!* – n-not *big* enough!').
Returning to the kitchen, he throws the offending fillet away,
and finds Terry heating up another one ('If *that's* the poisoned
one, these are all right'). Bolting back to the dining room, Basil
assures Mr Carnegie that a bigger, hotter veal fillet will soon be
brought to his table.

Confusing news awaits him back in the kitchen: both Sybil
and Polly have now confirmed that the cat is perfectly well. Basil
is incredulous, because, as he explains, he caught the cat making
vomiting noises. 'That's just fur balls,' Sybil assures him. 'He
does that all the time in the summer.' It begins to dawn on Basil
what this possibly means: 'But . . . if *he's* all right . . . *that* one
might . . .' He launches himself back into the dining room and,
yet again, confiscates Mr Carnegie's veal straight after Polly has

served it. 'We wouldn't want you to think that because you were one of Her Majesty's Civil Servants, we were showing you any excess favouritism. I'm sure you wouldn't want that.' He disappears back to the kitchen, where Terry will make up a dish from the cat's slice for the second time.

Meanwhile, in another corner of the dining room, Manuel catches sight of his precious rat nosing about by a female diner's feet. Her partner, spotting the waiter staring, is hugely offended by the supposed ogling of his partner's legs. 'Do you *mind?*' he moans. He is made even more angry when, after Manuel summons reinforcements, he finds that the manager has come out and joined the waiter in crouching down and, apparently, staring at his partner's legs ('Just doing my shoelace up . . .' says Basil from beneath table level). Seeing the rat so close, Basil sends Manuel off to get the bread box. The male diner, meanwhile, has ordered the veal, been told that it is off the menu, and then watches Mr Carnegie be served a plate of something that looks remarkably like veal. Basil tries in vain to placate him – 'It's a sort of Jappo-Scandinavian imitation veal substitute, but I'm afraid that's the last slice anyway' – but he and his partner flounce off, with the rat now nestling in the woman's shoulder bag. At reception, Polly prevaricates while Basil hovers discreetly over the bag, and, when she comes up with the excuse that there is a bomb scare, he has a proper feel – and is bitten for his troubles.

The rat leaps out of the bag, hurtles across the lobby, races across the dining room and back inside Manuel's jacket, and, then, with the assistance of his loving owner, straight down into a tin of biscuits. It is at this very moment, however, that Mr Carnegie, having finished his sensibly sized, moderately hot, Norwegian veal substitute fillet, asks the waiter for some cheese and biscuits. Manuel heads off to the kitchen, but, in his absence,

Basil appears, wheels over the cheese trolley and asks Polly to bring over the tin of biscuits. He serves Mr Carnegie a generous slice of Danish Blue, and then lifts up the lid of the biscuit tin. A rat is staring straight out at Mr Carnegie. Basil spots it. Polly spots it. Sybil spots it. A rat is definitely staring straight out at Mr Carnegie. Mr Carnegie, however, appears to be in some kind of trance. 'Would you . . . care for a rat, or . . .?' says Basil casually. Mr Carnegie continues staring, blank-faced, at the little creature. 'J-Just the biscuits, then, please, Polly,' says Basil, replacing the lid. Sybil pours the health inspector some coffee, and Polly returns with another box of biscuits. Mr Carnegie chooses a digestive. He is still in a daze. Basil, meanwhile, has fainted from all of the strain, and is dragged away by Manuel.

The episode was a fitting farewell for the character of Basil, and a fine valediction for *Fawlty Towers*. The superb script, brilliant performances and polished direction, allied to the fact that this was such a long-awaited finale, made the episode into an extraordinary viewing event. When it was over, one was entertained and grateful, but one was also rather sad: one wanted more.

The second series had done what neither John Cleese nor Connie Booth had ever been sure that it would really manage to achieve: it had actually surpassed the great expectations. The audiences, for BBC2, had been superb. The reviews, after an ambivalent opening week, had been good enough to cherish (one critic, for example, described Cleese as 'the Jacques Tati of British television', playing 'a man so harried by modern times that his efforts to please make a true comedy of survival'[23]). The show would go on to win BAFTAs for Bob Spiers and Douglas Argent (for Best Situation Comedy) and John Cleese (for Best Light Entertainment Performance), as well as a nomination for

Andrew Sachs. The key contributions by Prunella Scales and Connie Booth would also be widely, warmly and deservedly appreciated.

Fawlty Towers had come back, moved on, and now looked as though, if everyone involved was determined enough to see it all through, it still had the potential to progress even further up to another, unprecedented, level. The vital question was: would it actually happen?

12

Just Out of Waldorfs

That was quick, do I get another? Sorry, mate, that's your lot.

No one had said that the second set of episodes would definitely be the last. 'After this new *Fawlty Towers* series,' John Cleese had commented just before it started, 'we'll forget about it for a year and then decide if there's any juice left in it or whether we ought to try something completely different.'[1]

The fans were prepared to wait. After enduring the long gap between the first and the second series, there was greater patience this time around: diversions and delays were now almost expected, but, given the huge appeal of the show, there was still plenty of hope that, at some point in the not-too-distant future, it would return for a third run. This time, however, the fans of *Fawlty Towers* would wait . . . and wait . . . and wait.

The 1970s gave way to the 1980s, the 1980s were succeeded by the 1990s, a new millennium duly began, and still there was no sign of any fresh editions of *Fawlty Towers*. The twelve existing episodes went on seeming more or less ubiquitous, sometimes being re-screened by the BBC and sometimes repeated in whole blocks at a time on the newly emerging cable and satellite channels, and the audiences, far from fading

233

away, remained remarkably strong and stable: when, for example, the second series was first repeated, on BBC1 at the end of 1979, the audience actually rose to an estimated average of 14.6 million;[2] then in 1985, when BBC2 marked the tenth anniversary of the first series with a repeat run, the shows brought in an estimated 12.7 million viewers – at the time, the biggest single audience ever for the channel;[3] in 1988, another screening of 'Basil the Rat' was seen by 13.1 million people; and in 1995, repeats of all twelve episodes averaged an extremely impressive weekly audience on BBC1 of 12 million.[4] *Fawlty Towers* was clearly not just being viewed over and over again by the same group of loyal but ageing fans; like only the very best kind of sitcoms can do, it was also being discovered, and loved, by new generations of admirers (and some of the episodes were now being used by the likes of the Hyatt, Hilton and Holiday Inn hotel chains as 'what not to do' training films).

It was not like this just in the United Kingdom. It was like it in countless other countries, too: dubbed into a wide range of languages, its popularity spread and was then sustained by the same kind of regular repetition as in the UK. By 1984, *Fawlty Towers* was one of the BBC's top five worldwide TV exports,[5] and one could find firm fans of Basil and Sybil and Co. in, among many foreign places, numerous parts of North America and Australasia as well as the vast majority of Eastern and Western Europe (although, when the show was broadcast in Spain, Manuel, for predictable reasons, was re-described and re-dubbed as a Mexican, and in the Basque region he became a dim-witted Italian called Manolo).

The demand for a third series, therefore, continued to grow increasingly broad and intense. The wait, however, was destined to go on for good.

No definitive announcement would ever be made, but, in private, soon after the second run was over, John Cleese and Connie Booth had already agreed, discreetly, to move on. 'Connie and I were simply too busy making the show to start thinking about the future,' Cleese would recall. 'It was afterwards that we looked at each other and said: "We've *done* that, haven't we?" And we both felt: "Yes, we have." So there was no desire to do it again, ever, for any reason.'[6] Unofficially, but nonetheless emphatically, *Fawlty Towers* really had finished.

Certain traces of the show, however, would stay in sight to kindle the curiosity. Physically, for example, some of the famous locations would long remain. The familiar white-and-black building that viewers saw at the start of each episode – the Wooburn Grange Country Club in Buckinghamshire – is now, alas, no more (after an awkward phase in the 1980s of calling itself 'Basil's' and passing itself off as a restaurant and nightclub, it burned down, somewhat mysteriously, in 1991 and eight red-bricked residential homes were built in its place), but the actual establishment that inspired the creation of *Fawlty Towers* – the Hotel Gleneagles – is still standing in Torquay and remains very much open for business. In 2005, shortly after Torbay Council rejected plans to replace the hotel with twenty-five luxury flats, it went on the market and was purchased by a Bristol-based family of *Fawlty Towers* fans (Kumar Patel, his wife Panna and his brother Keethri) for a reported £1.5 million. It was then bought from them in April the following year by two local businessmen, Brian Shone and Terry Taylor, and, following a £1.5 million refurbishment, was officially reopened on 18 September 2006 by Prunella Scales (who, for her first-ever visit to the premises, arrived in a buffed-up replica of the Fawltys' faulty red Austin 1100).[7]

More pointedly, the actual scripts and shows themselves remain available in an increasingly rich variety of media forms. Following on from the first volume of scripts that was published in 1977, a second collection was compiled in 1979 and then all twelve scripts made it into print as, unsurprisingly, *The Complete Fawlty Towers* in 1988. The first vinyl album,[8] which consisted of the edited soundtracks to a couple of episodes, was released (after some prolonged prodding of the BBC's commercial wing by John Howard Davies) in 1979; the second album[9] followed in 1981, the third[10] in 1982 and the fourth[11] in 1983. Audio cassette versions were also made available during this period.[12] Both series were then released on video and laser disc in 1984,[13] and, in 2001, the episodes made it on to DVD.[14] Later the same year, the BBC released what would become an award-winning CD-ROM 'digi-pack' called *Fawlty Towers* (featuring, among other technical things, a desktop 'customiser' to create Fawlty-style cursors, icons wallpaper and screen savers; a selection of video clips; and some virtual interactive games).[15]

Back on the prosaic television screen, meanwhile, *Fawlty Towers* was beginning to tempt numerous US-based producers and entrepreneurs either to market or mimic the show in a more ambitious and dramatic way. The actual impact of the programme on the massive American market as a whole had, initially, been relatively modest but, in certain places, it had nonetheless been very intense ('I love *Fawlty Towers*, I'd like to be *in* that, you know,' John Lennon enthused about the sitcom in New York shortly before his tragic death in 1980. '*Fawlty Towers* is the greatest show I've seen in years. They have it over here now. God, it's *great!*'[16]). Screened since 1976 on several local public television (PBS) stations,[17] including the very popular W/NET 13 in New York, the two series had quickly acquired a large and very loyal cult following: in Miami, for example, there had been a 'Fawlty Festival', dominated by hordes of Basil 'lookalikes', while a New York journalist (who almost certainly wore a patterned bow tie) would go on to form a 'Basil Fawlty Brigade' which, in 1986, and then in 1987 as well, supported a 'Basil Fawlty for Prime Minister' campaign.[18] The nationwide network television audience, however, had still to make Fawlty's acquaintance.

Cleese and Booth had rejected the chance to write an 'Americanised' version of the sitcom for NBC – on the understandable grounds that, as it took them about a year to come up with six half-hour scripts, and a run during the typical American commercial TV season would require them to produce more than twenty 26-minute scripts, the workload would have been unbearable – but they did agree to sell the show's format rights.[19] These rights – which entitled another programme-maker to draw on the basic scenario, the original scripts and the production know-how to adapt the sitcom as closely or as loosely as he or she saw fit for another country's audience – had been sold early on to a Los Angeles-based packager called Herman Rush; he was looking to emulate the huge commercial success enjoyed in the early 1970s by Norman Lear (whose US adaptations of the British sitcoms *Till Death Us Do Part* as *All in the Family*, and *Steptoe and Son* as *Sanford and Son*, had soared to the top of the American ratings).[20] Rush, however, had been struggling to match Lear's shrewd sense of what to use, what to lose and what to revise in order to turn one country's crowd pleaser into another one's firm favourite. He had tried and failed in 1973 with ITV's popular ethnic-centred sitcom *Love Thy Neighbour*, which ABC cancelled twelve episodes into its first season,[21] and had fared even worse in 1976 with a spectacularly ill-considered alternative version of *Dad's Army*, called *Rear Guard*, which relocated the wartime situation from Walmington-on-Sea to Long Island, New York, and transformed Captain Mainwaring into a garrulous Italian-American and Sergeant Wilson into a wise-cracking Jew. The revamped show failed, unsurprisingly, to make it beyond the pilot stage – but only after a classic British script, involving a captured German U-boat captain ('Your name will also go on the list. What is it?') and a doughty home platoon ('Don't tell him, Henderson!'), had been well and truly butchered.[22]

So the portents for the *Fawlty Towers* format were, in the hands of a packager such as Herman Rush, fairly poor, and, sure enough, the package failed to sell. It was passed from one Los Angeles office to the next over the course of a couple of years, prompting plenty of admiring comments about the original material but plenty more doubts as to the potential for an American remake ('too English' and 'too cruel' were a couple of the common responses[23]). Eventually, however, the rights were redistributed and, during the period when Booth and Cleese were developing ideas back in London for their second series for the BBC, the format was picked up by the US syndication specialist Viacom Productions.[24]

The first American adaptation was called *Snavely* (sometimes billed as *Chateau Snavely*), which was piloted by ABC and Viacom on 24 June 1978. Featuring the fifty-one-year-old comic actor Harvey Korman (probably best known in the UK for the part of Hedley Lamarr in the 1974 Mel Brooks movie *Blazing Saddles*) in the Basil Fawlty role of Henry Snavely, and Betty White (who would later play Rose Nylund in *The Golden Girls*) as his shrewish wife Gladys, with support from Deborah Zon as a student-cum-waitress called Connie and

Frank LaLoggia as a waiter named Petro, the sitcom was set in a small off-highway hotel in middle America. Nothing further came of the show, however, and John Cleese would later put this down to the fact that 'the producers feared [the original version] was too mean spirited' and that there 'was a noticeable attempt to reassure the audience that the people in the show were all right, folks.' Pointing out that Basil, like the on-screen persona of W. C. Fields, was not meant to be remotely 'lovable' but rather 'a total bastard', Cleese criticised Korman's perform-ance for its reluctance to make him seem unsympathetic: '[He'd] give a slightly reassuring smile now and then. He'd allow little moments of warmth to creep in. Disastrous.'[25]

What happened next, however, would strike even the worldly-wise Cleese as one of the most extraordinary cases of format filleting that he, or anyone else, has ever encountered. 'I was at a house party in England,' he would recall, 'and two Americans introduced themselves. They said, "Our company owns the *Fawlty Towers* format. And we're just about to make six of them." My heart leaped to the sound of cash registers, and I asked, "How nice, but would a series about a small private hotel be understood in America?" "No problem with that," they said. "Have you made any changes at all?" I asked. "Just one," they replied. "We've written Basil out." And, you know, there's just this moment when you stand there smiling politely, thinking everything you've ever heard about Hollywood is true.'[26]

Sure enough, ABC and Viacom duly reworked the basic format a second time, in February 1983, as *Amanda's* (a.k.a. *Amanda's by the Sea*), starring Bea Arthur (who would be much better known in the UK two years later for playing Dorothy Petrillo in *The Golden Girls*) as Amanda Cartwright. The owner of a seaside hotel, she was assisted by her moody son, Marty

(Fred McCarren), her flibbertigibbet of a daughter-in-law Arlene (Simone Griffeth), a chatty cook named Earl (Rick Hurst) and a Mexican bellhop called Aldo (Tony Rosato) who struggled with his English. Her competitor next door, Krinsky (Michael Constantine), was her nemesis, waiting hopefully for the chance to buy her out in a distress sale. One-paced and laboured, with Bea Arthur delivering each comic line with all the grace and speed of an ageing oil tanker with 'Joke Coming Up' painted in large white letters on its side, the show lasted for ten episodes before being pulled prematurely from the schedules (the New York Times having dismissed the pilot as 'little more than an exercise in hysteria': 'What is the inspired lunacy of Mr Cleese in Fawlty Towers here becomes something resembling a sustained, vulgar shout'[27]). Cleese himself was so appalled at what had been done to the format of his show that he had refused to let his name be included anywhere among the credits. The shamefaced producers withdrew to lick their wounds, allowed the rights to run out, and there would be no sign of any more reformulated Fawltys, of either gender, for the next fifteen years.

The third – and, so far, last – American attempt at a remake of the format of Fawlty Towers came at the end of the 1990s, with a CBS show (overseen by the co-writers of the successful US sitcom, Coach,[28] Judd Pillot and John Peaslee) called Payne.[29] Set on the northern California coast in a restored Victorian inn called Whispering Pines, the proprietors of the hotel were the painfully named Royal Payne (John Larroquette) and his domineering wife, Connie (JoBeth Williams). Helping them run the establishment was a bellhop named Mo (Rick Batalla) and a chambermaid called Breeze O'Rourke (Julie Benz). Later instalments would also feature a couple of figures inspired originally by Miss Tibbs and Miss Gatsby, but remodelled here, somewhat bizarrely, as a pair of elderly dope smokers called Ethel and Flo. Screened between March and April 1999, it never appalled but patently failed to impress,[30] and expired with little more than a whimper after a mere eight episodes had been shown.[31]

In spite of these varying degrees of failure, few observers would be too surprised if, at some point in the future, another attempt was made by an American producer to fashion a new fiction for Fawlty. What did surprise many, however, was the news in 2001 that *Fawlty Towers* was being adapted by, of all people, the Germans. Produced in association with the BBC by a Cologne-based company called Clou Entertainment (with John Cleese acting as a consultant), a pilot episode of the show, called *Zoom Letzten Kliff* ('To the Last Cliff'), was broadcast by the RTL network in December 2001. Basil and Sybil became Viktor (played by Jochen Busse) and Helga (Claudia Rieschel), an unhappily-married couple – who presided over a chaotically awful hotel called 'Zum letzten Kliff' – which was relocated to a North Sea island, just off Germany's Jutland coast, called Sylt (pronounced 'Zoolt'). The hotel also featured a young waitress called Polly (played by Saskia von Winterfeld), while the Manuel character was reinvented as a waiter named Igor (Dimitri Alexandrov) from the Republic of Kazakhstan. A full-blown series has yet to appear, but at least Fawlty finally gained admission into Germany.

The repeats, and the revisions, go on, and so do the lives and careers of the original team. Not all of the old fans seem to have grasped this fact, so absorbed they remain in the ever-present world of TV reruns. One such admirer, for example, was pleased but somewhat bemused to encounter Andrew Sachs, many years after *Fawlty Towers* had ended, on a luxury P&O cruise liner, giving a talk about his long and distinguished career in the performing arts. 'I talked about *Fawlty Towers*, obviously,' Sachs would recall, 'but I also discussed lots of other things, like the repertory system, certain plays I'd been in – the whole range, really. And the next day, one of the members of the public who'd been in the audience approached me and said, "Mr Sachs, I'd like to just say that I found your talk very, very, interesting, I enjoyed it very much. But can I ask you a personal question?" So I said, sure, go ahead. He said, "Have you *always* been a waiter?" '[32] Something similar happened to the admirably tolerant – and chronically busy – Sachs a few years later in London, when a passer-by spotted him walking along Oxford Street: 'He'd recognised me and wanted my autograph, so I said fine, and while I was writing it we started chatting. And he was extremely surprised, like so many other people are, to hear that there had only ever been twelve episodes, and that they had gone out as long as thirty years or so ago. This guy seemed really genuinely concerned about this – that there had been so few shows so long ago. "Really?" he said, suddenly looking quite sorrowful for me. Then, putting his hand rather lovingly on my arm, he said: "How on earth do you *manage* these days, Mr Sachs?" I thought he was going to give me fifty pence for a cup of tea!'[33]

Other members of the old cast would experience the same kind of thing – it seemed destined to stick around with the territory. There would always be someone, somewhere, who expected Prunella Scales to look – and laugh – like Sybil, or John Cleese to thrash his car with the branch of a tree. It made perfect sense to some of these admiring outsiders. It just made less sense to the insiders who were busy getting on with the rest of their lives.

John Cleese, for example, went on to be, if anything, more active than ever, maintaining a mews house in London, an apartment in New York and a villa in Santa Barbara, California, as he moved from one new project to the next. He married his second wife, the American painter and television producer Barbara Trentham, in 1981, and had a daughter with her – Camilla, born in 1984 – before divorcing nine years later, then he married the American psychoanalyst Alice Faye Eichelberger in 1992. In 1995, on the happy occasion of his daughter Cynthia's Napa Valley wedding to the American-born screen-writer Ed Solomon, he is said to have greeted Connie Booth warmly with the words: 'Now let me see. Which wife were you?'[34] Relations with both of his former wives remain amicable. 'There is a lot of breast-beating about marriages breaking down,' he would say, 'but so what? If you are interested in that great middle-class ideal of making it to your grave without ever having been embarrassed, then it is not the way to live your life. But I can have no regrets about the way I've lived mine.'[35] He started to joke, as he sat back and quaffed another glass of Californian Merlot, that, as his wife Alice called him 'Jack' and his family name used to be 'Cheese', he would one day retire, move to Monterey and rename himself 'Monterey Jack Cheese'.[36]

There was never any danger, however, that he was ever going to really withdraw very far from social, commercial or even political life. In October 1989, for example, acting on the advice of merchant bankers, Cleese and his four partners sold their company Video Arts (which in April 1982 had won a Queen's Award for Export on the strength of two training films that featured material from *Fawlty Towers*[37]) for £50 million, but he would continue to contribute to some of its projects. Politically,

Cleese oscillated during the early 1980s between the left and the centre before becoming a vocal supporter of Britain's short-lived left-of-centre alliance the Social Democratic Party, and then he threw his weight behind the newly reformulated Liberal-Democrats (while in America he remained committed to the Democrats). Although no longer relying on regular sessions of psychotherapy himself, he retained a passionate interest in both the subject and the activity, and collaborated with his old friend and former therapist Robin Skynner on a couple of best-selling populist books, *Families and How to Survive Them* (1983) and *Life and How to Survive It* (1993).

As far as his more conventional professional activities were concerned, there would always be some kind of Monty Python project – such as the movie *Monty Python's Meaning of Life* (1983) or Eric Idle's comedy-musical *Spamalot!* (2005) – to discuss, contribute to, block or tolerate from afar, as well as plenty of other solo ventures to absorb the rest of his time. Inspired by a fascination with lemurs that dated back to 1954 (when, as a day student at Clifton College in Bristol, he used to sneak away every now and again to see them in the flesh and fur at the local zoo), he travelled to Madagascar to film a documentary about them called *Born to Be Wild: Operation Lemur with John Cleese* (BBC1, 1998)[38] – and ended up, as a tribute to his conservation work, with a new species of lemur named after him: the 'Avahi Cleesei'. Also on television, he wrote and presented the four-part series *The Human Face* (BBC1, 2001),[39] hosted an introductory guide to oenology on America's Food Network called *Wine for the Confused* (2004);[40] provided humorous links to *The Art of Football from A to Z* (2006);[41] and popped up as a special guest star on such US sitcoms as *Cheers* (5 March 1987), *3rd Rock from the Sun* (three episodes, 1988–2001) and *Will & Grace* (six

Bob Spiers: director of the second series of *Fawlty Towers*.

'Communication Problems' with Joan Sanderson as Mrs Richards: 'May I ask what you were hoping to see out of a Torquay hotel bedroom window?'

'The Psychiatrist': Martin Luther said that faith is under the left nipple. Basil Fawlty has a feel.

'Waldorf Salad': 'It's celery, apples, walnuts, *grapes!*'

'The Kipper and the Corpse': 'Our guests ... They give us trouble even when they're dead!'

'Basil the Rat': Strikes, Germans, more strikes, rained off cricket . . . and now the Major spots a dirty rat.

Harvey Korman – the first American incarnation of Basil Fawlty. 'He'd allow little moments of warmth to creep in,' Cleese complained. 'Disastrous.'

'Excuse me, there are no nuts here …': In 1983, Bea Arthur played an hotelier called Amanda in a strangely Basil-free Fawlty adaptation.

'Forgive and forget ...':
John Cleese with
Jochen Busse on the set
of the 2001 German
version of *Fawlty Towers*:
Zoom Letzten Kliff.

'Ich weiß, ich weiß ...':
Germany's Fawlty
couple – 'Viktor' (played
by Jochen Busse) and
'Helga' (Claudia
Rieschel).

Andrew Sachs alongside Manuel's waxwork double in 1990. When the first *Fawlty* series was screened Germany – minus one obvious episode – Sachs was dispatched to Munich to re-voice Manuel in German with a Spanish accent: 'An interesting fora into guesswork on my par But they seemed satisfied enough.'

At last, a higher class clientele: Prunella Scales at re-launch of the Torquay ho that inspired Fawlty Tower, the Gleneagles – in 200

Connie Booth, now leading a life away from show business, in 2002. 'She is not a recluse,' John Howard Davies explained, 'she has just chosen a different path.'

A contented-looking John Cleese in 2007: 'It is always good,' he said of the enduring popularity of *Fawlty Towers*, 'to hear how many people still enjoy the results of our efforts.'

No riff-raff here: the faultless ensemble.

episodes, 2003–4). He also contributed ideas to a graphic novel called *True Brit* (2004)[42] – an entertaining Superman spoof that had the Man of Steel raised not as Clark Kent in America's Kansas countryside but rather as Colin Clark on the outskirts of England's Weston-super-Mare (growing up to be a superhero who plays cricket, gets the trains running on time, shortens the wait for hip operations and reaffirms the old Reithian standards of the BBC).

In movies, Cleese played a foppish Robin Hood in Terry Gilliam's *Time Bandits* (1981); Major Giles Flack in *Privates on Parade* (1982); Sheriff Langston in *Silverado* (1985); suffered gloriously as the normally punctual but repeatedly delayed headmaster, Brian Simpson ('I can take the despair. It's the hope I can't stand'), in Michael Frayn's crafty minor classic *Clockwise* (1985); and appeared – in an unintentional name-check to the dreaded hotelier – as 'Donald Sinclair' in *Rat Race* (2001). He joined the James Bond franchise for a couple of instalments as the eccentric MI6 inventor 'R' and then 'Q', appearing in *The World Is Not Enough* (1999) and *Die Another Day* (2002); assumed the role of 'Nearly Headless Nick' in the Harry Potter movies, *Harry Potter and the Sorcerer's Stone* (2001) and *Harry Potter and the Chamber of Secrets* (2002); and provided the voice of King Harold in the second and third *Shrek* movies (2004/2007). He also co-directed as well as co-wrote two very successful comedies, *A Fish Called Wanda* (1988) – in which he appeared as a character named Archie Leach ('It was as near as I could ever get to being Cary Grant'[43]) – and *Fierce Creatures* (1997), and, in 2005, he collaborated with Kirk DeMicco on the screenplay of an animated feature, set in prehistoric times, called *Crood Awakening* (scheduled for release by DreamWorks in 2009).

There would be numerous more tributes and awards, including, in 1987, an Emmy for his cameo performance in *Cheers* and the London *Evening Standard*'s 'Peter Sellers Award for Comedy' for his role in *Clockwise*, and, in 1989, a 'Best Actor' BAFTA and a 'Best Screenplay' David di Donatello 'David' for his work on *A Fish Called Wanda*. In 1999, however, he was reported to have politely declined the offer of a CBE 'for services to entertainment', but he did agree the same year to become an A. D. White Professor-at-Large (and then a Provost's Visiting Professor) at Cornell University in Ithaca, New York, appearing there fairly regularly to lecture on, among other things, comedy, religion and philosophy.[44] In 2006 he told *The Times* that he was 'too tired to write new comedy' – claiming: 'I can never do better than *Fawlty Towers* whatever I do'[45] – but, in a Sinatra-style approach to his supposed 'retirement', he continued to commit himself to certain comedy projects while maintaining a lively personal website (www.thejohncleese.com) and producing a long-running series of audio and video podcasts.

Connie Booth, on the other hand, became increasingly private after *Fawlty Towers* ended, and (after one last indulgence, a 1982 feature in *The Times* on her fashion preferences – 'I stay away from browns with my blonde hair, but I have lots of pinks'; favourite designer, the Paris-based Sonia Rykiel; and favourite boutiques, Whistles, Crocodile and Browns[46]) eschewed all but the most essential of interviews and public appearances; but she, too, was as busy as she wished herself to be. There was more stage work, and more movies – including Jack Gold's remake of *Little Lord Fauntleroy* (1980), in the role of Mrs Errol; *The Hound of the Baskervilles* (1983), playing the suspicious Laura Lyons; a role opposite Peter O'Toole in *High Spirits* (1988); a performance, as the alluringly independent Caroline Hartley, alongside

Michael Palin's relatively unworldly Oxford academic in *American Friends* (1991); and the game gentile mother Yvonne Chadwick in *Leon the Pig Farmer* (1993) – as well as the occasional role on television – such as her portrayal of Miss March in the miniseries dramatisation of Edith Wharton's *The Buccaneers* (BBC1, 1995).[47] Eventually, however, she seemed to lose interest in performing, and started to explore other activities that absorbed her more – particularly those relating to psychology, psychiatry and group therapy. As a consequence, she spent five years during the 1990s studying psychotherapy under the auspices of the University of London, and qualified to practice in 2001. From that point on, she concentrated on working as a psychotherapist near her home (which she shared with her second husband, the distinguished *New Yorker* senior drama critic John Lahr) in Kentish Town. Some of those who met her socially would say that she seemed bright, charming and happy; she just had other things to discuss rather than *Fawlty Towers*.[48] 'She is not a recluse,' said John Howard Davies, 'she has just chosen a different path.'[49]

Prunella Scales, meanwhile, would continue to enjoy a contented home life in London with her actor husband Timothy West, and remain in almost constant work in the theatre and on radio, TV and movies. Among her many stage roles was a glorious *tour de force* as Queen Elizabeth II in Alan Bennett's clever and playfully insightful *A Question of Attribution* (1988 – the performance was repeated in a television version shown by BBC1 in 1991);[50] she also played the lonely and morphine-addicted Mary Tyrone (opposite her real-life husband as James Tyrone) in Eugene O'Neill's *Long Day's Journey into Night* (1991); appeared as Dorothy, an exasperating sixty-two-year-old matriarch, in *Mother Tongue* (1992); was spellbinding as the middle-class housewife Winnie, buried up to her neck with dirt and doubts, in Samuel Beckett's *Happy Days* (1993); led as Dolly Levi in *The Matchmaker* (1993); played the dim but doting landlady, Meg, in a revival of Harold Pinter's *The Birthday Party* (1999); made a fine impact as Ranevskaya, the widowed owner of a bankrupt estate, in *The Cherry Orchard* (2000); and toured Australia and New Zealand in 2004 with two musicians for her show, *An Evening with Queen Victoria*.

On radio, she was impressive as the widow Sarah France in *After Henry* (BBC Radio 4, thirty-five episodes, 1985–9); as Rosie in Simon Brett's *Smelling of Roses* (2000–3); and, alongside Patricia Routledge, in *Ladies of Letters* (BBC Radio 4, 1999–2006). She also continued to appear fairly often on television, including a much-praised portrayal of Elizabeth Mapp in an adaptation of E. F. Benson's Edwardian-era *Mapp and Lucia* (LWT/Channel 4, 1985–6);[51] she also took part in the radio-to-TV spin-off *After Henry* (Thames/ITV, 1988–92);[52] and John Cleese's documentary *The Human Face* (BBC1, 2001).[53] She found time for the occasional contribution to movies, too, including a role as Frau Pollert in *Wagner* (1983); Moira O'Neill in *The Lonely Passion of Judith Hearne* (1987); co-starred as Hannah Llewellyn, the sex-starved wife of a tyrannical amateur stage director, in *A Chorus of Disapproval* (1989); appeared as Aunt Juley, the surrogate parent of the Schlegel sisters, in *Howards End* (1992); as Rose in *An Awfully Big Adventure* (1995); as Lady Markby in *An Ideal Husband* (1998); and as Aunt Agnes in the Merchant-Ivory parody *Stiff Upper Lips* (1998). In addition to all of this, she fronted a successful TV advertising campaign for Tesco as a fussy mother called Dottie Turnbull (alongside a long-suffering daughter played by Jane Horrocks), campaigned for the Labour Party, became an ambassador for both the Howard League for Penal Reform and the SOS Children charity, served as President of the Council for the Protection of Rural England and, in 1992, received a CBE for services to drama.

Andrew Sachs was another former cast member who continued to enjoy a happy home life with his wife and fellow actor, Melody Lang, and, like his old friend Prunella Scales, he did not find it difficult to stay busy. There were numerous stage appearances, including a portrayal of the servant John Dory in *Wild Oats* (directed in 1995 by Jeremy Sams at the National Theatre). He also appeared regularly on radio, including a stint from 1984 to 1986 as Father Brown in one eight-episode and one five-episode BBC Radio 4 series based on the stories of G. K. Chesterton.[54] In 2001, he presented BBC Radio 4's critically praised four-part documentary series *The Jewish Journey*;[55] he appeared as Skagra in the webcast/audio version of the *Doctor Who* story 'Shada' in 2003. In 2004 he played Dr John Watson opposite Clive Merrison as the famous consulting detective in a series of original stories for BBC Radio 4, *The Further Adventures of Sherlock Holmes*;[56] and, in 2005, once again for Radio 4, he narrated a fifteen-part adaptation of Cervantes' *Don Quixote*.[57] On television, he took the starring role in James Andrew Hall's splendidly evocative five-part adaptation of the H. G. Wells classic *The History of Mr Polly* (BBC1, 1980);[58] he also contributed, as the jester Trinculo, to a production of Shakespeare's *The Tempest* (BBC2, 1980);[59] as Tadeus in the East–West satirical series *The Mushroom Picker* (BBC2, 1993);[60] the eponymous theoretical physicist in the absorbing *Einstein Revealed* (BBC2, 1996);[61] had a regular role as Murray Plaskow (the father of a character – Jake – played by David Walliams) in the dot.com drama *Attachments* (BBC1, 2000); and, alongside Prunella Scales, appeared in an adaptation of the Evelyn Waugh story *Mr Loveday's Little Outing* (BBC4, 2006). He also contributed to several children's television programmes, including *William's Wish Wellingtons* (BBC 1, 1994) and *Starhill Ponies* (BBC1, 1999–2001). His movie roles included Durdles in *The Mystery of Edwin Drood* (1993) and, performing all the voices, he worked on the English-language version of Jan Švankmajer's part-live and part-animated adaptation of *Faust* (1994). As one of the best-liked narrators in the business (and a winner of the Sony Radio Award for 'Best Actor' in 1989 and a Spoken Word Award in 1999), he was also hugely in demand to provide voice-overs for documentaries as well as a wide variety of 'talking books' for radio, digital television and internet download services.

The more mature members of the team kept on working at whatever pace they liked. Ballard Berkeley picked and chose his roles at his leisure. On television, he played various country gentleman types in episodes of *To the Manor Born* (BBC1, 1981),[62] *Terry and June* (1982/87),[63] *Are You Being Served?* (BBC1, 1983),[64] *Hi-de-Hi!* (BBC1, 1983)[65] and *Fresh Fields* (Thames/ITV, 1985/6).[66] In movies, he appeared alongside Connie Booth as the toff Sir Harry Lorrydaile in *Little Lord Fauntleroy* (1980); contributed a cameo as an hotel guest in *Bullshot* (1983); was glimpsed as an ultra-polite motorist in *National Lampoon's European Vacation* (1985); and provided the voice of the Head of the Army for the animated version of Roald Dahl's *BFG* (1989). Between 1982 and 1987, he also played another retired military man, Colonel Freddy Danby, in BBC Radio 4's long-running serial *The Archers*. He passed away, aged eighty-three, on 16 January 1988.

Gilly Flower and Renée Roberts were reunited in 1983 for one episode of another BBC sitcom, *Only Fools and Horses*,[67] shortly before both of them began to ease themselves into belated retirement. Flower's death, though recently confirmed,[68] was not reported, but Roberts died in 1996. Brian Hall's career, however, was cut sadly short due to illness, and he died of cancer, at the age of fifty-nine, on 17 September 1997.

As for the people behind the scenes, they lent their experience and expertise to several other projects. John Howard Davies, for example, would go on, as the BBC's Head of Comedy, to commission such programmes as *Yes Minister* (1980–84), *Not the Nine O'Clock News* (1979–82) and *Only Fools and Horses* (1981–2003), before being promoted again in 1982 to the post of Head of Light Entertainment. After spending three years behind a desk, however, he was tempted to return to 'hands-on' production duties, leaving the BBC in 1985 to join Thames Television as a producer. In 1987, he returned to the executive fold as the company's new Head of Light Entertainment (acquiring notoriety two years later when he decided to dispense with the services of Benny Hill), and then returned to the BBC in the mid-1990s, where he continued to make and advise on a wide range of popular comedy and drama productions.

Douglas Argent had reached a stage in his career where he was ready to ease up on his programme-making duties, but Bob Spiers went on to be busier than ever. Turning freelance at the start of the 1980s, he produced and directed the final series of *The Goodies* (LWT/ITV, 1982), as well as directing fifteen new episodes of *Are You Being Served?* for Australia's Channel 10. On the newly formed Channel 4, Spiers helped shape the television arena of the burgeoning so-called 'alternative comedy' scene. The channel's opening night, on 2 November 1982, featured his *The Comic Strip Presents . . . Five Go Mad In Dorset* (which promoted the creative talents of such up-and-coming performers as Rik Mayall, Adrian Edmondson, Jennifer Saunders, Dawn French and Peter Richardson), and he oversaw several more projects by the same team. He also directed – quite splendidly – two series of Steven Moffat's seriously under-appreciated sitcom *Joking Apart* (BBC1, 1993 and 1995); and was responsible for the first four hugely successful series of *Absolutely Fabulous* (BBC1, 1992–2001). Branching out into movies in the second half of the 1990s, he began with *Spiceworld: The Movie* and the Disney feature *That Darn Cat* (both of them released in 1997), before moving on to more challenging projects.

One other member of the team ended up doing something that must have felt slightly like following in the footsteps of the Fawltys. After a few more years working in television as a freelance, Peter Kindred, the original set designer, moved with his wife Bridget to Denbighshire in North Wales, where they opened an elegant Georgian country-house hotel, called Tyddyn Llan, in Llandrillo near Corwen in the Vale of Edeyrnion.[69] Unlike Fawlty Towers, however, the hotel would attract some enthusiastic reviews and its restaurant would win itself a positive mention in *The Good Food Guide* (and Gressingham duck was often on the menu, but never in the middle of a trifle).

For all of these multiple solo activities, however, there would still be the occasional Fawlty-related enterprise. In the late 1970s, for example, Andrew Sachs, in character as Manuel, recorded two comedy singles, followed in 1984 by a comical version of the Joe Dolce song 'Shaddup You Face' (backed with another song called 'Waiter, There's a Flea In My Soup'). The record did not quite make it to the relevant parts of the charts, because Dolce took out an injunction to delay its release until after he had issued (or inflicted) his own undeniably distinctive version on the people of Britain. In 1983, Sachs reappeared as Manuel for an Australian television advertisement for Carte D'Or Riesling wine ('Si, Señor, I got car door!'). There was also talk for a while of a *Fawlty Towers* spin-off sitcom featuring Sachs once again as Manuel. His son, John, had found a willing writer, and, in the summer of 1995, it was reported that a commission was due 'within months'.[70] 'John Cleese has given us his blessing,' said John Sachs, 'and will sit down with the creative team to point us in the right direction. He trusts us to preserve the memory of something as special as *Fawlty Towers*.'[71] The project, however, petered out before the pilot stage.

Even John Cleese, in his most capricious – and/or commercially-minded – of moods, could be persuaded to briefly reprise Fawlty for the odd event that caught his fancy. At the end of June in 2005, for example, he was reunited with Andrew Sachs in, of all places, the Norwegian town of Stavanger, where the set of the hotel restaurant was reconstructed and the characters of Basil and Manuel returned for six training films commissioned by the major Norwegian oil company Statoil (the idea was for them to experience a fresh set of calamities and then discuss how to stop them from ever happening again). Cleese also lent his voice, and a couple of Fawlty phrases, to an otherwise instantly forgettable ditty – called 'Don't Mention the World Cup' – designed to bring some mild amusement to followers of the 2006 tournament, which on this occasion was being held in Germany. In 2007, he even gave his blessing to plans to place a statue of Basil on show in the town of Torquay: 'I think this sounds like a splendid idea,' was his reported response. 'Can I assume it will be a conventional, realistic kind of statue, and not a tribute to Henry Moore? If so, let's get someone to sculpt it in a non-controversial style.'[72]

As far as the prospect of a fully fledged reprise of *Fawlty Towers* was concerned, however, Cleese would always remain firm and clear: without Connie Booth it could never happen.[73] 'I asked him about it once,' recalled Andrew Sachs. 'People had been coming up to me for so many years after the last series was over, saying, "Are you doing any more? Are you? Are you going to do any more?" And, obviously, I didn't know. All I could ever say was, "Probably not. No, I doubt it." But then I met John one day for lunch – this would have been some time in the early 1990s – and I said to him, "People keep asking me about the show coming back, John, and I never know what to say. Presumably it's finished, but would you ever consider writing any more?" And he said, "Um . . . y-yes . . . maybe . . . I think so, yes." That surprised me. So I said, "Well, would you do it without Connie?" And, without the slightest hesitation, he said, "No, never." So that's your answer, I think.'[74]

In 2007, there was one more attempt to bring the team back together – not to make any more shows, but just to reminisce about what a phenomenon it had become. The people behind BBC Radio 4's *The Reunion* – a series that reunited key players in certain notable social, political and cultural events – attempted to gather the key surviving members of the *Fawlty Towers* cast to reminisce about the chemistry that had made it such a success. John Cleese agreed to take part, along with Prunella Scales and Andrew Sachs, but Connie Booth maintained her refusal to have anything more, in public, to do with the show. David Prest, the producer of *The Reunion*, explained to journalists at the time: 'We had most of the *Fawlty Towers* cast lined up but Connie simply didn't want to have anything to do with it. We felt that as we didn't have everybody on board we had to abandon the idea.'[75]

The show was definitely over. *Fawlty Towers* was never coming back, but, as John Cleese would confirm, there had once been a time when it could have done.

It would not have been in the form of another series. That, he was quick to explain, would have been far too much of a strain: 'So many people have said, "Are you going to do any more *Fawlty Towers*?" And you're up against [such] an expectation – I couldn't win. I could not win.'[76] Noting that some fans had always hoped for a movie version of the show, he was similarly dismissive: 'Trying to make *Fawlty Towers* work at ninety minutes would be very difficult, because [. . .] in a movie there has to be a trough and then another peak and . . . it doesn't interest me.' He did admit, however, that he and Connie Booth had indeed toyed with the notion for a while: 'I had an idea for a plot. I love the idea of Basil finally being invited to meet Manuel's family, and getting to Heathrow and spending about fourteen hours there, waiting for the flight. Then finally getting on the flight, being furious, and then a terrorist pulls a gun and tries to hijack the plane. And Basil is so angry he overcomes the terrorist, and the pilot says, "We have to fly back to Heathrow." Basil says, "*No* – fly us to Spain or I'll *shoot* you!" Arrives in Spain, is immediately arrested, spends the entire holiday in a Spanish jail, is released just in time to go back on the plane with Sybil.' Cleese would admit that the premise struck him as attractively practicable – 'It's funny, isn't it?' he laughed – but then, alas, he added, 'I don't want to do it.'[77]

Even the most avid of fans will surely sympathise. Sometimes it really is best to leave well alone. When one looks back on what we did get to see – what a privilege it was to be present. As strong as the temptation was to ask for even more, it was surely never as strong as the inclination to reflect on the extraordinary contributions of John Cleese and Connie Booth, and all of the rest of the cast and crew, and just smile and say, for the two series, two words: thank you.

CHECKING OUT

Well, that was fun, wasn't it, dear? The odd moment like that, it's almost worth staying alive for.

It could have taken up just six hours of our valuable time. Two short series. Twelve little half-hour episodes. Six evanescent hours. That is all, in essence, that *Fawlty Towers* actually was. What it meant to us, however, was so much more than that. *Fawlty Towers* did not last a mere six hours. It will last us for all of our lives.

When, in the early 1950s, the BBC – in other words, in those days, British television in general – first started taking popular entertainment seriously, appointing a bright and decent man called Ronnie Waldman to oversee a new television department dedicated to creating programmes of this kind for the screen, there was a certain amount of doubt and anxiety. Is making people smile, some pondered, part of what public service broadcasting is, or ought to be, all about? Waldman, to his great credit, had a good and sincere answer to allay such nagging fears: some entertainment, he said, is poor, and some of it is mediocre, and some of it is good, and a little bit of it is truly wonderful, so if one can 'give the viewers what they want – but better than they expect it', and show them just how wonderful the very best kind of entertainment can be, then that, too, is a precious public service – not just to the viewers, but to the entertainment industry as well. Great entertainment, great comedy, great sketch shows and great sitcoms – they set the bar higher and higher, they make connoisseurs of us all, and they make us want more and more of the very best. They make the activity matter, and they make us care. That is some service; that is some goal.

Ronnie Waldman would have been so proud of *Fawlty Towers*. It epitomised all that he hoped to bring to the screen. It was intelligent, ambitious and hugely amusing. The scripts were supremely and consistently well written, the acting was playful yet precisely apposite, the production was subtle and unobtrusive yet impressively progressive, and the overall effect was richly and enduringly entertaining. Here was a television show that gave the viewers what they wanted – but was so much better than they had been expecting it to be.

Fawlty Towers would remain an inspiration to any programme-maker who wanted to do something that stood up to careful scrutiny and passed the test of time. There are plenty of other comedy shows these days – under-drafted, seemingly unedited and instantly, shamelessly, forgettable – that demonstrate just what one can actually get away with, but *Fawlty Towers* teaches one just how much can actually be achieved, provided that there is a team in place that has the talent, the discipline, the patience and the passion to see the project through to its proper conclusion.

The precise number of episodes or series is not what really matters most. It would be wrong to turn such a singular act of prudence into a generalised and unthinking gimmick. *Fawlty Towers* ran for twelve episodes and two series, while, at the other end of the spectrum, *Dad's Army* – with a different situation, set of characters and range of potential scenarios – ran for eighty episodes and nine series. Both of them were rare and lasting delights. The important thing is that both of these truly exceptional sitcoms knew when it was right for them, and them alone, to stop – and that was at the top, when they were still loved, widely watched and warmly admired. When a sitcom not only has a great situation, great material, great performances and great production, but also great taste and great judgment, it really does have it all – and so, as a consequence, do we.

John Howard Davies, the producer/director of the first series of *Fawlty Towers*, reflected on the achievement:

> I'm never exactly 'proud' of anything I do, but I do value the fact that we used to laugh so much when we made those shows. We worked very, very hard, it really was tough, but we really did laugh a lot, too. Some might say that the second series was better constructed than the first series – a bit more polished – and that's probably true. But I also think that, in a sense, the first series had a kind of eclectic brilliance, simply because it was so surprising and nobody had ever seen it before, and that gave it an edge – a spark – that some other episodes in the second series perhaps didn't quite have. And I suspect that's because it looked more spontaneous and immediate.[1]

Bob Spiers, the director of the second series, also looked back on the show as a whole with a great sense of satisfaction:

> I was relatively inexperienced at this stage, and relatively young, so this was a big, big, big programme for me to be doing, and very nerve-wracking. [. . .] Because there was always that kind of feeling, at that time amongst certain people, that the second series wouldn't be as good as the first, and one just had to be supremely confident that this one was the same standard as the first series. Which has [since] been proved, because now they're interchangeable.[2]

As for the members of the cast, there would never be any resentment about being associated with twelve half-hour shows that made such a remarkable and lasting impression. There was, on the contrary, only affection, gratitude and pride. Andrew Sachs, for example, reminisced:

> I've so many very pleasant memories. It was such a nice team, as well as such a funny and successful show, so I look back on the experience of being part of it with great fondness. People still want to talk about it, and still seem to have so much affection for it, and it's nice to think you've been involved in something that has had that effect. And it seems to keep finding younger and younger fans. That's quite amazing and very satisfying. So I'm pleased to say that I think, thanks to all the repeats, the show will live on and continue to make people laugh.[3]

Prunella Scales, with the same kind of warmth, reflected:

> I don't get bored talking about *Fawlty Towers*. I'm very proud of it, and have such happy memories of the series. It was a wonderfully professional team, and we've all remained dear friends. And I'm so pleased that the programme continues to stand up so well. Very often when you see an old comedy, you think, 'Well, it's still charming and funny but it has got very slow.' It isn't like that with *Fawlty Towers*. Even now, all these years later, it still has its speed. That's such an impressive achievement. And I do admire John and Connie so much for resisting all the pressure and stopping when they stopped. Originally, they had six things to say about anger and aspects of hotel management. Then they managed to find six more – and the second six were just as good and as true and as funny as the first six. And then they had the courage to stop. It was all so fine and so right.[4]

As for Connie Booth and John Cleese: the pair of them have always been content to let the high quality of their work speak on their behalf. On the odd occasion, however, Cleese has been known to express a happy sense of wonder at what the two of them managed to achieve – 'Shakespeare only got four hours out of Hamlet,' he once joked. 'We got six hours out of Basil' – and how enduring has been its appeal: '[Even] after all these years, I don't get offended by the fact that so many people remember *Fawlty Towers*, as if I've never done anything else. I would never say, "But don't you realise that it's just one of many things I've done?" No, it is always good to hear how many people still enjoy the results of our efforts.'[5]

Plenty of people – famous, infamous, healthily anonymous, the specific identities matter far less than the shared sensibilities – still enjoy and cherish the results of their efforts. Forget the demographics, the spreadsheets, the current executive spin and the latest buzz words in the broadcasting boardrooms: *Fawlty Towers* has lasted because good creative people were trusted to get on with their vision and, rather than being pressured into punching the right buttons or ringing the right bells, they were allowed to surprise, intrigue and delight. What Cleese and Booth, and Scales and Sachs and the whole of the team, achieved was something unforced, extraordinarily engaging and well worth returning to again and again and again.

There was so much about *Fawlty Towers* for us to enjoy. It was full of pain and violence and misery and cruelty and an unremitting air of failure. It also made us laugh. We so enjoyed our stay.

Episode Guide

THE TV SERIES

Series One (1975)

Regular Cast:
Basil Fawlty: John Cleese
Sybil Fawlty: Prunella Scales
Polly Sherman: Connie Booth
Manuel: Andrew Sachs
Major Gowen: Ballard Berkeley
Miss Tibbs: Gilly Flower
Miss Gatsby: Renée Roberts

1. A Touch of Class (19 September 1975)

Basil Fawlty is determined to attract a better standard of guest to his hotel. He is delighted, therefore, when a peer of the realm arrives for a brief stay. Appearances, however, can be deceptive.

Also featuring:
Lord Melbury: Michael Gwynn
Danny Brown: Robin Ellis

Sir Richard Morris: Martin Wyldeck
Mr Watson: Lionel Wheeler
Mr Wareing: Terence Conoley
Mr Mackenzie: David Simeon

(Running Time: 30:22)

2. The Builders (26 September 1975)

Sybil has picked a professional firm to make some alterations to the hotel. Basil, however, has another, secret, plan to hire someone considerably cheaper.

Also featuring:
O'Reilly: David Kelly
Lurphy: Michael Cronin
Jones: Michael Halsey
Kerr: Barney Dorman
Stubbs: James Appleby
Delivery Man: George Lee

(Running Time: 28:17)

3. The Wedding Party (3 October 1975)

Basil is battling against what he regards as an outbreak of moral turpitude within his hotel. Everyone appears to be in an unusually amorous mood – and he suspects certain guests of taking things far too far.

Also featuring:
Alan: *Trevor Adams*
Jean: *April Walker*
Mrs Peignoir: *Yvonne Gilan*
Mr Lloyd: *Conrad Phillips*
Rachel Lloyd: *Diana King*
Customer: *Jay Neill*

(Running Time: 33:21)

4. The Hotel Inspectors (10 October 1975)

When Basil hears that a hotel inspector is planning to make an unannounced visit, he suspects that one of his guests is working undercover. It might be the fussy man called Mr Hutchinson . . .

Also featuring:
Mr Hutchinson: *Bernard Cribbins*
Mr Walt: *James Cossins*
John: *Geoffrey Morris*
Brian: *Peter Brett*

(Running Time: 28:49)

5. Gourmet Night (17 October 1975)

Basil's continuing efforts to raise the standard of guests in the hotel lead him to organise a special gourmet night ('no riff-raff'). This time he has a top-notch chef called Kurt in the kitchen, expert advice from the local restaurateur André and a stylish menu in place. VIPs have been invited, black ties have been donned and everything looks promising. What can go wrong?

Also featuring:
André: André Maranne
Kurt: Steve Plytas
Colonel Hall: Allan Cuthbertson
Mrs Hall: Ann Way
Mr Twitchen: Richard Caldicot
Mrs Twitchen: Betty Huntley-Wright
Mr Heath: Jeffrey Segal
Mrs Heath: Elizabeth Benson
Master Ronald Heath: Tony Page

(Running Time: 28:38)

6. *The Germans (24 October 1975)*

Sybil is in hospital for her ingrowing toenail, but she is still monitoring Basil from afar. A moose head needs to be put up on the wall, the cheese needs scraping, a fire drill needs to be completed and a party of Germans needs to be welcomed. Basil is certain he can cope.

Also featuring:
Sister: Brenda Collins
Doctor: Louis Mahoney
Mr Sharp: John Lawrence
Mrs Sharp: Iris Fry

Large Woman: Claire Davenport
German Guests: Nick Lane
　　　　　　　Lisa Bergmayr
　　　　　　　Willy Bowman
　　　　　　　Dan Gillan

(Running Time: 31:17)

Series Two (1979)

Regular Cast:
Basil Fawlty: John Cleese
Sybil Fawlty: Prunella Scales
Polly Sherman: Connie Booth
Manuel: Andrew Sachs
Major Gowen: Ballard Berkeley
Miss Tibbs: Gilly Flower
Miss Gatsby: Renée Roberts
Terry: Brian Hall

1. Communication Problems (19 February 1979)

A troublesome guest causes problems when she refuses to turn on her hearing aid. Basil, meanwhile, has received a red-hot racing tip that he must keep a secret from Sybil.

Also featuring:
Mrs Richards: Joan Sanderson
Mr Yardley: Melvyn Pascoe

Mr Thurston: Robert Lankesheer
Mr Firkins: Johnny Shannon
Mr Mackintosh: Bill Bradley
Mr Kerr: George Lee

(Running Time: 31:26)

2. The Psychiatrist (26 February 1979)

Sybil is flirting with a young man who buys his fertility symbols from Colchester. Basil is scowling in the background. Then two doctors arrive for a brief stay. Basil is delighted – until he discovers that one of them is a psychiatrist.

Also featuring:
Mr Johnson: Nicky Henson
Dr Abbott: Basil Henson
Mrs Abbott: Elspet Gray
Raylene Miles: Luan Peters
Mrs Johnson: Aimée Delamain
Girlfriend: Imogen Bickford-Smith

(Running Time: 36:19)

3. Waldorf Salad (5 March 1979)

An American and his English-born wife arrive too late for dinner, but, after bribing Basil, a modest repast is arranged. The problem is that Terry the chef has gone home and Basil has never heard of a Waldorf salad.

Also featuring:
Mr Hamilton: *Bruce Boa*
Mrs Hamilton: *Claire Nielson*
Mr Libson: *Anthony Dawes*
Mrs Johnstone: *June Ellis*
Mr Johnstone: *Terence Conoley*
Miss Hare: *Dorothy Frere*
Miss Gurke: *Beatrice Shaw*
Mr Arrad: *Norman Bird*
Mrs Arrad: *Stella Tanner*

(Running Time: 32:06)

4. The Kipper and the Corpse (12 March 1979)

Mr Leeman is unwell. He checks in, orders breakfast in bed and then struggles upstairs. When he croaks by breakfast time, Basil can only think of one thing: was it the out-of-date kippers he was given?

Also featuring:
Dr Price: *Geoffrey Palmer*
Mr Leeman: *Derek Royle*
Mrs Chase: *Mavis Pugh*
Guest: *Len Marten*
Mr Xerxes: *Robert McBain*
Mr Zebedee: *Raymond Mason*
Miss Young: *Pamela Buchner*
Mr White: *Richard Davies*
Mr Ingrams: *Charles McKeown*

(Running Time: 31:34)

5. The Anniversary (26 March 1979)

It is the seventeenth of April – the Fawltys' fifteenth wedding anniversary. Last year, Basil forgot – and he paid for it. This year, he has remembered, and has planned a surprise party. The problem is, Sybil suspects that, yet again, he has forgotten, and she is furious.

Also featuring:
Roger: Ken Campbell
Alice: Una Stubbs
Virginia: Pat Keen
Arthur: Robert Arnold
Reg: Roger Hume
Kitty: Denyse Alexander
Audrey: Christine Shaw

(Running Time: 29:11)

6. Basil the Rat (25 October 1979)

Manuel's pet rat gets loose in the hotel on the same day that a health inspector is due to show up. If it eludes the poisoned veal in the kitchen and pops up in the dining room, Fawlty Towers could end up being closed down

Also featuring:
Mr Carnegie: John Quarmby
Guest: Stuart Sherwin
Mr Taylor: James Taylor

273

Mrs Taylor: Melody Lang
Ronald: David Neville
Quentina: Sabina Franklyn

(Running Time: 33:47)

The Merchandise

Scripts

Fawlty Towers (London: Futura, 1977, ISBN: 0-8600-7598-2)
Fawlty Towers 2 (London: Weidenfeld & Nicolson, 1979, ISBN: 0-7088-1547-2)
The Complete Fawlty Towers (London: Methuen, 1988, ISBN: 0-413-18390-4)

LPs/Cassettes

Fawlty Towers (1979: BBC Records REB 377/ BBC ZCF 377)
Fawlty Towers: Second Sitting (1981: BBC Records REB 405/ BBC ZCF 405)
Fawlty Towers: At Your Service (1982: BBC Records REB 449/ BBC ZCF 449)
Fawlty Towers: A La Carte (1983: BBC Records REB 484/ BBC ZCF 484)
Fawlty Towers Collection (1999: BBC Audio 0563553111)

CDs
Fawlty Towers: Volume 1 (2001: BBC Audio 0563478187)
Fawlty Towers: Volume 2 (2002: BBC Audio 0563536748)
Fawlty Towers: Volume 3 (2002: BBC Audio 0563528494)

Videos

The Germans, with The Hotel Inspectors and A Touch of Class (1984: BBC Enterprises, BBCV6635)

The Psychiatrist, with The Builders and The Wedding Party (1984: BBC Enterprises, BBCV6633)

The Kipper and the Corpse, with Waldorf Salad and Gourmet Night (1984: BBC Enterprises, BBCV6634)

Basil the Rat, with Communication Problems and The Anniversary (1984: BBC Enterprises, BBCV6632)

DVDs

Fawlty Towers: Complete Series 1 (2001: BBCDVD1064)

Fawlty Towers: Complete Series 2 (2001: BBCDVD1065)

Fawlty Towers: The Complete Set (2005: BBCDVD1794)

Fawlty Towers Revisited (2005: Iowa Public Television/BBC Worldwide Americas)★

CD-ROM

Fawlty Towers (2001: BBC Multimedia B0000507NA)

UMD

Fawlty Towers – Series 1 (2006: BBCUMD8012)

Fawlty Towers – Series 2 (forthcoming)

★Only available in the USA through PBS member stations.

Bibliography

A: Fawlty Towers

Bellamy, Guy, 'The Traveller's Unrest', *Radio Times*, 17–23 February 1975, pp.74–5

Bright, Maurice, and Robert Ross, *Fawlty Towers: Fully Booked* (London: BBC, 2001)

Bryson, Bill, 'Cleese Up Close', *New York Times*, Section 6, 25 December 1988, p.14

Chapman, Graham, *A Liar's Autobiography, Volume VI* (London: Magnum, 1981)

Chapman, Graham, et al., with Bob McCabe, *The Pythons' Autobiography* (London: Orion, 2003)

Cleese, John, 'My Local Hero', *Daily Mail* (Weekend section), 18 August 2001, pp.18–19

Gore-Langton, Robert, *John Cleese: And Now For Something Completely Different* (London: André Deutsch, 1999)

Holm, Lars Holger, *Fawlty Towers: A Worshipper's Companion* (Stockholm: Leo Publishing, 2004)

Johnson, Kim 'Howard', *Life Before and After Monty Python* (New York: St Martin's Press, 1993)

Johnstone, Iain, 'Falty Towers', *British Comedy Greats*, ed. Annabel Merullo and Neil Wenborn (London: Cassell Illustrated, 2003), pp. 71–5

Margolis, Jonathan, *Cleese Encounters* (London: Orion, 1998)

Nightingale, Benedict, 'One Pair of Cleese', *Radio Times*, 13–19 September 1975, pp.4–5

Norman, Neil, 'Fears of a Clown', *The Face*, no. 35, March 1983, pp.24–9

Ransome, Teresa, *Prunella* (London: John Murray, 2005)

Skynner, Robin, and John Cleese, *Families and How to Survive Them* (London: Methuen, 1983)

Thomas, David, 'Fawlty Memories', *Daily Mail* (Weekend section), 13 August 2005, pp.4–6

Viner, Brian, 'Just Don't Mention Fawlty Towers . . .', the *Independent*, 20 September 2000, p.7

B: General

Adorno, T. W., *Dream Notes* (Oxford: Polity, 1997)

Allen, Fred, *Treadmill to Oblivion* (Boston: Little, Brown, 1954)

Allen, Steve, *The Funny Men* (New York: Simon & Schuster, 1956)

Benny, Jack, and Joan Benny, *Sunday Nights at Seven* (New York: Warner, 1990)

Billington, Michael, *One Night Stands* (London: Nick Hern Books, 1993)

Black, Cilla, *Through the Years* (London: Headline, 1993)

Black, Peter, *The Biggest Aspidistra in the World* (London: BBC, 1972)

——*The Mirror in the Corner* (London: Hutchison, 1972)

Bradbury, David, and Joe McGrath, *Now That's Funny!* (London: Methuen, 1998)

Brandreth, Gyles, *Brief Encounters* (London: Politico's, 2003)

Briggs, Asa, *The History of Broadcasting in the United Kingdom* (Oxford: Oxford University Press, 1961–79):

——Vol. 1: *The Birth of Broadcasting*, 1961

——Vol. 2: *The Golden Age of Wireless*, 1965

——Vol. 3: *The War of Words*, 1970

——Vol. 4: *Sound and Vision*, 1979

Cardiff, David, 'Mass Middlebrow Laughter: The Origins of BBC Comedy', *Media, Culture & Society*, vol. 10, no. 1 (January 1988), pp. 41–60

Cotton, Bill, *The BBC As an Entertainer* (London: BBC, 1977)

——*Double Bill*, (London: Fourth Estate, 2000)

Craig, Mike, *Look Back With Laughter*, vols 1, 2 and 3 (Manchester: Mike Craig Enterprises, 1996)

Cryer, Barry, *You Won't Believe This But . . .* (London: Virgin, 1998)

——*Pigs Can Fly* (London: Orion, 2003)

Double, Oliver, *Getting the Joke: the Art of Stand-Up Comedy* (London: Methuen, 2005)

Emerson, Ralph Waldo, *Essays and Poems* (London: J. M. Dent, 1995)

Fisher, John, *Funny Way To Be a Hero* (London: Frederick Muller, 1973)

Frith, Simon, 'The Pleasures of the Hearth: the Making of BBC Light Entertainment', in Tony Bennett et al. (eds), *Popular Culture and Social Relations* (Milton Keynes: Open University, 1983)

Foster, Andy, and Steve Furst, *Radio Comedy 1938–1968* (London: Virgin, 1996)

Gambaccini, Paul, and Rod Taylor, *Television's Greatest Hits* (London: Network Books, 1993)

Goffman, Erving, *The Presentation of Self in Everyday Life* (London: Penguin, 1990)

Grade, Lew, *Still Dancing* (London: Collins, 1987)

Grade, Michael, *It Seemed Like a Good Idea at the Time* (London: Macmillan, 1999)

Greene, Hugh Carleton, *The BBC As a Public Service* (London: BBC, 1960)

Hudd, Roy, *Roy Hudd's Book of Music-Hall, Variety and Showbiz Anecdotes* (London: Virgin, 1994)

Hughes, John Graven, *The Greasepaint War* (London: New English Library, 1976)

James, Clive, *Clive James on Television* (London: Picador, 1991)

Jeffries, Stuart, *Mrs Slocombe's Pussy* (London: Flamingo, 2000)

Josefsberg, Milt, *The Jack Benny Show* (New York: Arlington House, 1977)

Kavanagh, Ted, *The ITMA Years* (London: Woburn Press, 1974)

Lewisohn, Mark, *Radio Times Guide to TV Comedy* (London: BBC, 1998)

McCann, Graham, *Cary Grant: A Class Apart* (London: Fourth Estate, 1996)

——'Why the Best Sitcoms Must Be a Class Act', London *Evening Standard*, 21 May 1997, p.9

——'An Offer We Can Refuse', London *Evening Standard*, 2 December 1998, p.8

——*Morecambe & Wise* (London: Fourth Estate, 1998)

——'Sit Back and Wait for the Comedy', *Financial Times*, 24 November 1999, p.22

——'Don't Bury Your Treasures', *Financial Times*, 28 June 2000, p.22

——*Dad's Army: The Story of a Classic Television Show* (London: Fourth Estate, 2001)

——'You Never Had It So Good or So Funny', *Financial Times*, 13 November 2002, p.17

——'How to Define the Indefinable', *Financial Times*, 20 March 2003, p.14

——'Bob Hope: The master of special delivery bows out', *Financial Times*, 29 July 2003, p.15

——'Steptoe and Son', *British Comedy Greats*, ed. Annabel Merullo and Neil Wenborn (London: Cassell Illustrated, 2003), pp.157–61

——'Johnny Speight,' *Dictionary of National Biography* (Oxford: Oxford University Press, 2004)

——*Frankie Howerd: Stand-Up Comic* (London: Fourth Estate, 2004)

——*Spike & Co* (London: Hodder & Stoughton, 2006)

McFarlane, Brian, *An Autobiography of British Cinema* (London: Methuen, 1997)

Mellor, G. J., *The Northern Music Hall* (Newcastle-upon-Tyne: Frank Graham, 1970)

——*They Made Us Laugh* (Littleborough: George Kelsell, 1982)

Miall, Leonard, *Inside The BBC* (London: Weidenfeld & Nicolson, 1994)

Midwinter, Eric, *Make 'Em Laugh* (London: George Allen & Unwin, 1979)

Monkhouse, Bob, *Crying With Laughter* (London: Arrow, 1994)

——*Over The Limit* (London: Century, 1998)

Morgan, David, (ed.), *Monty Python Speaks!* (London: Fourth Estate, 1999)

Muir, Frank, *Comedy in Television* (London: BBC, 1966)

Nathan, David *The Laughtermakers* (London: Peter Owen, 1971)

Perret, Gene, and Martha Bolton, *Talk About Hope* (Carmel, CA: Jester Press, 1998)

Pertwee, Bill, *Promenades and Pierrots* (Devon: Westbridge, 1979)

——*By Royal Command* (Newton Abbot: David & Charles, 1981)

——*A Funny Way to Make a Living!* (London: Sunburst, 1996)

Plomley, Roy, *Desert Island Lists* (London: Hutchinson, 1984)

Priestley, J. B., *Particular Pleasures* (New York: Stein & Day, 1975)

Richards, Jeffrey, *Visions of Yesteryear* (London: Routledge, 1973)

——*Films and British National Identity* (Manchester: Manchester University Press, 1997)

Silvey, Roger, *Who's Listening? The Story of BBC Audience Research* (London: Allen & Unwin, 1974)

Sloan, Tom, *Television Light Entertainment* (London: BBC, 1969)

Stone, Richard, *You Should Have Been in Last Night* (Sussex: The Book Guild, 2000)

Sykes, Eric, *Eric Sykes's Comedy Heroes* (London: Virgin, 2003)

Thompson, Joan B., *The Bleeding Obvious: A Brief Obfuscation of the Oeuvre of Sidney James Giddens* (Oxford: Peerage Press, 1996)

Took, Barry, *Laughter in the Air* (London: Robson/BBC, 1976)

——'Whatever Happened to TV Comedy?' The *Listener*, 5 January 1984, pp.7–8, and 12 January 1984, pp.8–9

Tynan, Kenneth, *Profiles* (London: Nick Hern Books, 1989)

Watt, John (ed.), *Radio Variety* (London: J. M Dent, 1939)

Wheldon, Huw, *British Traditions in a World-Wide Medium* (London: BBC, 1973)

——*The Achievement of Television* (London: BBC, 1975)

——*The British Experience in Television* (London: BBC, 1976)

Whitfield, June, *. . . and June Whitfield* (London: Corgi, 2001)

Wilde, Larry, *The Great Comedians* (Secaucus, New Jersey: Citadel Press, 1973)

Williams, Kenneth, *The Kenneth Williams Diaries*, ed. Russell Davies (London: HarperCollins, 1993)

Wilmut, Roger, *From Fringe to Flying Circus* (London: Book Club Associates, 1981)

——*Kindly Leave the Stage: The Story of Variety, 1918–60* (London: Methuen, 1985)

Windsor, Barbara, *All Of Me* (London: Headline, 2001)

Wyndham Goldie, Grace, *Facing The Nation: Broadcasting and Politics 1936–1976* (London: Bodley Head, 1977)

Notes

Checking In

1 Transcribed from the recording of the episode, 'A Touch of Class'. (All of the quotations from the show will be transcribed from the actual recordings rather than taken from the published versions of the scripts, as certain words and phrases were altered during the performances.)
2 'Waldorf Salad'.
3 'The Wedding Party'.
4 'A Touch of Class'.
5 The poll was conducted by BBC Worldwide, and the results were published online, on the BBC's website, on 10 October 2004. (The top ten were as follows: 1. *Fawlty Towers*; 2. *Keeping Up Appearances*; 3. *Blackadder Goes Forth*; 4. *Absolutely Fabulous*; 5. *Yes Minister*; 6. *The Vicar of Dibley*; 7. *Coupling*; 8. *Only Fools and Horses*; 9. *Are You Being Served?*; 10. *One Foot in the Grave*.)
6 'The Great British TV Survey,' *Radio Times*, 12–18 May 2007, p.19. (The top ten shows that viewers wanted to bring back to the screen were as follows: 1. *Fawlty Towers*; 2. *The Royle Family*; 3. *Prime Suspect*; 4. *Dad's Army*; 5. *The Likely Lads*; 6. *Tiswas*; 7. *The Generation Game*; 8. *Are You Being Served?*; 9. *Multi-Coloured Swap Shop*; 10. *Superstars*.)
7 The BFI 'TV 100' poll was chosen by members of the TV industry throughout the UK (1,600 programme-makers, critics, writers and

executives were invited to give their professional opinions and personal tastes). Each voter was given a 'big list' of 650 programmes in six genres, along with spaces for any titles not included. The resulting top ten – announced in September 2000 – were as follows: 1. *Fawlty Towers*; 2. *Cathy Come Home*; 3. *Doctor Who*; 4. *The Naked Civil Servant*; 5. *Monty Python's Flying Circus*; 6. *Blue Peter*, 7. *Boys From the Blackstuff*; 8. *Parkinson*; 9. *Yes Minister/Yes Prime Minister*, 10. *Brideshead Revisited*.

Chapter 1

1 Previous accounts – such as Morris Bright and Robert Ross's *Fawlty Towers: Fully Booked* (London: BBC, 2001), p.10 – claimed the year in question was 1971, which would have meant that a mere eight days after John Cleese checked out of the hotel (on 22 May), a *Doctor At Large* script inspired by his experiences there had been written, accepted, filmed and broadcast on television. Even more confusingly, in a 2005 PBS documentary (*Fawlty Towers Revisited* – Iowa Public Television/BBC Worldwide Americas, 2005), both John Cleese and John Howard Davies refer to the stay as happening in 1968 – which would mean that the Pythons were filming before *Python* existed. In fact, as Michael Palin's published diaries confirm, the Pythons definitely stayed in Torquay in May 1970.

2 Told to the author (24 November 2006) by a former guest at the Gleneagles.

3 *Ibid.*

4 See the *Independent*, 11 May 2002, p.5; *Guardian*, 11 May 2002, p.10; *Daily Mirror*, 11 May 2002, p.8; and the *Daily Mail*, 11 May 2002, p.29, and 22 May 2002, pp.20–1.

5 Graham Chapman, *A Liar's Autobiography, Volume VI* (London: Magnum, 1981), p.156.

6 See Kim 'Howard' Johnson, *Life Before and After Monty Python* (New York: St Martin's Press, 1993), pp.86–8, and John Cleese's interview on *Parkinson*, BBC1, 22 October 1980.

7 John Cleese, speaking on Disc 3 of *The Complete Fawlty Towers* DVD set (BBC Worldwide 2005: BBCDVD 1794).

8 See Chapman, *A Liar's Autobiography, op. cit.*, p.156.

9 See Brian Viner's article, 'Just Don't Mention Fawlty Towers . . .,' *Independent*, 20 September 2000, p.7.

10 *Ibid.*

11 John Cleese, speaking on Disc 3 of *The Complete Fawlty Towers* DVD set.

12 See Michael Palin, *Diaries 1969–1979: The Python Years* (London: Weidenfeld & Nicolson, 2006), pp.24–5.

13 Cleese, speaking at the Montreal Comedy Festival, 22 July 2006.

14 See *Radio Times*, 13–19 May 1995, p.6, and Cleese's interview on *Parkinson*, BBC1, 22 October 1980.

15 According to his death certificate, Donald Sinclair (who was born on 10 July 1909 in Eire) died at his home (Compass South, Ilsham Marine Drive, Torquay) on 5 September 1981.

16 Beatrice Sinclair, quoted by Richard Savill in the *Daily Telegraph*, 11 May 2002, p.9.

17 Beatrice Sinclair, quoted by Donna Watson, *Daily Record*, 11 May 2002, p.23.

18 Rosemary Harrison, letter to the *Daily Telegraph*, 18 May 2002, p.21. See also the accompanying article, 'Fawlty Hotelier was bonkers', same source, p.3.

19 Rosemary Harrison, quoted by Claire Gardner in *Scotland on Sunday*, 19 May 2002, p.3.

20 Roy Browning, quoted by Sarah Chalmers, *Daily Mail*, 22 May 2002, *op. cit.*

21 Richard Saunders, speaking on the *The Complete Fawlty Towers* DVD set extra feature, 'Torquay Tourist Office', *op. cit.*

22 J. Burl, letter to Torquay's *Herald Express*, 1 June 2002, p.8.

23 Christine Aitken, quoted by Claire Gardner in *Scotland on Sunday*, 19 May 2002, p.3.

24 *Ibid.*

25 Barbara DePaulis, reported by BBC Radio Devon, 18 September 2006.

26 Colin Bratcher, quoted by Sarah Chalmers, *Daily Mail*, 22 May 2002, *op. cit.*

27 See 'The Men Who Painted Trees', *The Times*, 3 November 1981, p.3.

28 *Ibid.* (See also 'Torquay Tourist Office', *The Complete Fawlty Towers* DVD, *op. cit.*)

29 'Come In and Lie Down', in *Six Dates with Barker*, recorded on 12 October 1970 and first broadcast on London Weekend Television/ITV on 5 February 1971.

30 Transcribed from 'No Ill Feeling', *Doctor At Large*, first broadcast on London Weekend Television on 30 May 1971.

31 Cleese, quoted by Johnson, *Life Before and After Monty Python, op. cit.*, p.86.

32 *The Ronnie Barker Yearbook*, BBC1, 20 March 1971.

33 *The Two Ronnies*, various sketches broadcast on BBC1 during 1971–3.

34 *Sez Les*, sixteen editions broadcast on Yorkshire/ITV between 1971–4.

35 *Elementary, My Dear Watson*, broadcast on BBC1 on 18 January 1973.

36 John Cleese, quoted by Johnson, *Life Before and After Monty Python, op. cit.*, p.86.

37 Video Arts was founded by Cleese, Jay, Robinson and Peacock at the start of 1972. The company was sold for £50m in 1989, from which Cleese received £7m.

Chapter 2

1 See Michael Palin's entry for 4 December 1972 in his *Diaries 1969–1979, op. cit.*, p.98: '[T]he thought of doing any more [series of *Python*],' Palin wrote of Cleese, 'makes his stomach tighten.'

2 John Cleese, quoted by David Nathan, *The Laughtermakers* (London: Peter Owen, 1971), p.183.

3 See Sheridan Morley's interview with John Cleese, 'Beastly Basil', *The Times* (Review section), 5 November 1977, p.11: '[I]t never to his dying day occurred to him that it might be his fault and not the magazine's,' Cleese recalled.

4 So opposed to the marriage was her strict and very religious father – Marwood Joseph Cross – he saw to it that the wedding, which took place on 21 October 1926 at the Bristol Register Office, was not even reported (as was traditional for the family's members) by the *Weston Mercury*.

5 Listen to John Cleese's comments in his Podcast no. 13, 30 June 2006.

6 John Cleese, quoted by Penelope Gilliatt, *To Wit* (London: Weidenfeld & Nicolson, 1990), p.239.

7 Cleese, quoted by Bright and Ross, *Fawlty Towers: Fully Booked, op. cit.*, pp.142–3.

8 Cleese, quoted by Bill Bryson, 'Cleese Up Close', *New York Times*, Section 6, 25 December 1988, p.14.

9 Recounted during Cleese's interview on *Parkinson*, BBC1, 22 October 1980.

10 Cleese, quoted by Hunter Davies, originally in the *Sunday Times* in 1977, and reproduced in the collection called *Hunting People* (Edinburgh: Mainstream, 1994), p.133.

11 Muriel Cleese, quoted by Roger Wilmut, *From Fringe to Flying Circus* (London: Book Club Associates, 1981), p.37.

12 Cleese, quoted by Bill Bryson, 'Cleese Up Close', *op. cit.*

13 Cleese, 'My Local Hero', *Daily Mail* (Weekend section), 18 August 2001, pp.18–19. See also the BBC1 profile of Grant, *Hollywood Greats*, broadcast 1 November 1999, and my *Cary Grant: A Class Apart* (London: Fourth Estate, 1996).
14 Muriel Cleese, quoted by Jonathan Margolis, *Cleese Encounters*, revised edition (London: Orion, 1998), p.15.
15 Clifton College archive.
16 *The Times*, 30 July 1957, p.12, and 31 July 1957, p.11.
17 See Cleese's entertaining account of the occasion in his 'Foreword' to Mike Brearley and Dudley Doust's *The Ashes Regained* (London: Hodder & Stoughton, 1979), pp.7–8.
18 Benedict Nightingale, 'One Pair of Cleese', *Radio Times*, 13–19 September 1975, p.4.
19 Cleese, quoted by Robert Hewison, *Footlights!* (London: Methuen, 1983), p.133.
20 The building has since been demolished and is now the site of the Lion Yard car park.
21 Cleese, quoted by Nathan, *The Laughtermakers, op. cit.*, p.185.
22 Cleese, quoted by Kim 'Howard' Johnson, *Life Before and After Monty Python, op. cit.*, p.5.
23 Transcribed from record *Cambridge Circus* (1963: Odeon PPMC 1208).
24 Tim Brooke-Taylor, quoted by Hunter Davies, *op. cit.*, p.135.
25 John Cleese, quoted by Margolis, *op. cit.*, p.94.
26 Cleese, quoted by Kim 'Howard' Johnson, *Life Before and After Python, op. cit.*, p.8.
27 Howard Taubman, *New York Times*, 7 October 1964, p.53.
28 Harry Gilroy, *New York Times*, 15 January 1965, p.22.
29 Connie Booth, quoted by Margolis, *op. cit.*, p.103.
30 John Cleese, *ibid.*, p.135.
31 Connie Booth, quoted by Hunter Davies, *op. cit.*, p.136.
32 Donald Zec, quoted by Margolis, *op. cit.*, p.119.
33 John Cleese, *ibid.*, p.103.

34 Connie Booth, quoted by Hunter Davies, *op. cit.*, p.136.

35 See *The Times*, 3 November 1970, p.5, and 30 March 1971, p.16.

36 Cleese's appearance on *Desert Island Discs* was broadcast on BBC Radio 4 on 17 July 1971.

37 John Cleese would tell Kim 'Howard' Johnson: 'It was an extraordinarily happy collaboration. Like all things that are small, cheap, and done more in a good spirit because people want to do it, rather than in terms of money, it was a success' (*Life Before and After Monty Python, op. cit.*, p.71).

38 Connie Booth referred to this project when interviewed by Guy Bellamy, 'The Traveller's Unrest', *Radio Times*, 17–23 February 1979, pp.74–7.

39 The critic Stanley Reynolds noted in *The Times* (1 November 1974, p.13) how the combination of scheduling the show in the BBC's late-night regional 'opt-out' slot (which allowed five BBC regions to ignore the show, leaving it to be seen only in London and parts of Northern England) and postponing certain episodes at the last moment in favour of show jumping or current affairs debates had 'made the show about as esoteric as a mass medium can get'. The team had, however, recently released a very successful live album – *Live at Drury Lane* (1974) – and had started receiving very positive reviews in America (see, for example, John O'Connor's review in the *New York Times*: '*Monty Python's Flying Circus*: A Soufflé of Lunacy', 10 November 1974, section AL).

40 Michael Palin, *Diaries, op. cit.*, p.149.

41 Cleese, quoted by Hunter Davies, *op. cit.*, p.137.

42 *Ibid.*, p.138.

43 Michael Palin, *Diaries, op. cit.*, p.98.

44 Alan Coren, *The Times*, 1 November 1974, p.13.

45 Cleese, quoted by Margolis, *op. cit.*, p.162.

46 Cleese, quoted by Bill Bryson, 'Cleese Up Close', *op. cit.*

47 John Cleese, quoted by Margolis, *op. cit.*, p.229.

48 *Ibid.*

49 Cleese, quoted by Barry Took, *Comedy Greats* (London: Equation, 1989), p.142.

50 Cleese, quoted by Morley, *op. cit.*, p.11.

51 Cleese, quoted by Hunter Davies, *op. cit.*, p.138.

52 John Cleese, speaking in the first of the three-part BBC1 *Omnibus* documentary, *Laughter in the House*, first broadcast 24 March 1999.

53 Cleese, quoted by Margolis, *op. cit.*, p.143.

54 Graham Chapman, quoted by Cleese, speaking at the Montreal Comedy Festival, 2006.

55 Barry Cryer, interviewed by David Bradbury and Joe McGrath, *Now That's Funny!* (London: Methuen, 1998), p.50.

56 Connie Booth, quoted by Margolis, *op. cit.*, p.144.

57 Cleese, quoted by David Thomas, 'Fawlty Memories', *Daily Mail* (Weekend section), 13 August 2005, p.4.

58 Carol Cleveland, quoted by David Morgan, ed., *Monty Python Speaks!* (London: Fourth Estate, 1999), pp.151–2.

59 Cleese, quoted by Simon Edge, *Daily Express*, 25 May 2007, p.34.

60 Cleese, quoted by Hunter Davies, *op. cit.*, p.138.

61 Connie Booth, *ibid.*, pp.138–9.

62 Cleese, speaking on Disc 3 of *The Complete Fawlty Towers* DVD set.

63 Cleese, quoted by Wilmut, *From Fringe to Flying Circus, op. cit.*, pp.243–4.

64 *Porridge* began as a pilot episode as part of Ronnie Barker's BBC1 series *Seven of One* on 1 April 1973; its first full series followed between 5 September and 10 October 1974.

65 The first series of *Some Mothers Do 'Ave 'Em* ran on BBC1 from 15 February to 29 March 1973.

66 The first series of *Man About the House* was shown on Thames/ITV from 15 August to 26 September 1973.

67 *Last of the Summer Wine* was piloted as part of BBC1's *Comedy Playhouse* on 4 January 1973; the first series followed between 12 November and 17 December 1973.

68 *Whoops Baghdad* ran on BBC1 from 25 January to 1 March 1973.

69 *Open All Hours* began life on BBC1 as an episode of Ronnie Barker's *Seven of One* on 25 March 1973; the first series – delayed because of Barker's other projects – was screened between 20 February and 26 March 1976.

70 The first series of *Whatever Happened to the Likely Lads?* ran on BBC1 from 9 January to 3 April 1973.

71 Cleese, quoted by Bright and Ross, *Fawlty Towers: Fully Booked, op. cit.*, p.25.

72 Georges Feydeau, quoted by Stephen Mulrine in his introduction to Kenneth McLeish's translation of Feydeau's *A Flea In Her Ear* (London: Nick Hern Books, 2000), p.xiii.

73 Cleese, quoted by Bright and Ross, *Fawlty Towers: Fully Booked, op. cit.*, pp.25–6.

74 Cleese, quoted by Hunter Davies, *op. cit.*, p.138.

75 Julian Doyle, production manager of *Monty Python and the Holy Grail*, was himself a member of the Communist Party, and had encountered Basil and Sybil in their capacity as subscription collectors. He mentioned them, in passing, to Cleese while on the set of the movie in Scotland during 1974.

76 Cleese, quoted by David Thomas, 'Fawlty Memories', *op. cit.*, p.6.

77 Cleese, quoted by Hunter Davies, *op. cit.*, p.138.

78 Cleese, quoted by Johnson, *Life Before and After Monty Python, op. cit.*, p.87.

79 *Ibid.*

80 Cleese, speaking in part two of the three-part *Omnibus* documentary series, *Laughter in the House*, broadcast on BBC1 on 31 March 1991.

81 Cleese, speaking on *The South Bank Show* profile of him, broadcast by LWT/ITV on 12 January 1986.

82 See Margolis, *op. cit.*, pp.159 and 198, and Morley, *op. cit.*, p.11.

83 Cleese, quoted by Guy Bellamy, 'The Traveller's Unrest', *op. cit.*, p.77.

84 Cleese, *Laughter in the House, op. cit.*

85 See Karen McVeigh, 'The Man Who Inspired Manuel', *The Scotsman*, 25 May 2002, p.7. (One should note, however, that neither Cleese nor Booth has ever said that Novak was, either partially or entirely, the inspiration for the character of Manuel – and, as Andrew Sachs also had a certain amount of input, Novak's certainty appears unfounded.)

86 Cleese, *Laughter in the House, op. cit.* (According to Penelope Gilliatt's *To Wit* – *op. cit.*, p.246 – Cleese had also been amused by certain Italian waiters because, he said, they were so courteous they treated each diner, immediately, like a confirmed member of the cognoscenti – 'I once went to a place and ordered veal saloppine and asked where the Gents was. "*Perfetto, Signore.*" The waiter made you feel that those were the only two things that any man of genuine taste could possibly have wanted' – but he concluded that the puzzled Spaniard promised more comedy in terms of communication problems.)

87 *Ibid.*

88 Cleese, quoted by Bright and Ross, *Fawlty Towers: Fully Booked, op. cit.*, p.19.

89 Cleese, quoted by Thomas, 'Fawlty Memories', *op. cit.*, p.4.

Chapter 3

1 See my *Dad's Army: The Story of a Classic Television Show* (London: Fourth Estate, 2001), pp.54–6.

2 See my *Spike & Co: Inside the House of Fun with Milligan, Sykes, Galton & Simpson* (London: Hodder & Stoughton, 2006), pp.283–90.

3 See BBC Written Archives Centre (WAC): *Fawlty Towers File* T12/1, 487/1 – General.

4 Apart from *All Gas and Gaiters* and the first series of *Monty Python*, Davies also directed several episodes of *Doctor Who* ('The Macra Terror', 1967) and *Z Cars* (1967); a four-part adaptation of Emile Zola's novel *Nana* (1968); *A. P. Herbert's Misleading Cases* (1967–71); *The World of Beachcomber* (1968–9); two series of *The Goodies* (1970–72); a series of *Steptoe and Son* (1972); and Frankie Howerd's series *Whoops Baghdad* (1973).

5 Cleese, quoted by David Morgan, ed., *Monty Python Speaks!* (op. cit.), p.27.

6 John Howard Davies, interview with the author, 31 May 2007.

7 John Cleese, quoted by Morley, *op. cit.*, p.11.

8 Cleese, interviewed by Richard Johnson, *Radio Times*, 13–19 May 1995, p.6.

9 Irving Wardle, *The Times*, 9 August 1974, p.9.

10 John Howard Davies, interview with the author, 31 May 2007.

11 *Ibid.*

12 John Howard Davies, commentary on series one, episode one, of *The Complete Fawlty Towers* DVD set.

13 Scales, interview with the author, 21 May 2007.

14 Scales, quoted by Ransom, *Prunella* (London: John Murray, 2005), p.132.

15 Scales, interview with the author, 21 May 2007.

16 *Ibid.*

17 *Ibid.*

18 *Ibid.*

19 *Ibid.*

20 Cleese, quoted by Ransom, *Prunella, op. cit.*, p.128.

21 Cleese, quoted by Bright and Ross, *op. cit.*, p.90.

22 Andrew Sachs' father, Hans Emil Sachs, was an insurance broker, and his mother, Katharina Schrott-Fiecht, a trained librarian. In September 1938, his father was arrested, but, thanks to a friendly police official, was saved from being sent to a concentration camp. Sachs Snr left immediately for London, where he obtained a job

with the insurance firm Leroy Flesch. He brought over his family in December, and they settled in West Hampstead.

23 One of Sachs' BBC radio plays, *Made In Heaven*, broadcast on 7 April 1971, featured Prunella Scales, her husband Timothy West and Peter Pratt.

24 Broadcast on 10 October 1970 under the banner of BBC2's *Chronicle* documentary strand.

25 Broadcast on 17 July 1971, again under the banner of BBC2's *Chronicle* documentary strand.

26 Cleese, quoted by Bright and Ross, *op. cit.*, p.82.

27 Andrew Sachs, speaking on Disc 3 of *The Complete Fawlty Towers* DVD set.

28 *Ibid.*

29 *Ibid.*

30 *Ibid.*

31 Ballard Berkeley would remain such a good friend and admirer of Cary Grant that he would give his son Peter the middle name of 'Cary' (source: conversation with Peter Berkeley, 22 May 2007).

32 *Here's Harry*, 'The Holiday', broadcast on BBC TV, 11 May 1961.

33 *Maigret*, 'A Man Condemned', broadcast on BBC TV, 29 October 1963.

34 *Sherlock Holmes*, 'The Illustrious Client', broadcast on BBC1, 20 February 1965.

35 *Dixon of Dock Green*, several episodes from 1956 to 1969, broadcast on BBC1.

36 See Ballard Berkeley, quoted by Joshua Levine, *Forgotten Voices of the Blitz and the Battle of Britain* (London: Ebury Press, 2006), p.400.

37 Cleese, speaking on Disc 3 of *The Complete Fawlty Towers* DVD set.

38 Some fans and commentators have placed doubt on these two actors being cast in time for the first episode of *Fawlty Towers*, as Miss Tibbs and Miss Gatsby were only seen briefly in the distance

and whoever actually played them were not included in the credits. John Howard Davies, however, told me: 'They *were* cast. That was them. It's a long time ago, and I suppose the memory can play tricks, and I haven't seen [that episode] for a while, but, no, I'm sure they were cast at the same time – during the same period – as the others' (interview with the author, 31 May 2007).

39 *Cabaret Kittens* was broadcast in London and the Midlands on 8 October 1927. (Incidentally: Roberts later found herself caught up in a controversial murder case, when she was called to give evidence during the inquest concerning the death of Violet McGrath, the mother-in-law of the actor Michael Rennie, who had been found strangled with one of her own nylon stockings on 9 May 1954. Roberts confirmed that a scar on a hand of the suspect, Walter Henry Hensby, had been caused by her ring when she had pushed him away during an unrelated meeting. The case was widely reported, but it remained unsolved. See *The Times*, 13 August 1954, p.3.)

40 Renée Roberts appeared in several editions of *Play for Today*, including 'Hearts and Flowers', broadcast on BBC1 on 3 December 1970; and an episode of the *Doctor Who* sequence 'The Daemons', broadcast on BBC1 on 5 June 1971; and she was also in three episodes of *The Prince of Denmark*, broadcast on BBC1 in 1974.

41 Gilly Flower appeared in *Steptoe and Son* as an unnamed relation in 'Oh, What a Beautiful Mourning', broadcast on BBC1 on 6 March 1972, and as 'Mrs Sheldon' in 'Séance in a Wet Rag and Bone Yard', broadcast on 10 October 1974.

42 *The Prince of Denmark* ran for six episodes on BBC1 between 10 April and 15 May 1974; the episode featuring both Roberts and Flower was the second one in the series, broadcast on 17 April 1974.

43 BBC WAC: *Fawlty Towers* File: T12/1,487/1 – General.

NOTES

Chapter 4

1 Overheard by Cleese's friend, Iain Johnstone; quoted by Bright and Ross, *Fawlty Towers: Fully Booked, op. cit.*, p.19.
2 Quoted by John Cleese, speaking on Disc 3 of *The Complete Fawlty Towers* DVD set, *op. cit.*
3 The address would be mentioned by Polly in the opening scene of the episode entitled 'The Builders'.
4 John Howard Davies, interview with the author, 31 May 2007.
5 John Howard Davies, speaking on Disc 3 of *The Complete Fawlty Towers* DVD set, *op. cit.*
6 John Howard Davies, interview with the author, 31 May 2007.
7 John Howard Davies, *ibid.*
8 John Howard Davies, *ibid.*
9 The sign changes were continued into the second series by Iain McLean when he worked as director Bob Spiers's assistant floor manager.
10 John Howard Davies, interview with the author, 31 May 2007.
11 Cleese, quoted in the *Daily Express*, 25 May 2007, p.34.
12 Cleese, quoted by Margolis, *Cleese Encounters, op. cit.*, p.201.
13 Cleese, speaking on Disc 3 of *The Complete Fawlty Towers* DVD set.
14 Andrew Sachs, interview with the author, 20 April 2007.
15 John Howard Davies, commentating on episode two, Disc 1 of *The Complete Fawlty Towers* DVD set.
16 Prunella Scales, interview with the author, 21 May 2007.
17 John Howard Davies, interview with the author, 31 May 2007.
18 Prunella Scales, interview with the author, 21 May 2007.
19 John Cleese, quoted by Margolis, *Cleese Encounters, op. cit.*, p.203.
20 John Cleese, quoted by Bright and Ross, *Fawlty Towers: Fully Booked, op. cit.*, p.33.
21 See series one, episode six: 'The Germans'.
22 See series one, episode five: 'Gourmet Night'.

23 John Howard Davies, interview with the author, 31 May 2007.

24 See Duncan Wood's interview in David Nathan's *The Laughter-makers* (London: Peter Owen, 1971), p.118.

25 John Howard Davies, interview with the author, 31 May 2007.

26 John Cleese, quoted by Johnson, *Life Before and After Monty Python, op. cit.*, p.87.

27 Prunella Scales, quoted by Peter Stanford, 'How We Met', *Independent on Sunday*, 6 November 2005, p.70.

28 Cleese, speaking on Disc 3 of *The Complete Fawlty Towers* DVD set.

29 Cleese, quoted by Bright and Ross, *Fawlty Towers: Fully Booked, op. cit.*, pp.140–1.

30 Benedict Nightingale, 'One Pair of Cleese,' *op. cit.*

31 The absence of advance screenings was actually a real cause for contention as far as the critics were concerned. The *Daily Telegraph*'s Sylvia Clayton, for example, announced ahead of the first episode: 'I would like to be able to recommend John Cleese's new series [. . .] but the BBC will not permit it to be previewed' (19 September 1975, p.29). Similarly, later on in the run, her colleague Sean Day-Lewis snapped: 'it would be good to think that those responsible might one day have sufficient faith in their product to show it to critics in advance' (24 October 1975, p.31). In those days, however, the BBC preferred to bypass the critics and reach the public with an 'un-spun' show.

32 Tim Ewbank, *Daily Mail*, 19 September 1975, p.21.

33 *The Observer*, Review Section, 14 September 1975, p.23.

34 Cleese, quoted by Wilfred De'Ath, 'John Cleese: a very private joker', *The Listener*, 5 February 1976, p.141.

35 *Ibid.*

36 See my *Dad's Army: The Story of a Classic Television Show* (London: Fourth Estate, 2001), Chapter XIII.

37 James Murray, *Daily Express*, 19 September 1975, p.12.

38 My calculations of these viewing figures are based on the per-
   centages included in the BBC's internal Daily Viewing Barometer
   for 19 September 1975.
39 Palin, *Diaries 1969–1979, op. cit.*, p.254.

Chapter 5

1 John Howard Davies, commentating on episode two, Disc 1 of
  The Complete Fawlty Towers DVD set.
2 Cleese, speaking on Disc 3, *ibid.*
3 *Beryl's Lot* starred Carmel McSharry as a former char who is
  determined to improve her mind. Now into its second series, it
  was reasonably popular with viewers, but its mix of comedy,
  drama and soap opera elements seemed to baffle or underwhelm
  the majority of critics.
4 BBC WAC: calculated from the relevant Daily Viewing Barometers.
5 Cleese, quoted by Bright and Ross, *Fawlty Towers: Fully Booked,
  op. cit.*, p.167.
6 Cleese, speaking in the US TV documentary, *Fawlty Towers
  Revisited* (Iowa Public Television/BBC Worldwide Americas,
  2005).
7 Andrew Sachs, interview with the author, 20 April 2007. (Sachs
  would suffer again in a scene in a later episode – 'Gourmet Night'
  – when Basil 'persuades' Manuel that a dessert spoon is slightly
  dirty and therefore needs to be replaced by rubbing it over his
  greasy hair and then hitting him with it on the forehead. The first
  take, said Sachs, went fine: 'I was expecting that, and it was all right
  because I've got a thick skull!' The problem was that Cleese then
  wanted an alternative take as an editing option, and, because the
  audience now thought that they knew what to expect, he decided

to surprise them – and Sachs – by banging him on the mouth as well as the head. 'So there I was,' Sachs recalled, 'staring at him, when he suddenly went *DOIIIING!!*, straight into my teeth! I could hear them swing on their hinges. They stayed in, but it was painful!')

8 Cleese, speaking in the documentary, *Fawlty Towers Revisited, op. cit.*

9 Bernard Cribbins, *ibid.*

10 John Howard Davies, commentating on episode four, Disc 1 of *The Complete Fawlty Towers* DVD set.

11 *Ibid.*

12 John Howard Davies, interview with the author, 31 May 2007.

13 Davies, commentating on episode two, Disc 1 of *The Complete Fawlty Towers* DVD set.

14 Davies, interview with the author, 31 May 2007.

15 'Oh, What a Beautiful Mourning', *Steptoe and Son*, first broadcast on BBC1 on 6 February 1972.

16 Cleese, quoted by Bright and Ross, *Fawlty Towers: Fully Booked, op. cit.*, p.158.

17 John Howard Davies, interview with the author, 31 May 2007.

18 Cleese, quoted by Bright and Ross, *Fawlty Towers: Fully Booked, op. cit.*, p.160.

19 John Howard Davies, commentating on episode six, Disc 1 of *The Complete Fawlty Towers* DVD set.

20 Martin Scorsese, quoted by Margolis, *op. cit.*, p.196.

Chapter 6

1 Oliver Pritchett, London *Evening Standard*, 22 September 1975, p.22.

2 Douglas Orgill, *Daily Express*, 26 September 1975, p.12.

3 Tony Pratt, *Daily Mirror*, 26 September 1975, p.17.

4 See John Cleese's interview on Disc 3 of *The Complete Fawlty Towers* DVD set.

5 See, for example, Richard Ingrams, *Independent*, 17 December 2005, p.41.

6 See Chapter 11 (an episode in the second series, entitled 'The Kipper and the Corpse', would include an in-joke about Ingrams involving a guest and an inflatable doll).

7 Tim Ewbank, *Daily Mail*, 3 October 1975, p.23.

8 *The Guardian*, 3 October 1975, p.4.

9 Peter Buckman, *The Listener*, 9 October 1975, p.478.

10 Douglas Orgill, *Daily Express*, 10 October 1975, p.12.

11 Kenneth Hughes, *Daily Mirror*, 17 October 1975, p.19.

12 Clive James, *The Observer*, Review Section, 5 October 1975, p.22.

13 Peter Fiddick, *The Guardian*, 18 October 1975, p.9.

14 Joan Bakewell, *The Listener*, 23 October 1975, p.541.

15 John Cleese, speaking on Disc 3 of *The Complete Fawlty Towers* DVD set.

16 The playwright Dennis Potter, for example, enthused in the *New Statesman* (31 October 1975, p.555) about the closing episode's almost 'indecently funny' goose-stepping finale: 'Orwell claimed that the British would never accept the continental varieties of fascism because the people would laugh in the streets at such brute ceremony. Cleese resoundingly proved the point.'

17 Douglas Orgill, *Daily Express*, 24 October 1975, p.12.

18 Michael Palin, entry for 11 November 1975, *Diaries 1969–1979*, *op. cit.*, p.264.

19 Scales, interview with the author, 21 May 2007.

20 Andrew Sachs, interview with the author, 20 April 2007.

21 John Howard Davies, interview with the author, 31 May 2007.

22 *The Guardian*, 6 January 1976, p.4.

23 *Daily Express*, 6 January 1976, p.10.

24 Tony Pratt, *Daily Mirror*, 3 February 1976, p.17.

25 Cleese, speaking on Disc 3 of *The Complete Fawlty Towers* DVD set.

26 See the *Guardian*, 6 September 1976, p.6.

27 Clive James, *Observer*, Review Section, 1 February 1976, p.24.

28 See, for example, 'Business Diary', *The Times*, 19 February 1976, p.19: 'Nabil Chartouni is smooth and composed for a hotelier whose experiences make Basil Fawlty's most frenzied crises look trivial.'

29 See *The Times*, 15 May 1976, p.16.

30 *The Times*, 4 September 1976, p.8.

31 Peter Tinniswood, 'Preview', *Radio Times*, 25 September–1 October 1976, p.21.

32 *The Guardian*, 4 September 1976, p.16.

33 *The Guardian*, 11 September 1976, p.20.

34 *The Listener*, 5 February 1976, p.141.

35 Peter Buckman, *The Listener*, 23 and 30 December 1976, p.843.

36 Video Cassette Recorders (VCRs) suitable for private and domestic use were first made widely available in the mid-1970s in two formats: Betamax or Beta (pioneered by Sony) and VHS (pioneered by JVC). After several years of notoriously fierce competition, during which time both the quality and the price improved rapidly, VHS drove Beta out of existence. In the process, video-cassette recorders gradually became more and more commonplace in UK households, rising steadily from about seven per cent of homes in 1981 to about fifty-one per cent by 1986 (see David Docherty, *The Last Picture Show?* [London: BFI, 1987], p.62). Commercially made video cassettes of popular movies only started to be released in the late 1970s. Television companies took longer to exploit the potential market and begin selling some of their most successful programmes on home video. *Fawlty Towers* would be one of the first of these releases in 1984 – see 'BBC set to tap home video sales boom', *The Times*, 26 June 1981, p.30: 'Some of the BBC's most popular programmes will be available on video

cassettes in High Street stores from next August. The corporation plans to launch its entry into the fast-growing home video market on Monday with details of an expensive advertising campaign and a list of about twenty initial takeaway programmes. BBC Enterprises, the corporation's marketing arm which is handling the project, refused to give any details yesterday. But fans of *Fawlty Towers* and *The Two Ronnies* who have not yet illicitly taped their favourites at home will probably find them among the first in the BBC's video lists' (and see, also, 'In a Fawlty World, Basil Is Still King', *The Times*, 22 September 1984, p.17, and Chapter 12 of this book).

Chapter 7

1 See the episode entitled 'The Wedding Party'.
2 'The Wedding Party'.
3 'The Hotel Inspectors'.
4 'A Touch of Class'.
5 'The Wedding Party'.
6 'The Germans'.
7 *Ibid.*
8 'The Hotel Inspectors'.
9 'The Wedding Party'.
10 'Waldorf Salad' and 'Gourmet Night'.
11 'The Hotel Inspectors'.
12 'The Hotel Inspectors'.
13 'The Hotel Inspectors'.
14 'Gourmet Night'.
15 'The Germans'.
16 'The Builders'.
17 'A Touch of Class'.

18 'The Hotel Inspectors'.
19 'The Wedding Party'.
20 'The Germans'.
21 'The Builders'.
22 'The Hotel Inspectors'.
23 'Gourmet Night'.
24 'The Hotel Inspectors'.
25 'The Wedding Party'.
26 'Gourmet Night'.
27 'Gourmet Night'.
28 'The Builders'.
29 'A Touch of Class'.
30 'The Hotel Inspectors'.
31 'The Germans'.
32 'The Wedding Party'.
33 'The Builders'.
34 'The Builders'.
35 'The Builders' and 'Gourmet Night'.
36 'Gourmet Night'.
37 'The Hotel Inspectors'.
38 'The Builders'.
39 'The Builders'.
40 'The Hotel Inspectors'.
41 'A Touch of Class'.
42 'The Germans'.
43 'The Wedding Party'.
44 'The Wedding Party'.
45 'The Hotel Inspectors'.
46 'The Hotel Inspectors'.
47 'The Hotel Inspectors'.
48 'The Builders'.
49 'The Germans'.
50 'A Touch of Class'.

51 'The Builders'.
52 'A Touch of Class'.
53 'The Builders'.
54 'A Touch of Class'.
55 Kenneth Robinson, *Radio Times*, 24–30 March 1979, p.23.
56 Clive James, *The Observer*, Review Section, 1 February 1976, p.24.
57 'The Builders'.

Chapter 8

1 See 'The Wedding Party'.
2 'The Wedding Party'.
3 Erving Goffman analysed interpersonal relations by discussing the active processes whereby people make and manage their social roles. Using metaphors from the stage (such as 'dramaturgy'), he described how ordinary individuals give performances, control their 'scripts' and enter settings that make up their lives. His research was first published in 1956 in a book entitled *The Presentation of Self in Everyday Life* (London: Penguin, 1990).
4 *Ibid.*, pp.210–11.
5 'A Touch of Class'.
6 'The Germans'.
7 'The Builders'.
8 'The Hotel Inspectors'.
9 'The Builders'.
10 'The Wedding Party'.
11 'The Builders'.
12 'Gourmet Night'.
13 'Gourmet Night'.
14 'The Builders'.
15 'The Germans'.

16 'Gourmet Night'.
17 'The Builders'.
18 Goffman, *The Presentation of Self* . . ., *op. cit.*, p.210.
19 See 'The Wedding Party'.
20 'A Touch of Class'.
21 'A Touch of Class'.
22 'The Builders'.
23 'The Hotel Inspectors'.
24 'The Germans'.
25 'The Builders'.
26 'The Builders'.
27 'The Builders'.
28 'The Germans'.
29 'The Germans'.
30 'The Hotel Inspectors'.
31 'The Builders'.
32 'The Wedding Party'.
33 'Gourmet Night'.
34 'The Hotel Inspectors'.
35 'Gourmet Night'.
36 'The Hotel Inspectors'.
37 'The Wedding Party'.

Chapter 9

1 'The Wedding Party'.
2 'A Touch of Class'.
3 'The Germans'.
4 'A Touch of Class'.
5 'The Germans'.
6 'The Builders'.

7 'The Builders'.
8 'The Wedding Party'.
9 'The Germans'.
10 'The Germans'.
11 'The Builders'.
12 'The Germans'.
13 'The Germans'.
14 'The Germans'.
15 'A Touch of Class'.
16 'The Germans'.
17 'The Germans'.
18 'A Touch of Class'.
19 Miss Gatsby is addressed by Miss Tibbs during series one as 'Ursula' in 'The Builders' and then as 'Angina' in 'The Germans'. Miss Tibbs is called 'Abitha' in 'The Builders'.
20 'The Builders'.
21 'The Wedding Party'.
22 'The Builders'.
23 'Gourmet Night'.
24 'The Builders'.

Chapter 10

1 See *The Times* (Review Section), 5 November 1977, p.11.
2 BBC WAC.
3 Cleese, quoted in Bellamy, 'The Traveller's Unrest,' *op. cit.*, p.75.
4 Cleese said in an interview for *The Times* (Review Section: 5 November 1977, p.11) that seven new episodes were planned for the autumn of 1978.
5 *The Glittering Prizes* was broadcast on BBC2 in six parts from 21 January to 25 February 1976.

6 *Spaghetti Two-Step*, broadcast on ITV on 18 January 1977.

7 *Off to Philadelphia in the Morning*, broadcast on BBC1 in three parts from 12 to 26 September 1978.

8 *Thank You Comrades*, broadcast on BBC2 on 19 December 1978.

9 *The Mermaid Frolics*, LWT/ITV, 11 September 1977; released as album by Polydor (2384 101) later the same year.

10 *The Strange Case of the End of Civilization As We Know It*, LWT/ITV, 17 September 1977.

11 *Tonight*, BBC1, 20 February 1976; *Read All About It*, BBC1, 14 November 1976.

12 *Three Piece Suite*, BBC2, 12 April 1977.

13 *The Muppet Show*, LWT/ITV, 21 October 1977.

14 Scales, interview with the author, 21 May 2007.

15 *The Importance of Being Earnest*, BBC Radio 3, 25 December 1977.

16 *Mistinguett*, BBC Radio 4, 27 January 1978.

17 *A Gallant Romantic*, BBC Radio 4, 9 August 1978.

18 *The Golden Trashery of Ogden Nashery*, BBC2, 14 July 1976.

19 *Mr Big*, thirteen episodes, BBC1, 7 January–11 February and 23 June–4 August 1978.

20 *Doris and Doreen*, LWT/ITV, 16 December 1978.

21 The episodes of *Call My Bluff* were broadcast on BBC2 on 10 and 17 June 1977.

22 *Took and Co*, seven episodes, Yorkshire/ITV, 7 August–18 September 1977.

23 *The Revenge* was broadcast on BBC Radio 3 on 1 June 1978.

24 The episode of *Rising Damp* was broadcast on ITV on 18 April 1978.

25 *Look – Mike Yarwood*, BBC1, 10 January 1976, and *The Mike Yarwood Christmas Show*, BBC1, 27 December 1976.

26 'Family Matters', *The Duchess of Duke Street*, BBC1, 4 September 1976.

27 *The Two Ronnies*, BBC1, 25 September 1976.

28 'Murder at Moorestone's Manor', *Ripping Yarns*, BBC2, 11 October 1977.

29 *The Fall and Rise of Reginald Perrin*, BBC1, 12 October 1977.

30 Connie Booth, quoted by Paul Callan, *Daily Mirror*, 2 June 1976, p.11.

31 Hunter Davies, *Hunting People, op. cit.*, p.131.

32 Ferry had recently ended his relationship with the model Jerry Hall. Cleese would remain at this address for twenty-four years, finally selling it in 2001 for a widely reported £5 million.

33 Connie Booth, quoted by Margolis, *op. cit.*, p.214.

34 Cleese, interviewed by Tim Satchell in 1977; quoted by Margolis, *op. cit.*, pp.213–14.

35 See *The Times*, 1 September 1978, p.3.

36 Connie Booth, quoted by Guy Bellamy, 'The Traveller's Unrest', *op. cit.*, p.76.

37 Cleese, quoted in *The Times* (Review Section), 5 November 1977, p.11.

38 John Cleese, quoted by Hunter Davies, *Hunting People, op. cit.*, pp.132–3.

39 Cleese, quoted by Guy Bellamy, 'The Traveller's Unrest', *op. cit.*, p.77.

40 Cleese, speaking on Disc 3 of *The Complete Fawlty Towers* DVD set.

41 Cleese, speaking on Disc 3 of *The Complete Fawlty Towers* DVD set. Confusingly, Cleese is quoted by Johnson, in *Life Before and After Monty Python* (*op. cit.*, p.87) as saying more or less the opposite (*viz.* 'a little less Alan Ayckbourn'). This, however, seems to contradict Cleese and Booth's known admiration for their fellow writer, as well as the evidence on the screen, so I have treated the other comment as the most reliable.

42 Note Cleese's comments on Disc 3 of *The Complete Fawlty Towers* DVD set.

43 'Communication Problems'.

44 'Waldorf Salad'.

45 'The Psychiatrist'.

46 'Waldorf Salad'.
47 'The Psychiatrist'.
48 'Communication Problems'.
49 'The Psychiatrist'.
50 'Communication Problems'.
51 'The Psychiatrist'.
52 'The Psychiatrist'.
53 'Communication Problems'.
54 'Communication Problems'.
55 'The Psychiatrist'.
56 'Basil the Rat'.
57 'The Psychiatrist'.
58 'The Psychiatrist'.
59 'The Psychiatrist'.
60 'The Psychiatrist'.
61 'The Psychiatrist'.
62 'Communication Problems'.
63 'The Psychiatrist'.
64 'The Psychiatrist'.
65 'Waldorf Salad'.
66 'The Anniversary'.
67 'Basil the Rat'.
68 'Basil the Rat'.
69 BBC WAC: *Fawlty Towers* File 1.
70 Andrew Sachs, quoted by Thomas, 'Fawlty Memories', *op. cit.*, p.6.
71 John Howard Davies, interview with the author, 31 May 2007.
72 'Waldorf Salad'.
73 'Trap', *The Sweeney*, ITV, 6 October 1975.
74 *Sweeney 2* (1978).
75 Brian Hall, quoted by Robin McGibbon, 'John Cleese Is Fawltless', *Daily Mirror*, 16 July 1996, p.15.
76 *Ibid.*

77 Brian Hall said: 'Terry didn't feature much in the first episode, so there was little for me to do except sit around and watch. This bothered John and, despite having a million things to think about, he found time to apologise to me. I told him I'd have paid to watch such a remarkable show, but he said he would make up for it by beefing up Terry's part in the sixth episode. And he kept his promise.' (*Ibid.*)

78 Cleese, quoted by Norman, 'Fears of a Clown', *op. cit.*, p.27.

79 John Cleese, quoted by Hunter Davies, *op. cit.*, p.138.

80 Scales, interview with the author, 21 May 2007.

81 *Ibid.*

82 Bob Spiers, commenting on episode one, series two, on Disc 2 of *The Complete Fawlty Towers* DVD set.

83 See, for example, the opening scene of 'The Psychiatrist'.

84 *Radio Times*, 17–23 February 1979, pp.74–5.

85 Tony Pratt, *Daily Mirror*, 10 February 1979, p.13.

Chapter 11

1 The *Radio Times* letters page (10–16 March 1979, p.71) would include a complaint from a viewer about this episode's supposed portrayal of the deaf. Cleese responded, pointing out that the show was mocking someone who was not deaf, but rather was using 'her slight deafness, as some people do, to her advantage'. He added: 'Ordinary, nice, kind people aren't funny: comedy has to have a critical edge to it.'

2 Mel Brooks, quoted by Kenneth Tynan, in his 1978 *New Yorker* profile of the comedian, reproduced in Tynan's *Show People* (London: Weidenfeld & Nicolson, 1980), p.232.

3 Paul Madden, *The Listener*, 1 March 1979, p.320.

4 Siân Phillips, *Radio Times*, 24 February–2 March 1979, p.21.

5 Roger Woddis, *Radio Times*, 3–9 March 1979, p.10.

6 One reason he was cast in the part, he later revealed, was that Cleese had written so many personalised insults for the character he could not face addressing them to a relative stranger instead of a familiar good sport (see the documentary *Fawlty Towers Revisited*).

7 Sean Day-Lewis, *Daily Telegraph*, 27 February 1979, p.15.

8 Michael Palin, *Diaries, op. cit.*, p.536.

9 BBC WAC: Daily Viewing Barometers.

10 Jack Waterman, *The Listener*, 15 March 1979, p.373.

11 See Margolis, *op. cit.*, p.217, and Cleese, speaking in the documentary *Fawlty Towers Revisited* (Iowa Public Television/BBC Worldwide Americas, 2005).

12 Spiers, commenting on episode four, series two, on Disc 2 of *The Complete Fawlty Towers* DVD set.

13 This line, for some reason, has been edited out of some prints of this episode, including the DVD boxed set.

14 Richard Ingrams confirmed that he recognised the joke in his column for the *Observer*, 14 April 2002, p.32.

15 Keith Waterhouse, *Radio Times*, 17–23 March 1979, p.23.

16 In 1978, the Labour Government's attempt to enforce its rule that pay rises must be kept below five per cent provoked the trades unions into rebelling – pushing for higher rates and using strikes to force a change. This prolonged period of industrial action, which lasted for much of the winter of 1978–9, was dubbed 'The Winter of Discontent'. Some months later, noting that many of these unions had ended up winning pay rises of 15–20 per cent, the Association of Cinematograph Television and Allied Technicians (ACTT) pressed ITV for a similar pay rise when negotiations commenced during the summer of 1979. ITV refused the ACTT's demands and, as a consequence, the union advised its members to walk out – thus effectively pulling the plug on the vast majority of the ITV network. On 10 August, all the ITV regions except Channel TV were officially on strike. (Channel kept going with a

heavily modified schedule consisting mainly of local programmes, and with much shorter transmission hours.) Programmes finally resumed at 5.45 p.m. on Wednesday 24 October, 1979. It had been the longest dispute in the history of British television.

17 What actually happened was as follows: on Thursday 8 March 1979, Terry Ryan, a BBC rigger who was also a union shop steward, got into an argument with John Carter, his departmental manager, at the BBC's transport depot in Kendal Grove, west London. Ryan ended up assaulting Carter, who was found later that day lying semi-conscious at the bottom of a flight of stairs; he required hospital treatment which included nine stitches in his forehead and eyebrow. Ryan, as a consequence, was dismissed on the spot, and, in protest, 360 of his fellow riggers, drivers and outside broadcast crew went out on strike, thus blacking out that evening's live *Song for Europe* programme and throwing the BBC schedules into chaos. The technical union met the following day and voted for the strike to be made official, and most studios at TV Centre ended up in darkness until 15 March, when a formula was worked out between BBC management and the union with the assistance of the conciliation service ACAS. Under the agreed formula, Ryan received his basic pay until a subsequent court case was over, and an internal inquiry was put into action. See *Daily Mirror*, 9 March 1979, p.1; *The Guardian*, 10 March 1979, p.1; and *The Guardian*, 15 March 1979, p.2.

18 Cleese, speaking on Disc 3 of *The Complete Fawlty Towers* DVD set.

19 *Daily Mirror*, 24 March 1979, p.12.

20 Spiers, commenting on episode six, series two, on Disc 2 of *The Complete Fawlty Towers* DVD set.

21 *Ibid.*

22 *Ibid.*

23 Andrew Sinclair, *The Listener*, 1 November 1979, p.509.

Chapter 12

1 Cleese, quoted by Tony Pratt, *Daily Mirror*, 10 February 1979, p.13.

2 BBC WAC: Daily Viewing Barometers.

3 BBC WAC: Daily Viewing Barometers.

4 BBC WAC: Daily Viewing Barometers: 24 July 1980 and 6 December 1988. See also *Radio Times*, 24–30 June 1995, p.78.

5 See *The Times*, 17 July 1984, p.4.

6 Cleese, speaking in the US documentary *Fawlty Towers Revisited*, *op. cit.*

7 See the *Daily Telegraph*, 19 September 2006, p.10, and the *Daily Express*, 19 September 2006, p.28. (Other surviving sights of Fawlty action include The Old Bank in Cookham High Street, near Bourne End in Buckinghamshire [where the rogue Lord Melbury was spotted in 'A Touch of Class']; Mentmore Close in Kenton, North London [where Basil thrashed his car in 'Gourmet Night']; 294 Preston Road in Harrow, Middlesex [the site of André's restaurant]; and Northwick Park Hospital in Harrow [where Sybil had her ingrowing toenail removed in 'The Germans'].

8 *Fawlty Towers* (1979: BBC Records REB 377).

9 *Fawlty Towers: Second Sitting* (1981: BBC Records REB 405).

10 *Fawlty Towers: At Your Service* (1982: BBC Records REB 449).

11 *Fawlty Towers: A La Carte* (1983: BBC Records REB 484).

12 *Fawlty Towers* (1979: BBC ZCF 377); *Fawlty Towers: Second Sitting* (1981: BBC ZCF 405); *Fawlty Towers: At Your Service* (1982: BBC ZCF 449); *Fawlty Towers: A La Carte* (1983: BBC ZCF 484).

13 Videos: *The Germans, with The Hotel Inspectors and A Touch of Class* (1984: BBC Enterprises, BBCV6635); *The Psychiatrist, with The Builders and The Wedding Party* (1984: BBC Enterprises, BBCV6633); *The Kipper and the Corpse, with Waldorf Salad and Gourmet Night* (1984: BBC Enterprises, BBCV6634); *Basil the Rat,*

with Communication Problems and The Anniversary (1984: BBC Enterprises, BBCV6632). Laser discs: *The Germans* (BBCL 703); *The Psychiatrist* (BBCL 7029); *Basil the Rat* (BBCL 7030); and *The Kipper and the Corpse* (BBCL 7031). In 1996, series one (EE1159) and two (EE1160) were released in laser disc form by Encore Entertainment.

14 *Fawlty Towers: Complete Series 1* (BBCDVD1064, 2001); *Fawlty Towers: Complete Series 2* (BBCDVD1065, 2001); *Fawlty Towers: The Complete Set* (BBCDVD1794, 2005).

15 *Fawlty Towers* digi-pack for Windows 98/95: Brummel Associates for BBC Multimedia Worldwide, 5032956104124.

16 John Lennon, interviewed by Andy Peebles, transcribed from the CD *The Lennon Tapes* (BBC CD 6002), also available in book form (London: BBC, 1981), p. 81.

17 Les Brown explained in the *New York Times* (Business & Finance Section, 3 March 1977, p.67) that the show had not been bought by the networks for two basic reasons: 1. There were not enough episodes to fill a full US-style TV season; 2. Syndicated shows in the US had to run for no more than twenty-six minutes because of commercial breaks, whereas *Fawlty Towers* ran for at least thirty minutes and Cleese and Booth had refused to allow the episodes to be cut.

18 Margolis, *op. cit.*, p.221.

19 See David Morgan, ed., *Monty Python Speaks!*, *op. cit.*, p.144.

20 See 'The Legacy of ALS' in my *Spike & Co* (London: Hodder & Stoughton, 2006), pp.331–46.

21 *Love Thy Neighbour* was broadcast on ABC between 15 June and 19 September 1973.

22 See my *Dad's Army: The Story of a Classic Television Show* (London: Fourth Estate, 2001), pp.201–3.

23 See Cleese's interview with Dick Lochte in *Playboy* (US), November 1988, vol.35, issue 11, pp.128–30 and 164–5.

24 Emerging from CBS Films – the syndication arm of the CBS network – Viacom (Video, Audio Communications) Productions

was founded in 1971. In 1973, following a change to federal regulations (since repealed) forbidding television networks from owning their own syndication companies, Viacom became independent. The company then became well known for distributing such old shows as *I Love Lucy*, *The Andy Griffith Show*, *The Cosby Show* and *Roseanne*. At the end of 2005, the company changed its name to CBS Corporation. A new, separate organisation – composed of those who had left the old company – calling itself Viacom was launched at the same time.

25 Cleese, interviewed by the *LA Times*; quoted by Margolis, *op. cit.*, pp.222–3.

26 Cleese, interviewed by Dick Lochte in *Playboy, op. cit.*

27 John J. O'Connor, *New York Times*, Section C, 13 February 1983, p.30. *Amanda's* ran from 10 February to 26 May 1983 (three additional episodes never made it to the screen).

28 *Coach* ran on ABC for 211 episodes between 28 February 1989 and 14 May 1997.

29 See the report in *The Intelligence Record*, 14 March 1999, p.D3.

30 Joel Stein, reviewing the pilot edition for *Time* magazine (29 March 1999), wrote: 'If *Payne* serves any purpose at all, it's to show what a genius Cleese is. In the wrong hands the characters are badly drawn cartoons, the jokes offensive stereotypes and the plots a bad cross of the *Keystone Kops* and *Three's Company*. Sure, *Fawlty Towers* was also based on silly misunderstandings and coincidences, but it carefully built toward a manic, slapstick conclusion. In the original show you felt bad about laughing at the mistreated bellboy's broken English; now you just feel bad.'

31 *Payne* ran from 15 March to 28 April 1999 on ABC. One additional episode remains unshown. ITV, for some obscure reason, screened the show in the UK between 2 August and 4 October in 2002.

32 Andrew Sachs, interview with the author, 20 April 2007.

33 *Ibid.*

34 Reported in the *Daily Express*, 25 May 2007, p.34.

35 Cleese, quoted by Thomas, 'Fawlty Memories' *op. cit.*, p.6.

36 Cleese, interviewed by Dick Lochte in *Playboy, op. cit.*

37 See *The Times*, 21 April 1982, p.17.

38 *Born to Be Wild: Operation Lemur* was broadcast on BBC1 on 23 August 1998.

39 *The Human Face*, broadcast on BBC1, 7–25 March 2001.

40 *Wine for the Confused*, broadcast on the Food Network on 21 October 2004 (also available as an NTSC format DVD: KOCH B0009NZ6P2).

41 *The Art of Football from A to Z,* broadcast on numerous stations, including Sky One in the UK, on 27 June 2006.

42 *True Brit* (New York: DC Comics, 2004) was written by Kim 'Howard' Johnson 'with some help by John Cleese'; the artwork was by John Byrne and Mark Farmer, the lettering by Bill Oakley and Jack Morelli and the colouring by Alex Blevaert.

43 Cleese, 'My Local Hero', *op. cit.*, p.19.

44 Cleese's decision to decline the CBE was reported widely at the time (see, for example, the *Daily Express*, 22 December 2003, p.8). He became an A. D. White Professor at Cornell in 1999, and remained in the office for a record eight years (two years longer than usual) before being appointed a Visiting Professor.

45 Cleese, quoted by Adam Sherwin, 'Let me guide young guns to the Holy Grail of comedy, says Cleese', *The Times*, 12 June 2006, p.5.

46 'Connie's Fawltless Dress Sense', *The Times*, 23 February 1982, p.9.

47 *The Buccaneers*, broadcast on BBC1 from 5 February to 12 March 1995.

48 Personal information; sources requested to remain anonymous.

49 John Howard Davies, quoted by Simon Edge, 'Fawlty Marriage Connie Doesn't Want to Re-live', *Daily Express*, 25 May 2007, p.34.

50 *A Question of Attribution*, broadcast on BBC1 on 20 October 1991.

51 *Mapp and Lucia* ran for two series on Channel 4 from April 1985 to May 1986.

52 *After Henry* ran for four series on Thames/ITV from January 1988 to August 1992.

53 *The Human Face*, BBC1, 21 March 2001.

54 The episodes of *Father Brown* were broadcast on BBC Radio 4 between 2 December 1984 and 27 January 1985; and 5 October to 2 November 1986; with one additional episode from series one finally broadcast on 29 November 1987.

55 *The Jewish Journey*, broadcast on BBC Radio 4, 8 February–1 March 2001.

56 *The Further Adventures of Sherlock Holmes*, broadcast on BBC Radio 4, 18 May–15 June 2004.

57 *Don Quixote*, broadcast on BBC Radio 4 between 3 and 21 January 2005.

58 *The History of Mr Polly* was broadcast on BBC1 between 2 and 30 March 1980.

59 *The Tempest*, BBC2, 27 February 1980.

60 *The Mushroom Picker*, BBC2, 3–17 February 1993.

61 *Einstein Revealed*, broadcast on US Nova TV and BBC2 on 1 October 1996.

62 'Connections in High Places', an episode of *To the Manor Born*, was broadcast on BBC1 on 22 November 1981.

63 'Swingtime' and 'They Also Serve', two episodes of *Terry and June*, were broadcast on BBC1, respectively, on 26 October 1982 and 3 August 1987.

64 'Memories Are Made of This', an episode of *Are You Being Served?*, was broadcast on BBC1 on 6 May 1983.

65 'Empty Saddles', an episode of *Hi-de-Hi!*, was broadcast on BBC1 on 11 December 1983.

66 'Alarums and Excursions' and 'Happy Returns', two episodes of

Fresh Fields, were broadcast on Thames/ITV on, respectively, 9 October 1985 and 26 October 1986.

67 The episode of *Only Fools and Horses* was called 'Homesick', and was first broadcast on BBC1 on 10 November 1983.

68 See Disc 3 of *The Complete Fawlty Towers* DVD set.

69 The Kindreds purchased the house in 1983, but sold it in 2002; it is now owned by Bryan and Susan Webb. Peter Kindred now mainly paints as a profession, and runs courses each summer in the south of France.

70 See Richard Johnson, 'Return Service', *Radio Times,* 13–19 May 1995, p.6.

71 *Ibid.*

72 See 'Just don't mention the Henry Moore . . .', *Western Morning News* (Plymouth), 20 January 2007, p.5.

73 Cleese remarked: '[I]t always slightly annoyed me when people used to come up to me on [the subject of] *Fawlty Towers* and say, "Well, how much did Connie Booth actually write?" And I wanted to say to them, "Certainly a lot more than Graham [Chapman] ever wrote." That used to annoy me, the assumption that because Graham was a man he was obviously making a bigger contribution than Connie as a woman' (quoted by Morgan, *Monty Python Speaks!, op. cit.,* p.63). We do not know Booth's reaction to such a defence, but one might conjecture that, while perhaps regretting such phrases as '*slightly* annoyed' and 'I *wanted* to say', she both appreciated and agreed with the basic sentiment.

74 Andrew Sachs, interview with the author, 20 April 2007.

75 See the *Daily Express,* 25 May 2007, p.34; and *Daily Mail,* 24 May 2007, p.49.

76 Cleese, speaking on Disc 3 of *The Complete Fawlty Towers* DVD set.

77 *Ibid.*

Checking Out

1 John Howard Davies, interview with the author, 31 May 2007.
2 Bob Spiers, speaking on Disc 2 of *The Complete Fawlty Towers* DVD set.
3 Sachs, interview with the author, 20 April 2007.
4 Scales, interview with the author, 21 May 2007.
5 Cleese, quoted by Thomas, 'Fawlty Memories', *op. cit.*, p.4.

Picture Acknowledgements

Plate Section 1
BBC Motion Gallery 12, 14, 15. BBC Photo Library 1, 3, 10, 11, 13. *Fawlty Towers Revisited*, Iowa Public Television 8. Mirrorpix 4. Popperfoto 2, 9. Rex Features 5, 6, 7.

Plate Section 2
AP Images 8. BBC Motion Gallery 3. BBC Photo Library 2, 4, 5, 6. *Fawlty Towers Revisited*, Iowa Public Television 1. Getty Images 7, 14. Paphotos 12, 13. Rex Features 9, 10, 11.

Index

67; locations for 67, 70–1, 235; set designs for 68–9; anagrams of hotel sign 70; theme tune of 71; reasons for delay between series 233, 234; used by hotel chain as training film169, 234, 253; second series of 182–9; demand for third series 233, 234; American versions of 236–41; available in other media forms 167, 236; sale of format rights 237–41; German version of 241; abandoned BBC Radio 4 *Reunion* 254; idea for movie version 255

Series one writing of 44–51, 73; budget for 68–9; casting of 53, 54–62; fees for 64; editing of 74, 90; recording of 74, 75–6, 89–90; scheduling of 83–4, 90,118; pre-publicity for 82–3; viewing figures for 83–4, 90, 126,127; reception of 84, 90, 114–15, 117–23, 125–7, 142–3; repeats of 125–6, 127, 167, 233, 234, 241; awards won by 126–7

Series two writing of 168, 172, 174–81, 184–5; weight of expectations 174–6,188, 231; evolution of characters 176–81, 216; changes to personnel 178, 182–6; fees for, 182; rehearsals for 182, 185–7; changes to filming of 187–8; recording of 187; publicity for 188; scheduling of 188–9, 222, 223; reception of 196–7, 203, 209–10, 215, 222, 231–2; viewing figures for 209, 234; industrial disputes and 216, 222; repeats of 233, 234, 241; awards won by 231

Feldman, Marty 35
Ferry, Bryan 173
Feydeau, 44
Fiddick, Peter 121
Fields, W. C. 239
Fierce Creatures 245
Fish Called Wanda, A 245, 246
Flea In Her Ear, A 45
Fletcher, Cyril 33
Flower, Gilly
  acting career of 63–4; in *Fawlty Towers* 63–4, 91, 157, 161–4; post-*Fawlty Towers* career 171, 250–1
Food Network (USA) 244